# BUCKET

## ~ TO ~

# GREECE

Volume 13

## V.D. BUCKET

Editor: James Scraper
Proofreader: Alan Wood
Cover Designer: German Creative
Interior Formatting: The Book Khaleesi

# Other Books in the
# Bucket to Greece Series

# Chapter 1

*Highfalutin Grecian Dreams*

omfortably ensconced on a balcony chair, Catastrophe lifted her head from the cushion. Fixing me with her beady eyes, she dared me to dislodge her from an indulgent catnap. Taking pity on the indolent feline, I scooped it up; claiming Catastrophe's seat, I settled the cat on my lap rather than slinging it over the balcony, thinking the puss clever enough to spot a sucker at fifty paces. Closing my eyes for forty winks, I made a mental note to rid my lap of my furry friend before Marigold returned from her gadding. It wouldn't do for my wife to catch me out showing a soft spot for one of her pampered imported domestics.

Woken from my nap by Marigold depositing a tender kiss on my cheek, I played the innocent, pretending to be irritated by the cat taking advantage of my good nature. Joining me on the balcony, Marigold thrust a large packet into my hands. Neatly wrapped in brown paper, the parcel was secured with intricately knotted string.

"What's this?" Recoiling from the disgusting touch of the sticky paper, I shuddered at the thought of what particular viscid substance may have contaminated the parcel. I sincerely hoped it didn't hail from Milton, the local purveyor of porn.

"I wouldn't dream of opening it, darling. It's addressed to you." Marigold's fingers hovered over the packet, just itching to rip the brown paper open. "I've just come back from Athena's. She picked it up at the post office yesterday."

"Your hair looks lovely," I belatedly complimented my wife on hearing she'd returned from the hairdresser's kitchen. Whilst my wife's raised eyebrows indicated she questioned the sincerity of my compliment, I reflected that if the parcel had been hanging around in Athena's kitchen, the sticky substance seeping into the paper was undoubtedly nothing more suspect than an overload of chemically laden hairspray.

"I only popped round there to help Doreen out. She got herself into a bit of a pickle trying to explain what she wanted Athena to do to her hair," Marigold tutted. "It's a good job I did. Athena started rummaging through her drawers in search of a pair of pliers when Doreen asked her to pull her nails out…"

"Pull her nails out? Has Athena branched into manicures now?"

"No, Athena's still only doing human hair. I've told her she's missing a trick there. Moira has Waffles up at the pet grooming place at least twice a month but Vangelis put his foot down about her doing pets in the kitchen…"

"So why the pliers?" I interrupted before Marigold could continue with her bizarre tangent. I was already familiar with Vangelis' vocal complaints about constantly finding hairs in his food.

"Well, now that Doreen is keeping company with a Greek man, she's been trying to get to grips with a bit of Greek vocabulary. I've told her that she needs to start with the basics but she found the alphabet a bit challenging. She copied down a few words from the dictionary and tried memorising them to let Athena know that she wanted to go blonde. Doreen's pronunciation was so terrible that her attempt at *xanthia* came out all wrong."

Making a mental note to look up the Greek for 'pull out my nails' to determine how it could possibly be confused with blonde, I quipped, "So,

Doreen has retained all her talons and gone blonde…"

"Such an improvement on the grey…"

"I thought that she'd coloured her hair red…"

"Yes, but that was out of a bottle." Since Doreen had now apparently transformed into a bottle blonde, Marigold's logic was patently absurd.

"So, what's in the parcel? Another hefty tome on hygiene management?" Marigold's sarcasm was on top form. "It certainly weighs enough."

Ripping the parcel open, I said, "No, James Scraper has finally returned the manuscript of 'Grecian Dreams' that I sent him. You may recall he offered to cast his eye over it and perform any necessary edits."

I considered my former colleague in the Food Standards Agency to be an excellent choice to proffer an honest opinion on my book about our adventures moving to Greece, since his reputation for punctiliousness was second to none; nary a typo nor misplaced comma in a food premises inspection report escaping his eagle eye. Finding himself a tad bored once he retired, Scraper offered his service gratis; naturally I had snapped his hand off at the price. After duly printing off a paper copy of my manuscript, I had mailed it to England, waiting a seeming eternity for its return.

Breezing out to join us on the balcony, my

brother-in-law, Barry, grabbed the parcel containing my manuscript, sneering, "'Grecian Dreams'. Couldn't you come up with something a bit catchier than that, Victor? I have to say it puts me in mind of Grecian 2000 rather than a book about up-sticking to Greece."

As Barry heaped scorn on the title of my book, I self-consciously touched my hair, hoping that the latest application of date expired gunk left behind in Harold's bathroom cabinet wasn't too obvious. It wouldn't do to be the butt of jokes if the locals got wind that I applied a lotion to cover the grey. Still, compared to the liberal application of boot polish that Vangelis slapped on his head and his chest hair, my own touch-ups were modestly discreet. Considering Vangelis is married to a hairdresser, one really would think that the builder wouldn't be quite so obvious about it.

"I didn't hear you knock, Barry," I said churlishly. I hadn't forgotten how Barry had fed the first few chapters of my book through the shredder, albeit at Marigold's instigation. Now here he was, barging in and mocking the title of my literary masterpiece.

"For goodness' sake, Victor, since when has Barry had to knock?" Marigold chided. "Just ignore him, Barry. He's obviously taken umbrage with you criticising the title of his precious book. I have to agree with you, it's not very imaginative."

"If the pair of you have quite finished. 'Grecian Dreams' is just a working title," I fibbed. In truth, I had considered it to be the height of wit until Barry had burst my bubble by pointing out it could well provoke unfortunate connotations of male hair potions.

"You'd be better off with a jocular pun as your title. And chuck in some alliteration," Barry suggested. "Something along the lines of 'Old Fogies in France with Felines'…"

"We moved to Greece, you numpty," I said dismissively.

"And less of the old fogies," Marigold snapped.

"How about 'Geriatrics in Greece'?" Barry was coming perilously close to inciting the wrath of his sister. Seemingly lost in a world of her own, Marigold shushed us, indicating by gesture that she was thinking.

"I've got it," she said after remaining pensive for another minute. "Bucket to Greece."

"That's not half bad, Sis. A play on Victor's pseudonym. I like it and it's catchier than that dreadful 'Grecian Dreams'. What do you think, Victor?"

"'Bucket to Greece'. I don't know. Let me mull on it."

Snatching the now grime smeared, sticky parcel

back from Barry, I unknotted the string and stripped my book of its wrapping. To my horror, I saw that the pristine white pages had been utterly defaced with purple scrawl.

"I don't believe it!" I exclaimed in annoyance.

"What's wrong, dear? You've gone a funny colour," Marigold observed solicitously.

Flicking through the pages, I replied, "James Scraper has tarnished my manuscript with an excess of purple jottings…"

"Ah, I expect he's added some much-needed exclamation marks to make your prose sound more exciting. I don't know how many times I've advised you that they're all the rage in 'up-sticking' books. It's a pity that you never listen to a word that I say."

Marigold's obsession with plings was as unrelenting as my loathing for the way they indiscriminately littered the pages of so many modern books, seemingly dropped with as much gay abandon as Tiffany's gratuitous use of the word like. "You should have just taken my advice in the first place instead of involving that pernickety Scraper fellow in your writing project. I never took to him. I still remember the time you invited him and his peculiar wife to dinner and left me to entertain them alone…"

"How many more times do I need to apologise for being late that evening? You know I had a potential public health emergency on my hands; there was no way of knowing how many people had been served from that contaminated vat of rancid sauce..."

"You should have got James Scraper on the case instead of dealing with it alone; he was technically your superior at the time. At least if you'd dragged him out for his opinion on that suspect sauce, it would have spared me from listening to him cast aspersions on the hygienic state of our kitchen."

"Well, you did practice exceedingly lax sponge hygiene at the time." Marigold's mouth gaped in imitation of a goldfish. Before she could protest, I insisted, "I'm sorry, darling, but you did."

"But you would never have been so rude to point it out to the hostess as your colleague did. He was supposed to be off duty. Anyway, your department had no jurisdiction over domestic kitchens, you told me that yourself." It must be ten years since we entertained the Scrapers in our Manchester home but Marigold could certainly carry a grudge.

"How was his wife peculiar?" Barry piped up.

"Aside from being rather stunted, she was one of those annoying mutterers. You know the type; one has to lean in really close to make out a single word. In Mrs Scraper's case, I risked being knocked out by a nasty case of halitosis," Marigold said.

"It's a pity we hadn't discovered Mastic Tears back in those days. A generous glass of that would have spared you her bad breath," I quipped.

Tuning out as Marigold continued to vent about how offended she'd been when James Scraper took it upon himself to cast aspersions on the state of her mophead and her cutlery drawer, I glanced at the first few pages of the purple splodged manuscript, my eyes drawn to the numerous 'Too Pretentious' comments littering the margins. I bridled as I read Scraper's considered opinion that any readers that I could manage to attract, would need to leaf through a dictionary in order to understand a single word that I'd penned.

Grabbing the first page from me, Marigold skimmed Scraper's comments. "Well, I can see his point about your written use of English being a bit pompous and pretentious…"

"Don't forget sophomoric and highfalutin," I added, Scraper's slurs on my writing style already embedded in my mind. Still bristling at such unjustified criticism, I demanded, "What do you mean, you can see his point?"

"Well, here, darling. Look. You've written 'it simply wouldn't make a good impression on the locals if Barry disembogued a stream of vomitus on them from the superior height of the roof terrace.'"

"What's disembogued when it's at home?"

Barry asked.

"I've no idea. I suppose that's why James Scraper said Victor's readers would need a dictionary," Marigold replied.

"It means to evacuate the contents of your stomach," I clarified.

"Nobody talks like that. Even you don't talk like that, Victor," Barry scoffed. "If you mean hurl, why don't you just say so?"

"And here, too," Marigold added. "Did you really need to add such an obscure definition of venereal disease to explain why your initials are so offensive to you? It sounds as though you've copied it out of a medical tome from the twelfth century."

"He'd have had a job to do that, Sis," Barry interrupted. "The printing press wasn't invented until 1476."

"Fancy you knowing that," Marigold said, sisterly pride suffusing her features.

"I'm not just a pretty face," Barry responded.

"If I didn't know better, I'd think that Victor had spent a day traipsing around that ghastly museum in Athens with that sexually infected Ashley that Geraldine had in tow. What was that place called again, dear?" Marigold asked.

"The Wax Museum of Andreas Syggros located in the Hospital of Cutaneous and Venereal Diseases." I shuddered at the recollection of the nylon haired

Ashley's obsession with moulage and wax models, depicting deformities derived from a dose of the nasty affliction bearing my own unfortunate initials.

Relieving Marigold of the pages, I muttered in annoyance as I absorbed some of Scraper's criticism. Perchance he had a valid point and my prose could benefit from being a smidge more succinct. On reflection, perhaps it had been a tad unnecessary to replace commonplace words with fancier ones gleaned from poring over my well-thumbed thesaurus. Readers may well be distracted if they had to consult a dictionary to decipher my meaning.

Despite conceding that Scraper may have a point when it came to my substituting straightforward words with more obscure ones, some of his other remarks riled me.

"He's got a darn cheek criticising my use of tad. It's just a figure of speech which I intend to retain since it reflects my own voice in the book."

"You're not wrong there," Barry agreed. "You might think on what he had to say about replacing all those turgid words with something folks can relate to, but your use of tad is a definite Victorism that you want to retain."

Amazed that Barry's vocabulary even encompassed the word turgid, I took his points on-board, knowing that it would entail a major re-write of my book. At this rate it could be years before my great opus was unleashed on the reading public. I reflected that at least it would give me plenty of time to try out the title 'Bucket to Greece' in my mind.

# Chapter 2

*Dangerous Scaffolding*

**W**ith the manuscript of my book safely stashed away in an office drawer well out of sight of Marigold's prying eyes, I changed into my gardening clothes ready to accompany Barry to the old ruin we were doing up in the evenings.

"Surely you're not going out in public looking like that?" Marigold challenged me. "You look such a scruff."

"Would you prefer that I tackle that overgrown garden in a dinner jacket and tie?" I didn't bother to hide the sarcasm in my rhetorical question. Having learned to my cost that gardening in a decent button down was a hazardous venture as far as my wardrobe was concerned, I now outfitted myself in my tattiest clothes before taking on any gardening tasks at the old ruin.

"Don't forget that we're having dinner with Doreen and her new man in the taverna later," Marigold reminded me as I prepared to leave with my brother-in-law.

"He must want his head examining," Barry muttered as the pair of us took our leave.

After collecting a hoe, a five-litre container of vinegar, and a spray bottle, we rounded up a half-comatose Guzim from his shed at the bottom of my garden, the Albanian muttering under his breath that I was turning into as much of a slave-driver as Nikos. After the three of us duly piled into Barry's van, we found our progress impeded by Panos' tractor blocking the road.

"I don't think Yiota has got the hang of reversing the tractor," Barry observed.

"It's early days yet. I'm impressed that she's even giving it a go," I said with genuine admiration.

Following Panos' unexpected death several weeks earlier, his granddaughter, Yiota, had inherited his farmhouse, land and animals. Despite not having a farming background, Yiota was considering making a permanent move to Meli, keen to rise to the challenge of running the farm. Unsure if she would be able to make a go of it with her lack of experience, she had been granted three months exceptional compassionate leave from her job at KEP in order to give her the necessary time to sort out Panos' farm and reach a decision regarding her future. Throwing herself into the farming life with gusto, she had willingly accepted the offer of the experienced local farmers to show her the ropes, reliant on their expertise to guide her.

"If Yiota finds the farm is too much for her to cope with, she might keep the house and sell off the land. She says that she can probably get a transfer to the local KEP," I told Barry, referring to Yiota's public sector job at the Citizen Service Centre.

"She needs to get some proper help with the farm if she's going to make a go of it," Barry opined. "I know she's got the local farmers rallying round helping out with the livestock, but it won't do on a permanent basis."

Barry made a valid point. Whilst Nikos and some of the other locals were helping Yiota out with the crops and the livestock, they had little enough free time to take on the additional burden long-term. Running the farm was a lot for a novice though eager farmer to take on alone, plus Yiota would need to get the hang of flogging her products on a market stall. At least I could offer some practical guidance with that, having clocked up some experience on Panos' stall.

If only from a selfish perspective, I was rooting for Yiota to take to farming like a duck to water, hoping she could make a go of it and take over her grandfather's legacy. In the wake of Panos' passing, Yiota had become as close as family to Violet Burke, the two women spending time together and offering each other mutual comfort. My mother had even done Marigold a favour by palming Mabel the goat off on her surrogate granddaughter. After Mabel had served his purpose by chomping through weeds in the overgrown garden at the investment property, Marigold had put her foot down when I attempted to return the goat to our garden, claiming it gave her anxiety every time she pegged out the washing.

"It looks as though Kyrios Stavropoulos is coming to Yiota's aid with the tractor," I said, observing the communistic pensioner climb into the cab to offer guidance to the young woman.

As we waited for Kyrios Stavropoulos to shift the tractor, Barry told me that he had managed to rope in a labourer to help with the pointing job on the ramshackle house which he and Vangelis were tackling in the evenings.

"Since Blat recently moved into a rented place in Meli, we've used him a couple of times on jobs where we've needed extra help. He's proved himself to be industrious and reliable, and he's eager to take on the extra work," Barry said. "He also speaks pretty good English which makes it easier for me."

"Blat. That's an odd sounding name," I commented.

"He has an interesting background. He's an ethnic Albanian hailing from the Kosovo part of Yugoslavia. He and his wife fled Yugoslavia during the NATO bombing campaign of March 99, settling with distant relatives in Albania."

"So, they were refugees from the conflict?"

"That's right. His wife, Blerta, was pregnant at the time. She gave birth a couple of months after they crossed the Albanian border. You'll never guess what they called the sprog," Barry said, his eyes fairly dancing with amusement as he nudged me in the ribs.

"Fatos," I guessed, recalling that Guzim had named his firstborn son after the Albanian prime minister.

"No, it's better than that. They only went and called him Tony Blair…"

"Tony Blair! Have you lost the plot, Barry? Who in their right mind would name their firstborn child after Teflon Tony?"

"Not Tony Blair." Adopting an uncharacteristic raspy tone, Barry repeated the name, enunciating each syllable slowly. "Ton-i-bler. You're pronouncing it all wrong, Victor. You need to say it in a guttural accent to do it justice."

"Tonibler," I repeated in my best imitation of Marigold's Albanian. Sounding out the ridiculous name incredulously, I realised that Guzim's head had fallen onto my shoulder, the dozy shed dweller in imminent danger of spreading his drool onto my shirt. As I shoved Guzim away from me, he snorted in his sleep, his head hitting the window before slumping over his chest. I shuddered as he dribbled down the front of his second-hand Lycra bodysuit. The visible wet stain he created had a distinctive tang of curry about it.

If Guzim had been stuffing his face with one of my curries the minute he got back to his shed from his day labouring, it would account for his somnolent state. I would need to have another word with Marigold about feeding Guzim's recently acquired addiction to curry. The last time I had broached the matter, Marigold had retorted it was no skin off my nose if Guzim preferred to draw some of his gardening wages in a tasty jalfrezi or vindaloo, rather than hard cash.

"About time," Barry said, steering the van through the village as the tractor finally pulled away. "By the way, Cynthia said it's fine if Benjamin and Adam want to stay in our spare room when they fly over on Sunday."

"That's a relief," I said, knowing that Marigold had been in a terrible tizzy wondering where she could cram in all our guests who were coming over from England for our vow renewal service.

With Benjamin and Adam staying with Barry and Cynthia, it would free up our spare bedroom for my half-brother, Douglas, and his wife, Elaine, leaving the sofa bed in my office free for Marigold's best friend, Geraldine. Douglas and Elaine were only staying for a few days, leaving the twins with Elaine's mother so the children wouldn't miss school. I was in two minds about Geraldine coming over alone. Whilst it would spare me enduring the company of whatever peculiar fellow she currently had in tow, it would leave my neighbour, Papas Andreas, exposed to her predatory charms. It wouldn't do his reputation as a man of God any good to be seen fraternising with the foreign tourist again.

As Barry parked the van at the old house, I nudged Guzim awake. "*Ela, nystagmenos.*"

"What's a *nystaga* whatsit?" Barry asked.

"Sleepyhead," I translated, watching in horror as Guzim took a hefty gulp from the five-litre container of vinegar to wake himself up.

Spitting the vinegar out on the road in disgust as he climbed down from the van, Guzim complained that the water had gone off. "*To nero eichei fygei.*"

"*Einai xydi re kritini. To efera na chrisimopolithei os oikologiko dolofono zizanion,*" I said, meaning, 'It's vinegar, you cretin. I brought it to use as an ecological weed killer.' Guzim didn't even have the good sense to spit out the vinegar on any actual weeds.

"I take it that you've had Cynthia bending your ear about ecological weed killers," Barry said.

"Your wife is very persistent on the subject," I confirmed.

Gathering my gardening stuff, I disappeared in the direction of the undergrowth with Guzim, whilst Barry headed over to join Vangelis and their new labourer on the make-shift scaffolding propped up against one side of the house.

Since the scaffolding had first appeared a week ago, I had given up on my attempts to lecture Barry and Vangelis about its lack of compliance with any safety regulations; it had proved a fruitless task, akin to banging my head on a brick wall. My reasonable expectation that sturdy scaffolding would be installed around the house by a professional engineer was laughingly foiled when I witnessed the pitiful substitute Barry and Vangelis rigged up in a dangerous exercise of cutting corners. Rickety wooden boards scaling the length of metal poles propped precariously against one stone wall of the house, wobbled dangerously as soon as one of the builder's put their weight on the sagging wood.

"It's designed to be portable," Barry had assured me when I first vociferously raised my concerns. "We don't need anything fixed solid. Not only does fixed scaffolding cost the earth to get set up, it can't be easily shifted. With this, we can just move these poles easily around the house to where we need them."

"But it looks neither solid nor secure. You won't get the job done any quicker by taking shortcuts if you fall off and break a limb."

"That's rich coming from the expert who reckoned we could just slap a bit of concrete on over the holes instead of doing a proper pointing job...I tell you what, Victor, why don't you save your opinion for any hygiene violations that might crop up in the kitchen. It's about all you're qualified to express an expert opinion on."

"I'm not as naïve as you think when it comes to safety standards," I'd argued. "I think if a newly mopped floor qualifies as dangerous enough to require a 'Caution: Wet Floor' sign, then working on wobbly scaffolding with no discernible guard rails is a hazardous venture."

"And since when have you ever seen a 'Wet Floor' sign in a Greek establishment? If we faff about with the sort of scaffolding that you're going on about, it will cost a packet and create delays. You're happy to cover the extra costs, are you?"

"Just make sure that your accident insurance is up to date," I countered before skulking back to my weeds, recalling my credit card was already feeling the pinch from our entrepreneurial property venture.

Raising the same issue with Vangelis, my pleas had fallen on deaf ears when he revealed he was as happy-go-lucky as Barry in the matter of lax safety standards. The only concession I had won from the pair of them was an agreement that they would wear safety helmets when scaling the rickety scaffolding. I should add that the concession was only won when I threatened to dob Barry into his sister if he refused to safety helmet up.

Directing Guzim as he sprayed the weeds with vinegar, I noticed he appeared to be in a particularly monosyllabic, sulky mood, sending vitriolic looks in the direction of Barry's new labourer. Worn down by his surliness, I finally rose to Guzim's bait, asking him why his nose was put out of joint.

Gesticulating with his thumb towards the labourer that I presumed was Blat, Guzim complained that he could have slapped some concrete on with a trowel, adding that labouring paid more than gardening. *"Tha borousa na to kano afto. I ergasia plironei perissotera apo tin kipourki."*

Having no intention of explaining that Vangelis had vowed never to be suckered into employing Guzim again due to his habit of tugging on the heart strings to loosen the purse strings, I came up with a convenient fib, telling Guzim that it was much too dangerous for him to risk working on hazardous scaffolding when he had five sprogs to support. Duped into thinking I was concerned about his safety, the Albanian shed dweller resumed his spraying with a bit more energy and a sight less grumbling.

# Chapter 3

*Victor is Mistaken for the Hired Help*

Noticing that the new labourer had climbed down from the scaffolding for a crafty cigarette break, I wandered over to introduce myself. The few details that Barry had given me about Blat had naturally piqued my curiosity about a Kosovar who had named his firstborn son Tonibler: it was just too delicious for words. Approaching the young man, I saw that although he was as slight of build as Guzim, his muscular arms hinted at superior strength. His almost black hair was cut in a short back and sides style reminiscent of the military, complimented with a neatly trimmed chin strap beard running from ear to ear, tracing his angular jaw. Since the young man appeared to be no more than twenty-years-old, I surmised it couldn't be the Blat that Barry had spoken of after all; according to my calculations, Blat had a six-year-old son and this youngster was barely out of short trousers himself. Nevertheless, I decided to proceed with the introductions since whoever he was, he was on my payroll.

"*Yassas. Vlepo oti ergazeste sklira*," I said in greeting, telling him that I noticed he had been working hard.

"*Douleveis sklira kai ston kipo*," he replied, saying that I worked hard in the garden too. As he offered me a cigarette, I realised that rather than twigging that I was in fact the owner of the property and his employer, he had mistaken me for the gardening help. I reflected that Marigold had been on point when she'd objected to my venturing out in my tattiest clothes. By spurning her advice, I only had myself to blame for the young man assuming I was the hired help. I made a mental note to ask Marigold to pick up a Panama hat for me when she was next in town. The addition of some natty headgear would surely send out the right message to any uninformed labourers.

Eager to clear up the likely mix up, I introduced myself, telling the young man that it was my house he was working on, mine and Mr Barry's. "*Eimai o Victor. Afto einai to spiti mou sto opoio douleveis, diko mou kai Kyrios Barry.*"

"You are the English, Mr Victor. I think you were the gardener, please to accept the apology." His wide amiable smile detracted attention from his prominent nose, exposing his equally prominent chipped teeth. "Please to converse in the English, Mr Victor. I am Blat. I want to speak in the great English language of your great nation, Great Britain. I spend many hours to learn the great language of the Great Britain."

"Your English is very good, it puts my Greek to shame," I praised him, noting that he had impeccable manners.

"I waste the time to learn the Greek language," Blat spat in contempt. "Luckily, he is very easy to pick up."

"That's a matter of opinion," I countered. Despite applying myself to studying Greek for almost three years, I still struggled with the language of my adopted country and had yet to master Greek pronunciation with an authentic accent. I was painfully aware that whenever I opened my mouth and spoke in Greek, I still sounded like a bumbling foreigner.

"I need to speak Greek to work in Greece until I can fulfil the dream of moving to the great nation of Great Britain."

"You want to move to Britain?" I parroted.

"Yes, to live in the great land of the Tonibler. Perhaps, Mr Victor, you could put in the good word in the ear of the great Tonibler. You know him, yes."

"Well, not personally," I admitted, stifling an involuntary snort at Blat's pronunciation of Tony Blair

Rifling through the pocket of his overalls, Blat produced a grubby looking envelope. "This is the photocopy of the letter the great Tonibler send to me. It is my most treasure possession. I have the original framed and it hang on the wall in our home."

Extracting the copy of the letter from the grubby envelope, I read it aloud. "Mr Blair was grateful to you for taking the time and trouble to write to him and very flattered you chose to name your son, Tonibler, after him."

"It was the great honour to receive the letter from the great Tonibler about my son, Tonibler. I am still waiting for the great Tonibler to reply to my many letters asking him when he will bring my family to live in the great nation of Great Britain. I tell myself, he must be the busy man to not reply."

"Well, this letter isn't actually from Tony Blair. It is from one of his minions," I pointed out.

"I do not know the English word minions.

Please to explain it to me, Mr Victor."

"The letter is from one of the prime minister's assistants," I clarified.

"This is why I am happy to work for you and the Mr Barry. You can help me to expand my English vocabulary, yes, and help me to take my family to the Great Britain."

"I'm afraid that I don't have any influence when it comes to British immigration policy," I admitted. "Don't you have any plans to return to Albania or Yugoslavia?"

"When we came from Albanian Kosovo, we settle in Kukes. It is a mountainous area of Albania and very poor. There is no work, nothing for us there. Most of the people must to migrate abroad for earning the living. I work as the labourer here and my wife, Blerta, clean the houses and iron the dresses. We work in Greece until the day when the great Tonibler invite us to move to the great land of Great Britain and bring up the Tonibler in the great capital city, Great London."

"It's just London, not Great London," I corrected him, noting his tendency to hyperbolically refer to everything to do with Britain as great.

"I dream of London ever since I hear about the great Dick Whittington. I tell my son, Tonibler, that one day he will follow in the footsteps of the great Dick Whittington and become the Mayor of the

Great London."

Realising that Blat had clearly fallen for the aspirational fantasy that the streets of London are paved in gold, I decided it would be prudent to disillusion him of such a foolish notion and explain how the myth came about. I told Blat that according to legend, Dick Whittington was a penniless orphan, born in the fourteenth century, who traipsed through the rat-infested streets of England to London where he had heard the streets were paved with gold. When he arrived, he discovered that in reality the streets were mucky and he needed a cat to control the mice and rats in his humble attic abode.

"It is not the problem. My son, Tonibler, has the cat. When I wrote to the great Tonibler about moving to the great land of Great Britain, I did not to tell him about bringing the cat. I must write again and tell him we are three the people and one cat. I have made the promise to Tonibler, that I will buy him a newt when we move to the great city of Great London."

"I'm not sure that bribing Tony Blair with the promise of a newt will do anything to facilitate your move to England," I said.

"You do not think a newt would be the great pet for my son?" As Blat spoke, I realised that I was beginning to confuse my Tony Blairs with my

Toniblers. It was all extremely surreal. "The great Ken Livingstone is the mayor of the great city of Great London and has the newt. Perhaps the Tonibler must leave the cat in Greece in case it eats the newt. I will ask the great Tonibler to advise when I write to him in the great Downing Street. Can I ask you the question, Mr Victor?"

"Yes, of course."

"Why do you give up the living in the wonderful Great Britain to come to live in the third world country of Greece?"

Bridling at the slur on my adopted homeland, I explained to Blat that I considered Greece a beautiful, warm and welcoming country, and that far from being third world, it was part of the great European Union.

"Great Britain is not quite the paradise you imagine," I warned him. "The roads are very congested and the weather can be pretty dismal."

"It is the paradise to me. It is the home of the great Tonibler. One day my son will have the opportunity to become the important rich mayor of the Great London"

"And you don't see any opportunities for your son in your homeland?"

"Too many Kosovars and Albanians are drawn into the life of crime. I teach Tonibler that if he work hard and learn good the language of the Great

Britain, one day he will be the great important man."

"Well, it's certainly an admirable ambition."

"Mr Victor, I have the proposing…"

"Proposal," I guessed.

"You would to give Tonibler the lesson in your great language so he can learn it perfect. My wife can bring him to your house and iron the dresses for no money for the payment for the lesson."

"Well, I'm not sure…" I faltered.

"With your instruction, Tonibler will be the equal of his peers in the great city of London when the great Tonibler sorts out the arrangement to move us there."

Although I had never contemplated teaching English on the side, it was hard to ignore the imploring look in Blat's eyes. I reflected that Marigold was always complaining about ironing in the heat; she had certainly been a tad remiss of late when it came to starching my collars and adding a snappy traveller's crease to my slacks.

Prostrating himself on the ground in a manner more than a little reminiscent of Guzim, Blat threw his arms around my shins, gushing, "Please to teach Tonibler the good English, Mr Victor."

"I suppose I could give it a whirl with the odd bout of instruction," I conceded, finding it hard to say no to Blat's supplicating look.

"Thank you, Mr Victor, thank you. Can I tell Blerta to bring Tonibler to your house tomorrow afternoon after the school finish?"

"That doesn't give me much time to prepare," I dithered. As the pressure on my shins increased, I reluctantly agreed, wondering what on earth I was letting myself in for. "I could fit him in tomorrow afternoon as I have some free time but it can't be a regular thing. I have my own work obligations as a rep several days a week."

"Tomorrow, Mr Victor," Blat repeated. As I watched him turn and scale the scaffolding with goat-like agility, I couldn't help but think that I'd been played by an expert manipulator. Still, I reflected, I was perfectly capable of tutoring one six-year-old boy for the odd hour and Marigold would be delighted to get out of the ironing. It wouldn't make too much of a dent in my day to spend some time with Blat's child and I must admit to being curious if the young Tonibler bore any resemblance to the British prime minister.

Returning to my gardening duties, I mentioned to Guzim that Blat seemed like a nice man. "*O Blat fainetai oraios antras.*"

My remark was met with a glob of spit flying past my foot and a volley of Albanian expletives. Clearly Guzim had the huff about something.

"*O Blat den einai sostos Alvanos. O Blat milaei*

*Gheg Alvanika, ochi katallila Toska Alvanika opos ego*,"
Guzim sneered. Telling me that Blat wasn't a
proper Albanian, he added that Blat speaks Gheg
Albanian, not proper Tosk Albanian like him. Slamming the hoe in the ground, Guzim opined that Blat
was probably in Greece without any papers. *"Mal-
lon einai stin Ellada choris chartia."*

Guzim's sullen complaints reminded me of the
petty jealousy he had harboured towards Sampaguita, until I had put him straight. Unwilling to
get into a heated argument with Guzim about Blat's
possibly illegal status in Greece, I retorted that Blat
had a work permit and Vangelis paid his insurance,
*"O Blat eichei adeia ergasias kai O Vangelis plironei tin
asfaleia tou."*

Although I was clueless about Blat's immigration status, I knew that Vangelis was a stickler for
ensuring he always paid his worker's insurance
even if he was a bit lax when it came to enforcing
safety standards.

Leaving Guzim to get on with the weeding, I
wandered over to the large prickly pear plants, examining their pads. Shielding my hands in a pair of
gardening gloves, I proceeded to pick the pads from
the plants. Having recalled that Benjamin had recommended utilising them in my cooking, I decided
to incorporate them in a large vat of curry that I
planned to knock up the next day. It would come in

handy to feed our houseguests on the cheap next week. I considered that I was perfectly capable of multi-tasking and intended to cook up the curry while tutoring young Tonibler in his ABCs.

# Chapter 4

*All Loved-Up*

V ictor, look at the time. We're going to be late meeting Doreen and her beau," Marigold chided as I dragged my weary body into the house after toiling in the garden at the investment property. "Do get out of those scruffy old clothes quickly and smarten up."

"Have I time for a shower or would you prefer that I just pass a wet sponge over my sweaty pits and spray some air freshener down the front of my pants?"

"There's no need to take that sarcastic tone, dear. You've obviously been spending too much time with Captain Vasos." In spite of her disapproving tone, Marigold's eyes sparkled with amusement. "You're the one that is always harping on about how you hate to be tardy."

"If I had my way, we'd be so tardy this evening that Doreen might have cleared off by the time we arrive," I muttered under my breath as I headed to the shower. I was in no mood for enduring Marigold's friend simpering all over her Greek boyfriend like a lovesick schoolgirl. The very thought of it was enough to put me off my food.

After I'd lingered under the hot shower until the water ran cold, Marigold nagged me to throw my clothes on at speed, practically dragging me out of the house with my body still damp and my tie unknotted. Although I had planned to tell her about my meeting with Blat and the arrangement for me to tutor his young son in return for his wife taking on the Bucket ironing, I could barely get a word in edgeways with Marigold chuntering on about Doreen's situation as we strolled along to the taverna.

Having finally rid the house of Doreen, she remained a frequent topic of conversation amongst the local expat community. After packing her bags, Doreen returned to her marital home but not to her marriage. Norman had been relegated to the spare bedroom to bed down with his traffic cones, while

Doreen and the cat took over the master bed. Whereas once Doreen and Norman had simply tolerated each other in their passionless marriage, now that they were back living under the same roof, they spent their waking hours sniping at one another. I had much preferred it when I had not been privy to anything pertaining to their personal situation. Presuming they muddled along like many married couples, I had been blissfully unaware of any cracks in their relationship until the cracks splintered into the gaping canyon which culminated in Doreen walking out and landing on the Bucket doorstep with her suitcase.

Slowing down to match my pace to Marigold's unsuitable heels, I basked in the greenery of the village. A sudden short burst of midday rain had revived the parched grass and wild herbs, leaving the air replete with the intoxicating scent of nature's freshness. If the summer was long and dry, it could be an age before my olfactory senses were treated to such delights again. Pickles shot past us on the street; having gained our attention, the cat hurled itself on the ground, rolling about in the dirt before stopping to lick itself. I marvelled that the cat didn't suffer from a permanent bad stomach from ingesting every bit of grime and muck that attached to his fur.

Marigold tugged my sleeve, demanding my

attention. "Can you believe that Norman has drawn up a colour coded rota to avoid the two of them coming to blows in the kitchen?"

"It sounds like an eminently sensible arrangement to me. There are sharp knives and cast-iron frying pans to consider," I pointed out.

"At least Doreen doesn't have to clean up his experimental patisserie messes anymore. Norman pays Theo to go in for an hour each morning..."

"Which has done my mother out of a job..."

"Well, Doreen's quite relieved about that. Your mother was rather vocal about what she considered Doreen's slovenly housekeeping skills..."

"To be fair to Doreen, she did always keep the place as neat as a pin," I concurred. My mother could be a tad harsh towards anyone that failed to keep pace with her exacting hygiene standards.

"Which wasn't easy considering how messy Norman is. Anyway, Doreen is too timid to stand up to Violet Burke. I think she's more than a little afraid of her. Doreen says that she can put up with the kitchen arrangement tolerably well as long as Norman keeps out of her garden."

The unhappily married couple had reached an impasse in their relationship, each refusing to move out of the marital home and risk relinquishing it to the other. Doreen regularly bent Marigold's ear with her complaints; in turn, Marigold insisted on repeating everything to me, even though I wasn't remotely interested in the minutiae of her friend's life.

Norman had finally grown something resembling a jellied backbone: putting his foot down when Doreen had taken up with her new Greek fellow, Norman point blank refused to allow Doreen to let his replacement over the threshold. Norman insisted that if she wanted to flaunt her new chap, she must do it elsewhere. Personally, I considered Norman's attitude short sighted. For all he knew, he could possibly have bonded with Doreen's new love interest over a shared fascination with traffic cones or cake recipes. Stranger things have been known to happen.

Despite my recent best efforts to hide behind the toilet roll display in the village shop, Norman had managed to corner me. Droning on in my ear, he aired his hopes that Doreen would simply waltz off into the sunset with her new chap and leave him to the newfound delights of the bachelor life. Whilst Norman claimed that he didn't have the remotest interest in what his estranged wife got up to, he considered that if she got up to it under his roof, it would make him a laughing stock. It appeared to have escaped his notice that he was already a figure of ridicule due to his obsession with traffic cones.

Still, their marital stand-off left Marigold in a

bit of a quandary as we all had to muddle along in Meli: whilst insisting we couldn't be seen to be taking sides, she naturally sided with Doreen. Marigold's solution was to insist I remain pally with Norman despite my never having considered the tedious bore a pal in the first place. Marigold was still in two minds over whether or not to extend an invitation to Norman for our imminent vow renewal service, since Doreen and her boyfriend would be attending. Whilst of the opinion that Norman's dull presence would do nothing to enhance any social gathering, I kept my own counsel, leaving my wife to make the decision. I knew from experience that if I proffered my two penn'orth on the matter and things didn't go according to plan, I would be the one to end up in the doghouse again.

As we reached the taverna, I squared my shoulders, mentally girding myself for a dreary evening ahead. I had endured quite enough of Doreen's company when she'd occupied the Bucket spare bedroom for what felt like a seeming eternity. Hoping that one of my Greek friends would put in an appearance and join us, thus diluting Doreen's cloying company, I sorely felt the loss of Panos. My farmer friend could always be relied upon to spice up a dull evening with his scintillating chatter about root vegetables and sheep.

Peering inside the taverna, I noticed that apart

from the loved-up couple, the place was empty with no sign of Nikos or Dina.

"They look awfully lovey-dovey," Marigold hissed as we approached the table where Doreen and her new chap were gazing into one another's eyes, oblivious to our arrival. "I hope we don't have to suffer through yet another recounting of the moment they met."

As Doreen prised herself apart from her new boyfriend to air-kiss Marigold, Manolis greeted me with a hearty slap on the back, his Texan twang quite prominent as he pulled out a chair for me, saying, "Victor, I hope you're hungry. My treat tonight. We're planning a blow out on chicken and all the fixins." As if to emphasise the point, he rubbed his round stomach in a familiar gesture that reminded me of Spiros' similar habit, a practice which always put me in mind of him cultivating a miniature undertaker in his belly.

I hoped that Manolis didn't have any expectations that the fixins would be anything other than the standard bread, cheese, salad and chips. Nikos could be very touchy when it came to suggestions about how he could expand and improve on his menu. I couldn't imagine he would react well to any ideas about giving his traditional Greek food a Texan twist.

Dear reader, I confess to leading you on,

allowing you to believe that we were meeting Doreen and Christos. I must have forgotten to mention that Doreen and Manolis were newly besotted with each other, the Greek-Texan implant replacing his oily brother, Christos, on Doreen's romantic radar the moment the two of them clapped eyes on one another. Allow me to press the rewind button and bring you up to date.

Christos, the oily Greek with a weakness for redheads, particularly my wife, had invited the newly Titian dyed Doreen to join him for Easter Sunday lunch at his house several weeks earlier. Doreen, in two minds whether to accept the invitation or not, had confided in Marigold that she was reluctant to join Christos as she suspected that he had designs on seducing her. After enduring Norman's neglect of her womanly needs, Doreen was flattered by Christos' attention even though she admitted she had only encouraged him to provoke Norman's jealousy. Even though her ruse was a dismal flop because Norman was completely indifferent to his wife's antics, Doreen continued to string Christos along; she found anyone showing an interest in her, a welcome novelty.

It had been so long since Doreen had attracted any male attention that she wasn't sure if the vibes she was picking up from Christos were lascivious or not, though she had certainly been forced to remove more than one of his unwanted hands when they landed with a bit too much enthusiasm on unmentionable parts of her anatomy. On the offchance that Doreen's sexual radar was on-point, Marigold had advised her friend to enjoy the lunch date but to carry a can of hairspray in her handbag. When Doreen fluffed her hair in confusion, Marigold explained that the hairspray was to use as a chemical weapon to fight off Christos' advances if he became overly amorous over the Easter *kokoretsi*. I still flinch at the thought of amorous being used in the same sentence as offal wrapped intestines.

Doreen confided in Marigold that whilst she was flattered by Christos' apparent interest, she supposed that she ought to consign her dreams of romance to the dustbin. Rather than going out of his way to woo Doreen romantically, Christos seemed only intent on making a conquest and Doreen wasn't too keen on the idea of being conquered.

"I just wanted a man to make me feel good about myself," Doreen whined to Marigold, who in turn repeated everything verbatim to me. Having witnessed Christos' lame seduction technique when he had turned his charms on Gordon at Milton's fancy dress party, before realising the tart had a hairy chest, I suspected that Christos' intentions towards Doreen were not in the slightest bit honourable. If she succumbed to his crude *kamaki*, I considered that she was in danger of becoming nothing more than a notch on his bedpost before he wantonly discarded her.

"And does Christos make you feel good about yourself?" my wife had prodded her friend.

"Some of the time. But he definitely has a roving eye and I think he's still infatuated with you." It had taken a lot for Doreen to admit the truth that she was only playing second-fiddle to Marigold in Christos' straying eyes. Unfortunately, the oily Greek remained infatuated with my wife.

With no other Easter Sunday invitations on the cards, Doreen had duly armed herself with a can of hairspray and accepted Christos' offer of lunch at his house, worrying she may be walking into a lion's den full of her Greek suitor's non-English speaking relatives. It turned out Doreen need not have worried about making a good impression on any of Christos' family. She was the only guest present, a situation that made the hair on the back of her neck stand on end when she realised that Christos had managed to get her alone. Moreover, he had an unmistakably lecherous look plastered on his face.

Fearing that she may need to utilise the chemical weapon in her handbag, the sight of the wood-fired cooking spit alarmed her. Even Doreen realised it would be going over the top if Christos' frisky advances were met with an explosion from her waving the aerosol canister around in too close proximity to the naked flames. Fortunately, Doreen's honour was spared when Christos' brother Manolis put in an appearance and she met what is now her new boyfriend for the very first time.

"We thought that the two of you had stood us up this evening." Doreen's words brought me back to the present as we joined her and Manolis at the taverna table.

"It's Victor's fault that we are late." Although Marigold put the blame squarely on my shoulders, she redeemed herself in my eyes by adding in a sarcastic tone, "But surely the pair of you wouldn't have noticed if we never turned up. You seem to only have eyes for each other these days."

I groaned inwardly when Marigold's words prompted Doreen to go all mushy on us. Grabbing Manolis' hand and pressing it to her cheek, she gushed, "Do you remember the moment we met, darling?"

"How could I ever forget it, my sweet?" Manolis replied, leaning in to tenderly drop a kiss on the top of Doreen's newly bottle-blonde perm.

Preening like a cat that has got the cream, Doreen said, "Did we tell the two of you how we met?"

"Just the odd time or two…" I said, hoping Doreen would get the hint and not bore us all over again with her account of how she had met the love of her life.

"It was fated." Manolis encouraged Doreen to continue even though it was patently obvious that he was well up on the circumstances that threw them together.

"Well, it's not as if Marigold hasn't mentioned how the two of you met in B&Q more than once," Doreen said, targeting me with one of the withering looks that she'd picked up from my wife.

Feeling the pressure of Marigold's hand on my thigh, I interpreted the look she was sending me, letting me know we ought to indulge Doreen if she wanted to rehash her life-changing first meeting with the Greek-Texan yet again.

"It was over Easter Sunday lunch," Doreen began.

"I was not invited even though I am forced through circumstance to live in the same house as my brother…" Manolis added.

"But fate intervened and brought us together…" Doreen twittered on. Since by then I was reluctantly intimately familiar with every last sentimental detail, I will condense their recollections, omitting the excessive mush they regurgitated when recounting their first meeting.

Fortunately, Christos' unwanted advances were tamed when his brother, Manolis, strode into the courtyard. It was the first time that Manolis and Doreen had ever met one another, though it later transpired that Manolis had admired the English woman from afar, considering her a fine figure of a woman. When Manolis walked into the courtyard where Christos had set up the lamb on the spit, Doreen's attention had been drawn to the stocky Greek with the luscious pornstache. Cradling three cats in his arms, Manolis succumbed to such a bout of violent sneezing that even his moustache quivered. Passing the cats to Christos, Manolis shouted something in Greek that was indecipherable to Doreen's ears. However, she was able to interpret Christos' shocking intention when he grabbed the cats and marched them over to the spit, making a skewering gesture.

The cat-hating Christos had hatched a cunning plan to rid the house of his brother by giving house room to three strays that he had picked up from the bins, hoping the cats would exacerbate Manolis' allergic reaction to felines and force him to leave. The flaw in Christos' plan was exposed when despite Manolis suffering from the close proximity of the cats, he bore them no ill-will: unlike his brother, Manolis was quite fond of the creatures.

When Christos threatened to skewer the cats,

he revealed his misothery, a trait which Doreen, as a cat lover, found deplorable. With Christos' true nature outed, the scales instantly fell from Doreen's eyes and she saw him for the oily lech he was. As Doreen and Manolis bonded over their mutual contempt of Christos using the cats for his own despicable ends, they decreed that Christos wasn't a fit person to have custody of the cats. Between them, they vowed that they would find the strays a new home. Since Doreen knew that Norman would never tolerate any feline additions once she moved back to the marital home, a plan was hatched to palm the cats off on Edna. In spite of the Hancocks' home already being overrun with too many cats to count, Edna was always a sucker when it came to taking in any felines going spare.

Tuning out, I reflected on the irony of Doreen and Norman sharing their marital home being quite similar to the situation of the two brothers, Manolis and Christos, living together yet loathing the other. Each of the four refused to move out of their respective homes, preferring to suffer an intolerable living situation in order to prevent the other person from getting their hands on the property and making some legal claim as the resident in situ.

"Manolis inherited the house jointly with his brother but Christos is trying to claim the house as his alone." Doreen filled us in on the sibling quarrel that I was already party to. Although the newly smitten couple would be inseparable given the choice, their opportunities to meet in private were severely curtailed by Norman's stubborn refusal to admit Manolis over his threshold and by Christos' equally stubborn refusal to grant houseroom to Doreen. Christos' attitude was particularly dog-in-the-manger: he had not only lost his potential female conquest to the brother he detested, but his cunning plan to rid the house of Manolis by using the cats to exacerbate his brother's allergies had been foiled when the two of them had joined forces against him by forcing him to hand over the felines or risk being reported to animal welfare for animal cruelty.

With nowhere to meet and consummate their passion, Doreen and Manolis were limited to meeting in public places, but the awkward situation had clearly done nothing to douse their ardour.

As Doreen delighted in regurgitating every detail of how she had discovered true love when she met Manolis, I was distracted by the sight of a familiar figure outside the taverna. Realising that if Marigold and I had the misfortune to encounter the fellow again, it would be highly embarrassing, I yanked my wife's arm, instructing her, "Quick, duck under the table."

# Chapter 5

*Not All Rumpled Like Richard Burton*

V ictor, what on earth are you playing at?" Marigold demanded as I yanked her arm and dragged her under the table.

"I just spied that unspeakable Nordic estate agent outside… it would be terribly embarrassing if he spotted us in here."

"Oh, my goodness. Not the cold-fish who tried to sell us a bridge?" Marigold gasped.

"The very same," I confirmed, pulling the paper tablecloth over the edge of the table and adjusting it to better conceal our presence. I was grateful that Marigold complied with my warning with such alacrity, without any regard for the unmopped state of the dusty taverna floor. Like me, she had no wish to run into the slimy agent that we had so un-ceremoniously dumped after engaging his services to find us a house in the Mani. By any polite stand-ards, the way we had ditched him would be consid-ered rude beyond measure; rather than informing him that we were dispensing with his services, we had simply given him the slip, hiding behind a handy bougainvillea in the taverna where we fortu-itously chanced upon Spiros.

Manolis' head appeared beneath the table. "You two can come out now, the coast is clear," he informed us, his lips curled in suppressed amuse-ment beneath his pornstache. "I bet you were hid-ing from that shyster estate agent…he's just driven off."

"You know him?"

"Christos had him round to value the house… we soon sent him packing with a flea in the ear when we found out how much the con artist in-tended to beef up the price so he could earn himself a hefty commission," Manolis explained as we emerged from under the table in a slightly dishev-elled and dusty state.

"I didn't realise the house was up for sale. I thought you wanted to turn it into a guesthouse," I said, vigorously brushing the dust from my slacks.

"The house isn't for sale. Christos reckoned we should flip a coin and the loser could buy the other out. Stupid idea. It turns out neither of us can afford to buy out the other, at least with the price tag that foreigner agent reckoned it was worth. I can't do anything about turning the house into a guesthouse unless Christos moves out. He would put off the guests."

"Christos shouldn't be let loose anywhere near women," Marigold opined. "His persistence borders on the creepy."

"Isn't that Barry outside?" Doreen said, waving enthusiastically to attract my brother-in-law's attention.

As Barry stepped into the taverna, he immediately earned a dressing down from his sister. "Really, Barry, I know this place is a bit spit and sawdust but surely you could have changed out of your scruffy overalls."

"I'm not stopping, Sis, so you can stop worrying that I'll lower the tone."

"You're working late," I noted.

"I'd only just got home when Vangelis phoned and dragged me out again. An estate agent had some English bloke looking at a house near the square...it was his second viewing and he was keen to get a builder's estimate on the work that needs doing. They were planning to grab a bite to eat in here and talk figures but the estate agent reckoned it was a bit of a dump. They've gone off to find somewhere posher. I don't want to miss Anastasia's bedtime so I've left Vangelis to deal with the schmoozing."

"We had a narrow escape, Victor," Marigold hissed, relieved that we had avoided an embarrassing encounter. In defence of our deplorable behaviour, the estate agent had played on our naivety, relegating us to the category of gullible foreigners. He would undoubtedly have ripped us off if we hadn't taken evasive action to escape his clutches.

"That's excellent, Barry. Going into business with Vangelis was a shrewd move," I said, reflecting that the two of them were never short of work.

"It will be very handy if you land a renovation job in the village. It will cut down on any travel," Marigold enthused.

"There is that, I suppose, but I'm not so sure that the bloke who has his eye on the house will be easy to work for," Barry said in a despondent tone. "I thought Sherry was bad enough when we did her place up but this potential buyer takes the biscuit."

"How so?" I enquired.

"He's a right know-it-all, completely full of himself. He's been living in Greece for years and doesn't he just want everyone to know it. The way he was harping on, you'd think he knew more about the country than Vangelis."

"Has he been living locally?" I asked.

"No, he's been living on one of the islands. Corfu, I think he said. According to him, the place has been overrun with so many British expats that he may as well have been living back in old Blighty. He started every sentence with 'I've been living in Greece for sixteen years.'"

"But surely that's good," I posited. "If he's been in Greece for so long, he must speak the language and should find it a doddle to integrate into village life."

"Well, he rubbed me up the wrong way and no mistake. Still, if he buys the place, we won't turn down the job. The house he's got in mind needs a fair bit of work. The cash will come in handy towards the renovations on our place."

Barry perked up a tad at the prospect of earning some surplus cash to put towards our joint venture. Thus far, he had saved us some money by claiming a second-hand bathroom suite we could use but he hadn't managed to luck out on a used kitchen that he could fix up.

"With a bit of luck, that Macey bloke will think he's too good to eat in here. I couldn't stomach him looking down his nose at me when I'm tucking into Dina's chips. Right, I'd best be getting back if I want to see my daughter before bedtime."

"Give little Ana a kiss from us," Marigold called out as he left.

"Dag nab it, we've been sitting here for ages without any sign of service," Manolis complained.

"Dag nab it?" I parroted, raising my eyebrows questioningly.

"It's Texan for flipping heck," Doreen said, giggling girlishly. "I've been picking up a bit of American from Manolis."

"Surely it would be more useful if you picked up some Greek from him," I pointed out.

"I'm having a go. *Suga suga*," Doreen protested, botching the Greek for slowly, slowly.

Smiling indulgently at Doreen, Manolis took her hand. "Your pronunciation is a bit out of kilter, my love. It's *siga siga*. 'Suga Suga' is a song by Baby Bash, Doreen *mou*. It used to come on the radio back in the gas station. A catchy tune."

"*Siga siga*," Doreen repeated. "I do love the way you are so patient with me, Manolis. Tackling a foreign language at our age is quite the challenge, isn't it, Marigold? I do admire you for keeping at it."

"I think you have a few years on me, Doreen," Marigold bristled at the implication she was anything past middle-aged.

"Well, if you'll excuse me, I'll just pay a visit to the little girls' room. I do hope your mother has been in with the bleach, Victor. The facilities here leave a lot to be desired."

Dropping a kiss on the top of Manolis' head, Doreen headed off to the lavatory, practically walking on air when Manolis told her that her outfit set off her curves nicely. In truth, the way that Doreen's mauve blouse strained tightly over her ample bosom brought home her striking resemblance to Roy Barraclough dressed up as Cissie Braithwaite in the comedy double act, Cissie and Ada: the similarity was certainly more pronounced now that Doreen's hair had been doused in hairdresser's bleach.

"I think it's cute the way Doreen calls the restroom the little girls' room. I never to hear anyone call the gas station restroom that in Texas," Manolis said. His observation surprised me since I considered the phrase pretty universal.

"Actually, Doreen's use of the term 'the little girls' room' is completely redundant since there is only one toilet to service all the customers," I said.

"Victor's right. We ladies tend to avoid it if we can. Doreen must have been caught short," Marigold said. "Whenever we voice our complaints that the toilet door lacks a lock and anyone could just barge in and catch us out in a compromising position, Nikos just dismisses us by saying, 'Put the foot on the door.'"

"He seems to overlook the fact that it is a bit of a stretch, even for someone of my elevated height with long legs," I quipped.

"Doreen is certainly blooming," Marigold said to Manolis, before adding a backhanded compliment. "Going blonde has taken years off her."

Having managed to avoid Doreen for the last fortnight or so, I had to admit that I agreed with Marigold's assessment. Finding love in her autumn years had softened Doreen's demeanour and her new delicately coiled permed hairdo suited her. It struck me that the way in which Manolis flattered her figure with endless compliments had allowed Doreen to embrace her recent weight gain; she seemed quite comfortably content with the extra pounds that she had only recently been desperate to lose since binge eating Norman's patisserie concoctions as though she could eat her way out of her boring marriage. Marigold had mentioned that Doreen had dropped all mention of embarking on a diet because Manolis appreciated a woman with a fuller figure.

"The service is terrible in here tonight," Manolis reiterated. "Not so much as a crust of bread to keep us from starving."

"I wonder where Dina has got to," I said, thinking it wasn't like her to fail to put in an appearance. "I'll pop outside and ask Nikos if he knows what's keeping her."

I found Nikos hard at work outside, hosing down the courtyard and the plastic chairs. Narrowly avoiding drenching my slacks with the spray from the hosepipe, he grumbled, "People will to want to eat in the outside soon. I must to clean. Everywhere the dead insect and the cat mucky."

I suppressed a snort at Nikos' words, noting how my mother was beginning to influence his choice of English vocabulary. Looking around the courtyard, I shuddered at the sight of wasps dive-bombing into the bloated stomach of a disembowelled mouse. Insects that were likely lower down in the pecking order, crawled over the severed tail of the mouse, no doubt hurled to one side by whatever predator had been at work dissecting the rodent. Perchance Cynthia's vile mutant tom, Kouneli, had been making its early evening rounds, engaging in a spot of murder before turning its thoughts to ravaging strays.

Turning my back on the scene of nature's carnage, I asked Nikos, "What's happened to Dina? She isn't inside..."

"She went to visit Violet Burke. Is she not back? No matter, I not to fire the grill yet."

"Manolis is making noises about wanting some service..."

"You can to make the start on the salad and

cheese, yes, Victor? I know how you love the woman's work."

"I'm here as a customer, not as a kitchen skivvy," I retorted before reflecting that if I got stuck into a bit of kitchen work, it would at least spare me from listening to yet more saccharine accounts of how Doreen and Manolis had been fated to meet. "On second thoughts, I'll give you a hand."

Taking refuge from the love-birds in the kitchen, I set to chopping tomatoes and slicing red onions for the salad. Waving a greeting as Spiros entered the taverna, I was pleased to see that he joined Marigold and the others at the table. Spiros would give short shrift to any of Doreen's mushy reminiscences.

I hadn't got very far with the salad when my chopping and slicing was interrupted by a call on my mobile. Listening as the woman spoke, I had a sinking feeling, anticipating Marigold's hysterical reaction to the news that the celebrant we had engaged to officiate at our vow renewal service was forced to cancel because she'd tripped over and broken her ankle. Realising that I had no choice other than to break the news to my wife, I grabbed a plastic bottle of *spitiko* wine from the fridge and approached Marigold with a well topped-up glass.

"You're not going to like what I have to tell you. You'd better have a glug of this wine to calm your nerves," I said, pressing the glass onto my wife.

"You could have got the rest of us some wine," Doreen complained.

"Marigold's need is greater," I said. Deciding there was no point in beating about the bush, I broke the bad news to Marigold. "Try not to get too worked up, darling. The celebrant has been forced to cancel."

"She can't do that. Our vow renewal service is next week." Marigold's eyes widened in outrage at the presumption of the woman, letting us down at the last minute.

"I'm afraid she had no choice; she's broken her ankle…"

"Oh, is that all? I thought it was something serious. Surely, she can hobble down to the beach on a pair of crutches?"

"Not from her hospital bed. She has to have it pinned."

"I don't believe it. It's just terrible," Marigold cried. The shock she voiced was transparently directed at the inconvenient loss of the celebrant, rather than sympathising with the poor woman's plight. In defence of my wife's callousness, I should point out that she had spent months organising the service, fussing over every minute detail with as much enthusiasm as a first-time bride. "Are you sure she won't be mobile by next week?"

"They aren't doing the surgery until next Monday. She won't be discharged from the hospital in time to do her thing."

Slapping her hands on her face, Marigold's eyes widened in panic. "Where on earth are we going to find someone else to officiate at such short notice? It's impossible."

"You want the someone to speak when you to marry the Victor again?" Spiros asked. Wiggling his bushy eyebrows expressively and throwing his arms out expansively, he proclaimed, "You will to be like the Elizabeth Taylor and the Richard Branson of Meli."

"It's Burton, not Branson. Richard Burton," I corrected.

"Victor's certainly no Richard Burton," Doreen scoffed.

"And no one could mistake me for Richard Branson," I added, annoyed at the very suggestion that I could be considered in any way comparable to someone bearded with a pullover habit.

"Victor had a look of Richard Burton when he was younger," Marigold snapped at Doreen. "Of course, Victor has aged much better. Richard Burton looked awfully rumpled when he got older."

"That would be from the booze," Doreen said. "Norman started to take on that creased look when he began hitting the bottle."

I was touched that Marigold compared me favourably to the former heartthrob. Of course, in my eyes, Elizabeth Taylor couldn't hold a candle to my wife.

"Spiro, I'm not marrying Victor again. We're still married. We are renewing our vows," Marigold clarified for his benefit since the undertaker didn't appear to grasp the concept of renewing one's vows.

"It is the strange foreign custom. I not to hear of any the Greeks that remarry unless they to make the divorce first," Spiros said, confirming my suspicion that he found the whole rigmarole confusing.

"It is a celebration of their marriage," Doreen explained.

"It's all moot now. Without a celebrant, we'll have to cancel," Marigold lamented, tearing up as she knocked back the wine and demanded a refill.

"The celebrant is the person who to remarry you?" Spiros asked.

"We aren't getting remarried because we are already married," I explained again. "During the service, we will reaffirm our commitment to one another. The celebrant was meant to say a few words before inviting us to read the vows we have written."

As I spoke, it occurred to me that I hadn't actually got round to writing my vows yet. Marigold would have my guts for garters if I came up empty on the big day. Tempted as I was to see the celebrant's broken ankle as a blessing that would allow me to get out of writing my vows or making a fool of myself by going barefoot in the sand while suited up, I realised a practical solution was needed. I couldn't bear the thought of Marigold's disappointment if we were forced to cancel so near to the day.

"Then the celebrant is like to the Papas Andreas?" Spiros persisted.

"No, there's no religious aspect to it…"

"Then the celebrant is more like the mayor at the *Dimarcheio*? You want that I ask him if he is the free next Tuesday?"

"He's a bit scruffy. He'd ruin the photos," Marigold objected, dashing my hope that I could take the evasive mayor to one side and have a quiet word about improving the sanitation of the public bins. I could swear the mayor went out of his way to avoid me, pulling a disappearing act every time I ventured into the *Dimarcheio* with my bulging file containing suggestions on cleaning up the local eyesore of overflowing bins.

Marigold's voice took on a high-pitched tone as the hysteria took hold. "Where are we going to find someone suitable before next Tuesday?"

"I am the used to the speaking at the formal occasion. I can to do it," Spiros offered.

"But you officiate at funerals. It might be a bit morbid," Marigold said.

"Spiros does scrub up quite nicely in a suit and tie," I pointed out.

"I have much the experience. It would be the good change to smile at the service instead of always to be the sombre," Spiros said persuasively.

"I suppose it's a better option than cancelling," Marigold mused. "After all, we do have guests flying over from England to help us celebrate and it's too late to put them off now. They fly in this Sunday."

"Marigold, you can to tell me what you want me to do. We can to do the practice race, yes."

"Practice run, that's a good idea. Yes, I suppose it's the ideal solution now that I think about it. As you are such a good friend to us both, it will add a much more personal touch to the occasion." Marigold's ready acquiescence surprised me but I reflected that she had always had a soft spot for Spiros; apart from the time he cluttered up our kitchen by lounging around in his vest and instilling bad habits into the cats.

"Yes, the more I think about it, the more I like the idea." I could see the cogs of Marigold's brain turning as she mulled the notion of Spiros officiating. "I never really took to that woman celebrant, anyway. Did you notice how she was always crossed eyed, Victor? I found it a bit unnerving, if I'm honest. And I did worry that she might try to upstage me by turning up in a glamorous dress. Every time I met her, she was flaunting the latest look from Marks and Spencer."

"Well, there's certainly no danger of Spiros up-staging you," I said, relieved beyond measure that Marigold was adopting a pragmatic approach, turning this negative turn of events into a positive. She'd done nothing but sing the praises of the celebrant until this moment, even going so far as to suggest we could include her in one of the expat dinner parties.

"Well, my pink won't clash with that posh frock you've bought," Doreen reassured Marigold.

"So, we are the agree? I to remarry the you and the Victor," Spiros pressed.

"Just make sure that you get Sampaguita to scrub out any lingering scent of embalming fluid from your suit," Marigold warned.

"But you to remarry on the beach. The fresh sea air will to blow any the smell away," Spiros declared.

# Chapter 6

*An Emerald Engagement Ring*

With the lack of a celebrant crisis averted by Spiros' timely offer to step into the breach, Marigold visibly relaxed. I attributed her slightly giddy state to tipsiness after knocking the heady *spitiko* wine back so quickly. Apostolos, the local barber, came into the taverna, nodding in greeting as he took a seat. He was soon joined by a couple of Greek pensioner chaps who rolled up, the three of them wasting no time in venting their annoyance at Dina's absence. Whilst they were more than happy to help themselves to some wine from the fridge, they baulked at the idea of venturing into the kitchen to grab some bread and olive oil: in their chauvinistic eyes, such woman's work was beneath them.

Since I find nothing shameful in getting stuck into the woman's work, I was about to return to the kitchen to dish out the bread to the grumbling pensioners when I was spared the role of playing skivvy by the arrival of Dina and Violet Burke. Walking into the taverna arm in arm, they were quite the picture in green, my mother's emerald tweed overshadowing in brightness the dullness of Dina's rather drab moss coloured frock. The budding friendship between the two women warmed the cockles of my heart. Knowing they had each other to lean on for mutual support was comforting, particularly in light of Violet Burke's recent bereavement.

As Dina headed straight to the kitchen, Spiros called out to her, *"Ela, koritsi mou, ela,"* ready to swirl her off her feet before she got stuck into her kitchen duties. Dina duly blushed, delighted to be referred to as Spiros' girl.

Since Manolis was deep in conversation with Apostolos, Doreen grabbed my sleeve, hissing, "Victor, why does the undertaker keep calling that woman Ela? I could swear her name is Dina."

"Yes, of course it's Dina…"

The penny dropped and I twigged that Doreen

thought that *ela*, the Greek way of saying come here, was a name. After I cleared up Doreen's misunderstanding, she shared with me how completely baffling she found the Greek language.

"The first time that Manolis called me Doreen *mou*, I must admit that I got the hump. The way he kept saying *mou* convinced me that he was having a dig at my weight. It was such a relief when he explained that *mou* was an endearment and he was really saying Doreen mine, or is it my Doreen? Either way, it would be so romantic if it didn't have cow-like connotations."

"The connotations are all in your mind, though it can take a while to adapt when you first learn the language. The amount of non-Greek speaking expats that I have seen nearly faint in disgust when a waiter asks them, *ti pineis*, is too many to count."

"I'm not surprised that they look disgusted if the waiter starts discussing his privates…"

"You're missing the point I was making, Doreen. *Ti pineis* means 'what are you drinking?' It just takes the English by surprise in the same way that you were disturbed by *mou* until you understood the context."

"Ah, I see, I get it now. It's a good job that Manolis speaks such good English. I don't imagine I'll ever be able to make sense of Greek. I must say, I do love it when Manolis calls me *apagi mou*. That means my love, you know."

"Yes, I do know that. It may have escaped your notice, but unlike you, I've been grappling with Greek ever since I first moved here."

"I'm so lucky that I have Manolis to translate for me. I might be able to get away with nothing more than throwing the odd *mou* into the conversation and people might mistake me for fluent."

It came as no surprise to hear that in spite of her much shorter sojourn in Greece than Doreen's, Violet Burke's attempt at basic Greek was more on the ball. Although her words were nothing approaching grammatically correct and she never paid any attention to tenses, when she called out to Dina "*Voitheia patates?*" her meaning was clear. She was asking Dina if she wanted any help with the chips.

Even more remarkably, Violet Burke took Dina's reply in her stride, nodding in agreement and claiming the seat next to me when Dina told her in Greek to sit with her son and she'd bring her some bread to go with her mucky fat: "*Ochi, kathesia me ton gio sou kai tha fero psomi gia na pas me to chonto lipos sou.*"

Sinking into a chair with a weary sigh, my mother delved into the depths of her ginormous handbag. I winced when she produced a packet of lard, the semi-solid white fat oozing out of the edges of the paper wrapping. Having relocated to the celebrated land of superlative extra virgin olive oil, Violet Burke refused to have any truck with that 'horrible greasy stuff that's only fit for shifting ear-wax', preferring to stick with her mucky fat.

"Vi, what's that on your ring finger? It looks like an emerald." Gasping in amazement, Marigold grabbed Violet Burke's hand for a closer look.

"Aye, lass, it looks like an emerald though 'appen it might be a fake. 'Appen it's not right to be flashing it off but Yiota insisted I wear it."

"Yiota?" Marigold queried.

"Aye, I was giving the lass a hand sorting out Panos' house. It's hardly speaking ill of the dead to say he could be a right messy bugger and Yiota can hardly be expected to settle in a tip. Anyway, we were having a clean out of Panos' kitchen drawers; you wouldn't believe the junk he collected, and Yiota came across this ring in a box. She reckoned that Panos must have bought it for me as an engagement ring because there was a receipt with it dated from the day before he croaked it."

"He did talk of proposing marriage," I said.

"But with an emerald, *mou*," Doreen butted in, indiscriminately tagging her one Greek word onto her sentence even though it made no sense. "Everyone knows that it's terribly bad luck to propose with an emerald. They say that if a woman accepts an emerald engagement ring, then the wedding is doomed not to happen and the woman will die an old maid."

"Really, Doreen," Marigold chided. "Could you be any more insensitive?"

"What? What did I say?"

"In case it escaped your notice, Panos dropped dead before he got the chance to put the emerald on my mother's finger," I said in exasperation.

"Yes, but it's not as if Violet is going to end up an old maid. How many times did you say your mother has been married, Victor?"

"I didn't," I snapped. "My mother's private life is none of your business…"

"And he's hardly likely to gossip about it behind my back when I'm sitting right here, you meddling dunce." Doreen visibly reddened at Violet Burke's insult. "I might have tied the knot with a few ne'er do wells in my time, but at least I didn't saddle myself with a crashing bore like your Norman."

"I'm seeing Manolis now…" Doreen stuttered.

"You might be playing fast and loose with this fella now, but you're still saddled with that traffic cone prat, aren't you? You haven't managed to divorce him or have the nous to do away with him, have you? He was still hanging round Meli like a bad smell this morning." My mother does love to have the last word.

"Well, I think it's a lovely ring, Vi," Marigold interjected, attempting to diffuse the tension.

"Indeed," I agreed, following Marigold's cue. "Yiota was quite right to insist that you wear it. Panos fully intended it should grace your finger."

"'Appen not everyone thinks like that. Look at the way that miserable lot over there are giving me daggers," Vi said with a hearty sigh, gesticulating towards the table of pensioner men. Swivelling round in my seat, I intercepted the disapproving stares that the three old men were firing in Violet Burke's direction. Clocking my frown, they looked away, embarrassed to be caught in the act.

"They to look the disapprove because you to not observe the Greek custom of the forty-day mourn," Spiros said, his words softened by the tender way he rubbed Violet Burke's arm solicitously. "I tell to you the before, Violet. After the death, you are expect to stay in the house in grief and to wear the black dress."

"And I told you that I've never been one to be ruled by convention," Vi fired back. "Dina's spuds are hardly going to peel themselves, nor will Nikos' lav start scrubbing itself with the toilet brush, if I took to extended weeping."

Whilst the local old-timers might frown on Violet Burke for not adhering to the tradition of going into full-blown mourning until the memorial service which served as a gratitude commemoration of Panos' life, my mother's approach was a sight more practical. I was pleased that Nikos and Dina weren't inexorably bound by tradition, appreciating that it would do my mother much more good to keep busy with her cleaning jobs rather than gnashing her teeth, pulling her hair out, and pummelling her breast behind closed doors.

"As for black, it's never been my colour. It puts years on me and makes me look all washed out," Vi stated.

Indeed, my mother had eschewed the customary black even for Panos' funeral, defiantly standing over the grave in some lurid purple number paired with a clashing red hat. Her only concession to the solemnity of the occasion had been to pluck a feather from one of my chicken's and dye it black before attaching it to the brim of her hat.

"That shade of green looks lovely on you, Vi, and it sets off the emerald nicely," Marigold flattered her.

Barely acknowledging Marigold's compliment, Violet Burke continued to voice her opinions. "You can keep your local custom of stopping indoors for forty-days, Spiros. When you get to my age, you'll have seen that many folk buried that you'd realise there isn't any time to waste on daft customs that mean nowt in the real world."

"I bet Spiros has seen more people buried than you have. He's an undertaker," Manolis piped up. Spiros' eye roll indicated it wasn't the first time he had heard the hardly original quip.

"Spiros was telling me a right load of old cobblers about how the Greeks drag everyone back for another depressing service forty-days after they've buried someone. 'Appen they aren't up on the expression 'let sleeping dogs lie,'" Vi opined.

"I believe that you are referring to the customary forty-day memorial service, Mother," I said.

"Ain't it enough that we've buried the old bugger without having to go digging through it all again?" Vi groaned.

"I think you may have got the wrong end of the stick, Vi," Marigold told her, adopting a patient tone. "I'm almost certain that it's too early to dig Panos up yet. I thought they waited a couple of years. Victor, you probably know more than me about Greek burial customs."

"I would have thought that you'd be an expert, darling, considering how many Fridays that you've spent beautifying the cemetery," I pointed out.

"There's no need to be sarcastic."

"Well, why ask me about the nitty-gritty of Greek burial customs when we're dining with the local undertaker?" I said, deferring to Spiros' greater knowledge. "You wouldn't ask Spiros about keeping a clean kitchen when you're married to a retired public health inspector."

"The Sampaguita keep the lovely clean kitchen," Spiros said proudly. "But I not to like her the habit of frying the tipaklong in the house."

"What's that?" Manolis asked.

"*Akrides*," Spiros translated, offering the Greek word for the Filipino delicacy.

"Fried grasshoppers," I clarified.

"A dreadful pest in Texas but we kill them with insecticides, we don't fry them."

"'Appen the Texans save that one for the electric chair," Vi shot back, sharp as a tack. "Anyhow, I doubt that grasshoppers would survive a chip pan. I was right surprised to discover how tasty they are."

Marigold and I stared at my mother in open-mouthed amazement that a woman who turned her nose up at most of the delicious Greek food on offer, dismissing it as foreign muck, had willingly snacked on grasshoppers.

"Course, Sampaguita never let on what I was eating until after I'd polished off a plateful of seconds," Vi added.

# Chapter 7

*Violet Volunteers Victor's Help*

The conversation came to a halt as Dina filled the table with bread and a huge bowl of salad brimming with juicy red tomatoes, red onions, green peppers, and black olives. Oregano dappled *feta* cheese doused in extra virgin was a welcome addition to the tantalising fare. While the rest of us dipped our bread into Nikos' superlative olive oil, looking on with disgust as Violet Burke slathered a heel of bread with lard, Manolis broke ranks and asked my mother if he could give it a try, shocking us all when he proclaimed the mucky fat to be quite delicious.

As chatter resumed around the table, it reverted to the topic of the forty-day memorial service. Violet Burke adamantly declared, "I'm not dragging out to the graveyard again; I reckon it's morbid. Burying Panos once was enough for me to stomach."

"Yiota may appreciate your support," I suggested.

"The lass hasn't got time to be faffing about with running to church when she's got to get to grips with running that farm."

"Speaking of Yiota, I haven't seen much of her around lately," Marigold said. "Has she been shamed into adhering to the forty-day mourning tradition? We really should have called round to see her, Victor. It can't be much fun for a young woman if she's expected to stay indoors for over a month."

"Did you not just hear me say that she's got a farm to be running? The reason you haven't seen Yiota out and about is because she's fair knackered after putting in a full day on the farm. It doesn't come natural to the lass, what with her being used to a cushy desk job, but she's determined to do her granddad proud and make a success of it."

"An admirable ambition," I agreed.

"I'm right glad that you can see that, Son. Panos was always banging on about how much of an asset you were on his stall." Vi's words, suffused with motherly pride, brought a lump to my throat and I reflected that she was finally beginning to get the hang of this mothering business. "Poor Yiota got herself in a right old tizzy at the thought of flogging her veggies to the public. She's never done 'owt like that before. So, I told Yiota that you'd be happy to give her a hand on Panos' market stall the day after tomorrow."

Thinking that my mother was as bad as Marigold when it came to volunteering my services without bothering to consult with me first, I mulled the idea, recalling that my time as the Del Boy of Meli on Panos' market stall had indeed been a roaring success.

"I'd be more than happy to show her the ropes," I agreed. "But the day after tomorrow could be a tad awkward. I'm already committed to leading the Greek Gastronomic Tour in town."

"You don't start until eleven, dear. Don't the stall holders start trading at some unspeakable hour? I'm sure you can put in an appearance and show Yiota the ropes before you pick up your tourists," Marigold urged.

"Yes, that could work."

"Panos would be right chuffed that you're there to support his granddaughter," Vi said. "You know how he doted on the lass."

I reflected that while Vi had no time for

maudlin sentiment, whenever she spoke of Panos, it was always in a positive light. I admired her attitude: it would certainly mean far more to Panos to know that the woman he had planned to marry was more concerned with offering practical assistance to his beloved Yiota, than shutting herself away in a darkened room and playing the hypocrite at some religious rite she had no time for. Panos had been in his element holding sway on his market stall. He would have liked nothing more than to see Yiota filling his wellies.

"Victor, when you're on the market stall with Yiota, you must be sure to tell her that we'd love her to be a guest at the celebration to renew our vows next week. And don't forget to mention that I've invited Giannis too," Marigold urged, unable to resist the opportunity for a spot of matchmaking.

Chatter ceased as Nikos arrived, bearing a laden platter of grilled chicken wings and thighs glistening with juices and sea salt, closely followed by Dina carrying a plate of her legendary chips.

"The chicken he so fresh he running round in the dirt this morning," Nikos boasted.

"I hope you give them a right proper washing," my mother said, bristling at the mention of dirt.

"You question my cooking?" Nikos snapped before telling Spiros, "I put the feet of the chicken in the bag for you to take to the wife."

"What's Sampaguita supposed to do with a bag of manky chicken feet?" Vi questioned, creasing her nose in repugnance.

"She to make the Panlasang Pinoy. It is the Filipino delicacy of the chicken feet with the garlic and the chilli," Spiros said, attempting to hide his grimace.

"That should be right up your alley, Mother, considering how much you enjoy fried grasshoppers."

"I reckon I'll give them feet a miss, lad. I don't reckon that chickens are up on feet hygiene. Anyway, I can't be doing with garlic. It doesn't half make me flatulent."

Noticing the flash of emerald adorning my mother's figure as it caught the fluorescent light, I hastily changed the subject. Any talk of feet would inevitably lead into an unwanted grumble about the state of Violet Burke's swollen appendages. For once, my mother had been mercifully quiet on the subject of her potentially exploding feet. "Your new ring will compliment that Jackie O dress you plan to wear for our vow renewal."

"Aye, you're right there, lad," Vi said before turning to Marigold to ask, "Have you had any luck finding a frock for your big day, lass?"

"Didn't I tell you? I found a lovely, fitted lace dress…"

"Ooh, what colour?"

"It's cream," Marigold revealed.

"I did offer to run up a dress for Marigold on my sewing machine…" Doreen began.

"Speaking of your sewing machine, I've a favour to ask of you," Vi bluntly interrupted.

"A favour from me?" Doreen looked suitably shocked, more used to my mother's put downs than requests for her help.

"It's not for me, it's for Panos' granddaughter, Yiota. 'Appen you've heard how she's moved into Panos' farmhouse. I don't mind telling you that the place isn't what you'd call inviting. It's right rough and ready, lacking what you'd call the feminine touch," Vi confided.

"About par for the course for a wellie wearing farmer," I suggested, thinking Panos had never struck me as the type to be in touch with his feminine side.

"Yiota's too worn out after all that chasing around after livestock and seeing to crops, to have time to do 'owt about it. I hate to think of her bedding down there without any proper home comforts. 'Appen you could knock up some cushions or some such on that sewing machine of yours?"

"I could come round with Doreen and we could get some ideas," Marigold volunteered. Even before my wife had worked her magic and transformed the

Albanian shed dweller's slum of a home into the pink palace of love, she had harboured grandiose pretensions of being something of an expert in interior design.

"I'm thinking throws and rag rugs to give the place a homely feel," Doreen suggested.

"And lampshades and cushions. One can never have too many cushions," Marigold enthused.

"'Appen some nice, crocheted antimacassars," Vi suggested.

"They're dreadfully old fashioned, Vi. Yiota's too young for anything so fussy."

"I'd be delighted to help," Doreen piped up. I considered it was no wonder she was so eager to assist as it would give her an opportunity to get out from under Norman's feet and finally do something productive.

"And I've got loads of fabric left from those curtains we brought over from Manchester, so it needn't cost a cent," Marigold volunteered, demonstrating a decidedly uncharacteristic frugal streak. She had obviously been paying attention when I complained about the obscene amount of my cash that she was throwing at the vow renewal service. Time and again, I had warned her that we needed to be watching the pennies in light of the renovation project I was sinking my money into along with Barry.

Fortunately, I was spared extensive cushion talk by the ringing of my mobile phone.

"If it's that celebrant woman calling to say she's changed her mind, tell her not to bother," Marigold instructed. "Now that I've had time to think it over, I'm over the moon that Spiros will be doing it. It will give it a more personal touch to have a good friend officiate."

Since I consider it the height of bad manners to engage in telephone calls at the table, I took the phone outside, careful to avoid stepping on the disembowelled mouse. Struggling to put a face to the Greek caller speaking in broken English, he finally jogged my memory by describing the occasion of our meeting. He reminded me that we had got chatting a few months ago in a coastal taverna when he had shared his ambition to purchase a taverna of his own.

I recollected that Takis, the caller, was a serious young man in his early thirties who had formally trained as a chef at culinary school. As he'd described the plans that he hoped to one day bring to fruition, I had encouraged Takis to call me if ever found a suitable venue to purchase, assuring him that I would be delighted to offer my professional opinion on the state of whatever kitchen he took over.

After listening as he filled me in about the

taverna he was considering purchasing, I agreed that I would drive down to the coast the next morning to give his prospective kitchen the once-over.

Returning to the table to join the others, I groaned in annoyance when I realised that my absence had given the others the opportunity to polish off all the chicken.

"I saved you a wing, darling," Marigold cooed, dropping the morsel of chicken onto my plate to accompany Dina's by now stone-cold chips. "Now, who were you chatting to for so long?"

"A fellow called Takis that I met a few months ago is considering purchasing a taverna as a going-concern. The owner wants to retire. Anyway, Takis requested that I bob down and give the kitchen the once-over, sound it out in my professional capacity."

"But you're retired." Marigold does love to state the patently obvious.

"I may be retired but that doesn't devalue my professional opinion. If the kitchen isn't up to scratch in my experienced eye, Takis might be able to barter the price down."

"Victor will be like the Gordon Ramsay..." Manolis began to say.

"Oh, no, you've got the wrong end of the stick, Manoli. Victor isn't a chef...he just plays at it," Marigold interrupted.

"If you've quite finished belittling my skills as a chef," I said to my wife before turning my attention to Manolis. "Although I sometimes lend a hand cheffing in the kitchen here, I spent my career as a public health inspector. My expertise lies in detecting gross violations of hygiene standards…"

"That's what I said, like the Gordon Ramsay. He plays the health inspector on the television programme 'Kitchen Nightmares.' My cousin in London sent me the video. It is very funny."

"That's a new one on me," I admitted. "I didn't know that Gordon Ramsay had taken up acting."

Nikos appeared at my elbow, carrying another small platter of freshly grilled chicken. "I see you the outside so cook you some more the chicken."

"You're a life-saver, Niko."

"I listen the conversation. In all my years of running the taverna, never the health inspector come into my kitchen. You should to tell your friend that he more to fear the tax inspector."

"Well, he's really just after my expert opinion on if the kitchen has been kept in good order," I said, quite looking forward to the prospect of dusting off my professional skills. Skivvying in the taverna kitchen, repping and offering cooking classes, didn't quite live up the illustriousness of my former career.

"The Nikos is right. Who to care if the kitchen

is clean if the tax inspector turn up?" Spiros said.

"It's a strange state of affairs in Greece where a taverna owner would quake in his boots at the prospect of an unannounced visit by a tax inspector yet give nary a thought to the far more important business of a hygiene inspection," I observed

"I've certainly seen some quaking by café bar owners in town when they get the call that the tax inspector is doing his rounds," Marigold said. "You remember how the waiters suddenly appear with printed receipts when they never usually bother, Victor."

I smiled in amusement at Marigold's words, recalling the first time we had questioned the frantic activity that suddenly resulted in a shot glass containing a printed receipt appearing on our table. The waiter took the time to explain that his boss had just had a phone call alerting him that the tax inspector was in the vicinity and the lack of a printed receipt accompanying our coffees would result in a hefty fine. I doubted that the way in which Nikos typically scrawled the bill for our evening's repast on the paper tablecloth would ever pass muster if the tax inspector should happen to drop in, but I had long resigned myself to the state of the slapdash kitchen.

# Chapter 8

*Milton Spouts Bollocks*

Full of the joys of spring, I crept out of the house after downing my coffee and feeding the cats, careful not to disturb Marigold's lie-in. I was brimming with excitement at the prospect of meeting Takis in the coastal taverna that he was considering purchasing. I don't mind admitting that I had missed the thrill of having a good poke round in a grubby kitchen since hanging up my hairnet when I took early retirement from my glittering career as a public health inspector.

It felt marvellous to know that my professional expertise was once again in demand. My efforts to keep up-to-date with all the latest hygiene regulations had not been a complete waste of time, an opinion which Marigold frequently voiced whenever she caught me with my nose buried in the latest literature on the subject. I couldn't recall if I was familiar with the taverna that I would be inspecting; no doubt the sight of it would jog my memory. It would be horrendous to discover that any taverna I had frequented flouted strict hygiene standards and was a breeding ground for bacteria, even if I hadn't succumbed to a virulent dose of food poisoning after eating there.

Before moving to Greece, I had been overly concerned, nay even a tad obsessed, with the possibility of dining anywhere that may be in violation of the stringent standards I enforced on a daily basis. Since landing in Meli, I was less anxious about such matters, adopting a more relaxed attitude.

A couple of times in our earliest days in the Mani, I had attempted to sneak into the odd kitchen, but such furtive moves on my part had done nothing but earn me Marigold's scathing disapprobation. My wife was quick to rebuke me with a stern reminder that it was none of my business since I was pensioned off. With invariably friendly hospitable service on offer in the area, I think my wife was worried on two counts: firstly, that I may be perceived as a bit of an odd-bod, leading us to being slung out on our ears and publicly banned; secondly, that she would earn a bad reputation by association with said odd-bod if her husband was caught in the act of sticking his nose in a refrigerator where it had no official business.

Making a final check of my satchel to ensure the requisite white coat and hairnet were neatly folded inside, I headed down to the Punto, stopping dead in my tracks at the bizarre sight that caught my attention. Milton, supported by his walker, was attempting to keep a grip on a stocky fellow, who in turn, was trying his best to maintain his handle on a pair of crutches. Seeing the pair of them wobbling precariously in what could be mistaken for a lover's embrace, I rushed forward to lend my assistance, just as one of the crutches clattered to the ground. Steadying the stranger clinging onto Milton, I retrieved the fallen crutch and helped him to regain his balance, receiving a hearty *efcharisto* in thanks for my trouble

"Blasted cat, shot out of nowhere. Nearly had the pair of us over, what," Milton complained.

"It's not like you to speak ill of a feline," I pointed out.

"I make an exception when it comes to Cynthia's dratted mutant, what. Nearly came a cropper when I tried to kick the blasted creature," Milton huffed. "I say, where are my manners? Terribly remiss of me, what, not to introduce you. Victor, this is my new friend, Kyriakos. Kyriakos, this is my good friend, Victor. I met Kyriakos at the hospital when he was having the casts taken off his legs. Discovering we are neighbours, we decided it made good sense to take our therapeutic exercise together. It's certainly motivated me to get out and about, what."

The name Kyriakos rang a bell. I recalled Nikos telling me about a local chap that had broken both his legs whilst in the grip of a delusion that he could fly off his balcony. The absurd notion that he could fly had taken hold of his mind whilst he was under the influence of too many antidepressants, prescribed due to the misery of an intolerable living situation. Caught in the crossfire of his wife and mother, both of whom he lived with and who each hated the other, his flight of fancy hadn't earned him any respite from their bickering. The two women simply continued their verbal rallies over his hospital bed.

Apparently, before his flight, Kyriakos had been a bit of a recluse; now, with his legs free of the casts, he told me that he was keen to escape the house. Palling up with Milton, who was still recuperating from the latest op on his dodgy hip, had motivated the two of them to stick to the exercise routines ordered by their respective doctors. I was interested to make Kyriakos' acquaintance now that he had decided to escape his intolerable home situation by limping around in the company of Milton.

Careful to include his new Greek friend, Milton continued his patter, peppering his chat with a few unexpected Greek bloopers. "I say, *malaka*, it's dratted difficult for Kyriakos to get used to those pesky crutches. Slippery things, especially when he tries to manoeuvre them over the cobbles, *boulonia*. He'd be better off with one of these wheeled walkers, *boulonia*."

I was taken aback, nay shocked, to hear the terribly proper Milton, who despite penning porn never used vulgar language or uttered anything coarser than a drat or a darn, punctuating his speech with Greek expletives.

"Milton, why on earth are you swearing in Greek?" I demanded to know.

"What? I'm doing no such thing," Milton protested. "Kyriakos has been teaching me the odd bit of Greek....only seemed fitting that I try to pick up a bit of his language. Jolly decent of him to make the effort to converse in English, *malaka*. I'm trying my darndest to respond with the bit of Greek he's drumming into me. Not easy to pick it up at my age, *boulonia*."

"I don't know what you think you're saying, Milton, but I can assure you that the Greek you are coming out with is not the sort of thing you want to be dropping in the hearing of the fairer sex. I rather suspect that Kyriakos has been pulling your leg."

"Surely not…"

Adjusting his crutches so that he could face me whilst turning his back on Milton, Kyriakos fired a broad wink in my direction, the corners of his lips turning up in amusement. "I was the confused by the Milton habit of always saying the 'what' when he was not to ask the question… I teach the Milton some the Greek words he can to use instead of always saying the 'what' and the 'old chap.'"

"You taught him the sort of obscenities that he would be embarrassed to utter…"

"I not to say the words mean the 'what' and the 'old chap.' I only tell the Milton that he can to replace them with the Greek words…" Kyrias began.

"There's no need to repeat them. We're not on a building site," I interrupted, conscious that the window to the *apothiki* was open just behind me. I had no desire for Violet Burke to overhear such foul language and add it to her increasing repertoire of Greek vocabulary. She was certainly in no danger of ever picking up such filthy language in Dina's kitchen.

"*Oti itan ena asteio.*" Saying it was just a joke, Kyriakos accompanied his words with a gesticulation; lifting his arms from his crutches, he almost came a cropper, losing his balance again.

As I assisted Kyriakos in readjusting his weight on the crutches, Milton told him, "I think you'd better fess up, Kyriakos, and tell me what you've been having me saying, old chap."

"I not to know the words in the English…" Kyriakos replied.

"Victor?" Milton questioned.

"Well, instead of coming out with your usual 'old chap', you've been spouting 'bollocks.'"

"I say, that's not too bad…might have uttered the odd bollocks once or twice in my air force days. Never in the company of the ladies, of course, *boulonia*. Darn, I'm doing it again, it's going to be a hard habit to break now I've picked it up. To think, I've been swearing all week and never knew it. I suppose you'd better tell me what *malaka* means since I'm guessing it doesn't translate as 'what.'"

"It certainly doesn't, but it's not a word that I care to repeat in either Greek or translated English."

"But…I say, I ought to know what I've been saying…"

"I'll whisper it."

Milton looked suitably shocked when he heard the translation of the common Greek expletive. I admit that I may have toyed with Milton's gullibility just a tad since the word in question, *malaka*, whilst meaning wanker, is often used in Greek as a term of friendly banter without its masturbatory connotations. One can often hear groups of youngsters bandying the term as an alternative way of saying mate or friend. However, it wouldn't do for a foreigner to use the word as a form of salutation when addressing a Greek. If Milton adopted it and tried it out on a stranger, his advanced years may not spare him a thumping.

"So, what's what in Greek?" Milton asked.

"It's very simple. It's *ti,*" I told him.

"*Ti.* I can manage that and it's nice and easy to remember. And old chap?"

"I suppose you could use *filarakos* as chap; it roughly translates as bloke, chap or chum. And stick a *palios* in front of it for old. Now that you seem eager to try out some Greek, perhaps you could get the hang of dropping the S from the end of male names when you address someone. When you're chatting to Kyriakos here, just call him Kyriako."

"Ah, I wondered what that was all about. Heard you calling the undertaker Spiro when I was pretty sure his name is Spiros."

"Well, I'm just happy to hear you making an effort at last."

"Least I can do when Kyriako here is so obliging to converse in English, even if he has been having a laugh at my expense," Milton said.

"Put the S back on the end of his name when

you're talking about him," I advised. Really, the concept wasn't that difficult to grasp but it seemed to elude the capabilities of most of my expat neighbours.

Addressing his new Greek friend directly, Milton added, "Can't blame you for having a bit of a leg pull, Kyriako. Bit of a hoot, what, old chap."

"*Ti*? *Palios filarakos*," I reminded him, wondering how long it would take to sink in. Milton wasn't the brightest bulb in the box. "So, Kyriako, are there any more clangers that Milton is coming out with that he ought to know about?"

"I teach the Milton to say *grafo vromika vivlia*," Kyriakos admitted, his guilty expression not quite wiping the smirk off his face.

"I say, old chap, don't tell me that it doesn't mean 'I write erotica.'"

"Close enough," I said. "It means 'I write dirty books.'"

"If think it better for the Milton to say that, than to say *grafo porno*…"

"I write erotica, not porn, old chap," Milton protested, having correctly guessed that *porno* was the Greek word for porn, the two words being almost identical.

"Actually, the word pornography is derived from combining the Greek words for prostitute and write, *porni* and *grapho*. I found that an excellent way to expand my Greek vocabulary when I first arrived was to find English words that are derived from Greek. You could try the same. Memorise a few Greek words which are similar in English and then test them out on Kyriakos during your walks."

"I don't suppose you could set the ball rolling with a few examples, old chap?"

"Well, let me think. Hygiene is *ygieni* in Greek and philosophy is *filosofia* …"

"Anything I'd be more likely to drop in a conversation? Can't say I go around prattling on about philosophical things and hygiene."

"Let me think. Off the top of my head, the Greek word for spider is *arachni*…"

"That's nothing like spider. You've lost me, old chap."

"Do I have to spell it out? Just think arachnophobia."

"Ah, got it. Anymore."

"*Omprela, theatro, tragodia*…"

"I ought to use the last one to describe the state of my Greek, what," Milton said, chortling in a self-deprecating manner.

"Well, much as I'd love to stand around chatting all day, work beckons," I said. "Good meeting you, Kyriako."

"And the you, Victor. You must to join us for the walk sometime."

"I'll do that," I replied, not bothering to voice my thought *if I'm ever reduced to shuffling around on a Zimmer frame.*

# Chapter 9

## *In the Mood for a Hygiene Inspection*

Hitting the road, I reflected that it was a perfect day for a drive. My senses felt heightened, appreciative of all the glorious colours of nature surrounding me. Imposing flint greyness merged with shades of brown in the rocky Taygetos range in the distance, meeting the lush greenery of fields and olive groves, the sky blue and cloudless. I must confess that on days such as this, I felt just a tad jealous of Gordon Strange's snazzy sports car, imagining it would be quite delightful to drive along with the roof open and feel more of a breeze in my hair than the side-on draught offered by the open windows. Of course, I would never voice such a sentiment to Marigold; she would drag me off to trade in the car for some flashy impractical number before I could say Punto.

Driving along, I anticipated various scenarios concerning what I may likely encounter in the taverna kitchen that I had agreed to critically examine. It struck me that after so many years spent inspecting kitchens, I doubted there was anything that could still shock me: there had certainly had some gruesomely memorable moments. Thinking back to some of the most shocking conditions I had encountered, I recalled a particular pigeon encounter that had left me gob-smacked.

The office was inundated with constant complaints concerning a certain Chinese takeaway that had been going for a number of years in a residential area comprising primarily terraced houses. Despite numerous inspection visits from myriad inspectors, nothing untoward had been uncovered, yet the complaints continued to flood in, necessitating yet another visit. Caution was required since the owner insisted that he was the victim of a concerted effort to close him down, orchestrated by a ruthless competitor making baseless and scurrilous accusations. A couple of anonymous letters concerning the business had been sent to the owner. Fashioned from words cut out of magazines and glued onto a sheet of notepaper as though cobbled together by some not very original criminal mind, they shed no light on the matter, simply spelling out the name of the takeaway above the words Coo Coo. To date, nothing insanitary had been uncovered; granted, it wasn't a shining example of the cleanest takeaway establishment, but it met basic standards.

Determined to get to the bottom of things, I duly turned up for a surprise inspection, convinced that the owner had something to hide. With the kitchen receiving the usual reluctant pass, I turned my attention to the paved back yard leading onto the typical cobbled ginnel so prevalent in the area. Drums of cooking oil were neatly lined up outside the back door; the original shelter that had housed the outside loo was now devoid of an actual toilet, the space piled high with plastic wrapped takeaway containers and bulk packages of kitchen rolls. As I stared around at the innocuous surroundings, nothing rang any alarm bells in my mind until a pigeon suddenly dive-bombed into the adjacent yard. Seconds later, the sound of a Chinese voice shouting something incomprehensible was followed by a loud thwack and a triumphant cry.

Climbing atop one of the oil drums, I peered down into the neighbouring yard, coming eyeball to eyeball with a manic looking Chinese man clutching a machete in one hand and a headless pigeon in the other. After some pressing, the takeaway owner finally came clean, admitting that he used the neighbouring terraced property for staff accommodation. It transpired that one of his chefs had been enticing pigeons into the yard with tasty titbits, the lured pigeons meeting their untimely demise by having their heads severed with a meat cleaver. Following a bit of random feather plucking, the pigeon corpses had been tossed into a huge vat of curry, left open to the elements, and passed off as chicken. It seemed that the anonymous Coo Coo letters had been a clue after all.

Even after the takeaway was summarily closed down before being taken over, it never recovered from its reputation of serving up suspect pigeons, despite the best efforts of the new management.

Slowing down to avoid hitting a couple of scraggy looking sheep grazing at the side of the road, put me in mind of a restaurant on my Manchester patch that had gained an acclaimed reputation for its superb garlic encrusted rack of lamb. When the owner-chef sold the business as a thriving going-concern, it wasn't long before the restaurant was beset with problems. The new owner, Dominic, despite being culinary challenged when it came to any actual hands-on kitchen experience, fancied himself as a bit of a gourmet and an expert sommelier. Taking charge of the front-of-house, he devised a fancy new wine list, selecting the perfect wine to accompany every dish on the menu.

The restaurant may have continued to run smoothly but Dominic couldn't control his hemophobia, having a fit of the vapours if even a hint of blood accompanied a dish as it left the kitchen. The moment a waiter attempted to serve a rare steak, Dominic would snatch the plate from their grasp, returning it to the kitchen. Tutting loudly, he would shout the word No, the sound coming out as a long drawn-out Nooooo, before instructing the chef to char the meat until any lingering trace of blood was completely eradicated. Racks of lamb were snatched away before outraged diners could begin to tuck in and returned to the kitchen where Dominic demanded the chef cremate the pink meat. I always considered it odd that the sight of a ruby red Burgundy or a full-bodied Bordeaux didn't trigger Dominic's irrational fear of blood.

Since no self-respecting chef would tolerate such behaviour, the business soon became known for disgruntled customers and its high staff turnover of, an unfortunate situation that often resulted in the restaurant closing on short notice until Dominic could rustle up a new chef, ignorant to his boss's phobia. The experience had underscored my belief that restaurants should be run by chefs rather than dabbling amateurs with gourmet pretensions.

Fortunately, Takis, the young man that I was on my way to meet, was a trained chef. He certainly ought to know his way around a kitchen. I expected that he would be as keen as I was to sniff out any hygiene violations in the establishment that he had a mind to purchase.

Locking up the Punto in the coastal village, I spied the familiar figure of Takis heading towards my car, brimming with energy. Although I had only met him once before, he was easily recognisable; short, slightly plump and genial of appearance, with a prematurely receding hairline. His sagging jawline sported what I believe is referred to these days as designer stubble, though Violet Burke would be likely to opine that he needed a good shave.

"*Ela*, we take coffee before we look at the taverna," Takis invited, grabbing my arm and pulling me into a café bar a few doors down from the restaurant I would be inspecting. I was appreciative of his thoughtful gesture; it would be terrible to drink coffee at the taverna I was about to inspect, only to then uncover some hygiene violation that left little to the imagination. Such a scenario would make me spend the rest of the day regretting imbibing said coffee and leave me feeling decidedly queasy.

"I hope your inspection, he will to go smoothly," Takis said. "I have many the plan for the taverna. The current owner, Vasilis, he only open for the tourist season. With so many the foreigns moving into the area, I plan to open all the year and to experiment with the foreigns food."

"That's an unusual move. I can't think of any local tavernas that serve anything other than authentic Greek food, not unless you count things like pizza and full English breakfasts," I said.

"The *pitsa* is Greek," Takis reminded me. "The ancient Greek, he invent the *pitsa*." Considering the typical Greek trait of taking credit for most inventions, I was surprised that Takis didn't insist that the ancients lay claim to coming up with a full English too.

"What kind of foreign cuisine are you thinking of introducing?"

"I think the foreigns like spice. I will to put the Thailand green curry on the menu and the Thailand skewer satay chicken...you like?"

"It would certainly be worth driving down for if my wife fancies a change from our local taverna," I said, imagining Nikos' contemptuous reaction if I tried to persuade him to start serving Thai food. "As you're thinking of opening beyond the tourist season, have you considered that traditional British Sunday lunches could be a big draw in the winter amongst the local Brits?"

"You to think?"

"Well, there is a growing contingent of British expats living here for much of the year. It may well be worth sounding them out to see if there would be any demand for roast beef and Yorkshire pudding. If it proved popular, you could do a roaring trade with a traditional Christmas dinner. I haven't met any Brits that are too enamoured with the idea of eating pork and celery at Christmas, rather than a turkey and all the trimmings."

"Perhaps you could to consult on the menu, Victor? I think that your input could be the useful."

"I'd be delighted to. As I may have mentioned last time we met, I run Greek cookery classes for British expats during the winter months and I have dabbled with cheffing in my local taverna." I considered that it couldn't hurt to drop my credentials beyond the hygiene sphere. I liked to keep myself busy over the winter and Takis may well require assistance with his new venture. A taverna full of captive Brits could present a wonderful opportunity for me to sign up a classful of the culinary inept. "Nikos, the owner of my local taverna, won't countenance making any changes to his menu."

"The same with the Vasilis. He only to serve the Greek food. His the wife do all the cooking with the recipe from the *yiayia*." Takis' words didn't surprise me. Most of the tavernas operated much like my local, the owner's wife taking charge of the kitchen and cooking recipes passed on from her grandma. "My cooking repertoire is the broadened from the culinary school, more the adventurous. The menu he will to include the traditional *pastitsio* and *kleftiko*, but I think to experiment with the rabbit *stifado* and the roast squab dish."

"I can point you in the direction of an excellent rabbit breeder in my village," I offered. Mentioning that Giannis also produced the most divine local honey, I attempted a quip that played on the Greek language, saying, *"To meli apo Meli einai amvrosia."*

Takis duly chuckled at my observation that the honey from my village, named for honey, was ambrosia. However, with the recollection of decapitated pigeons fresh in my mind, I thought it best to advise Takis that I didn't think squab would go down too well with the local Brits. I didn't envisage much demand for eating flying vermin.

"Perhaps I to experiment with the, how to say, the *tsichla*, instead."

"Chewing gum?" I queried.

*"Tsichla bird,"* Takis responded.

Belatedly remembering that *tsichla* also translated as thrush, I voiced an inspired thought. "Actually, I know a chap that's handy with his gun in the hunting season."

It would be better to have Kostis occupied taking out thrush with his gun than firing off pot shots at Marigold's cats.

# Chapter 10

*The Unmarried Daughter's Pension*

Draining our coffees, the two of us headed off to the taverna which Takis was considering purchasing. Situated across the road from a pebble beach, it offered fabulous sea views. I immediately recognised it as a place where Marigold and I had dined on a rather uninspired and unappetising *moussaka* over a year ago, its overly dry consistency leading me to conclude that it had been hanging around for a few days before making its way to our plates. I recalled that I had crossed the taverna off our list, marking it as a place to avoid in the future. Not only had the food been lukewarm and dismal, the staff had been at logger-heads with one another in the kitchen, the constant stream of Greek expletives emanating from the back only punctuated with the sound of breaking plates. Since plate smashing as entertainment isn't really a thing beyond the imagination of tourists these days, having been banned on health and safety grounds due to the hazardous risk presented by flying shards, I suspected that the staff were hurling plates at one another with gay abandon. My suspicion had been reinforced when the owner appeared with a bloody gash on his forehead when he presented our bill.

Determined not to let our previous disappointing experience of dining there cloud my judgement when it came to advising Takis, I assessed the taverna with impartial eyes. It was certainly picturesque. Ceramic pots bursting with vibrant blooms were dotted around the outdoor seating area. Stones scavenged from the beach had been painted with nautical themes to add a decorative touch, soothing elevator music playing quietly in the background. Spotting a couple of ceramic buckets in vibrant colours serving as floral hanging baskets, I had a flashback to the moment I had first clapped eyes on Marigold in the bucket aisle of B&Q, an unforgettable moment that had instantly transformed my life for the better. Thinking the buckets were a new addition since my previous visit, I decided to view them as a good omen.

A couple of tourists feeding the cats scraps from a full English breakfast were the only customers at such an early hour. A weary looking gent in his late sixties, shoulders slumped over a table, sipped coffee in a desultory fashion. He immediately perked up on seeing Takis, rushing forward to embrace him and greet him with a stream of Greek words uttered so quickly that I could barely comprehend them. Ushering the pair of us to a table, the gent, Vasilis, disappeared in the direction of the kitchen, telling us he would get his wife to bring us coffee. *"Leo sti gynaiko mou na ferei kafe."*

The peace of the morning was instantly disturbed by the sound of an argument emanating from the kitchen at full volume. Shouts reached a crescendo, culminating in the sound of breaking crockery. The elevator music was turned up to a head-thumping decibel level, presumably in a desperate effort to drown out the din from the kitchen.

Vasilis returned, rubbing his ear and looking like butter wouldn't melt. Sinking into a chair, he addressed Takis with an expectant look on his face. *"Tha agorasete tin taverna? Eipate oti tha parete mia apofasi simera."*

"Victor, you to understand?" Takis asked me. "Vasilis, he want to know if I to buy the taverna. He remind me that I say I will to make the decision to-day."

Switching to Greek, Takis introduced me to Vasilis, telling him that I would be offering him my professional opinion on the state of the kitchen before he reached his final decision.

"Ah, then we must to speak the English," Vasilis said, stroking his angular nose thoughtfully. "You are another the student of the culinary school?"

"No, I was a public health inspector before I retired."

"*Ti?*" Vasilis looked confused.

"I used to inspect kitchens to ensure that they complied with the requisite hygiene standards as laid out in the Food Standards Act," I clarified.

"Ah, yes. I to hear there are many the dirty kitchen in the England," Vasilis chortled, apparently unfazed by the thought of my poking around in the dark recesses of his kitchen. "My wife keep the kitchen the clean. You can to eat the *moussaka* off the floor, yes."

"I prefer mine on a plate," I quipped.

I instantly regretted my joshing remark when Vasilis replied, "I tell my wife to bring you the *moussaka*."

"No, please don't. I've only just eaten breakfast," I protested. Admittedly his wife may have just been having an off day on the *moussaka* front on my previous visit, but I remained resolutely determined to avoid consuming or imbibing anything emanating from the kitchen until it been given my professional seal of approval.

Eager to change the subject, I asked Vasilis, "Do you receive regular visits by health officials inspecting the kitchen?"

"No. The health official never to make the visit, never. This season, I take on the new waiter and he must to deliver the, how to say, the *deigma kopranon*, to the health official? They not to collect it, he must to deliver it in the glass jar from the pharmacy. He was much the, how to say, *dtrepotan*, to buy it?"

"The embarrass," Takis translated.

"*Deigma kopranon*?" I queried, openly gaping as I questioned my understanding of the Greek words. If my translating abilities were up to scratch, it appeared that the waiter had to deliver a stool sample.

"I see you to confuse, Victor. It is the true. For the new waiter to make the permit to work in the taverna, he must to give the faecal sample," Takis confirmed.

"How utterly bizarre," I said, wondering if it was a recently introduced rule. Certainly, Nikos hadn't demanded that I provide a stool sample before I stepped into Dina's shoes in the kitchen during my first winter in Meli, nor had he mentioned such a requirement when I'd taken over the grill more recently. More likely, Nikos had just flouted any such ordinance, perchance leaving me exposed to unwittingly breaking some hygiene edict. I shuddered at the thought that I may have unwittingly flouted the kind of ordinance that I had once been paid to enforce.

It seemed that whilst I was accustomed to inspecting kitchens in England in a quest to uncover lurking bacteria, in Greece they do things differently, testing the actual staff to ensure they don't have a gutful of anything nasty. The rules back in my homeland were hardly comparable. Restaurant employees in England were obliged to sit a short multiple-choice examination pertaining to food hygiene practices. The test covered familiarity with such details as not washing one's feet in the kitchen basin reserved for hand washing, and testing staff knowledge concerning the dangers of cross contamination of raw and cooked meat. They were, thankfully, spared the indignity of producing a stool sample.

"*Po*, the rule he is the many. To work in the taverna, the waiter must to have the testing the ear and the teeth at the hospital, and to make the X-ray of the breast."

"I can see the rationale behind testing for communicable viruses, but why on earth would a waiter need a dental check and a hearing test to work in a restaurant?" The only reason that sprang to mind was an effort to spare the customers from inhaling an overpowering case of halitosis from a hovering waiter or being stuck with a server who was so auricularly challenged that he was incapable of hearing the orders.

"The tests is to make the job for the hospital bureaucrat, what else?" Vasilis scoffed, as though it was patently obvious. "The, how you to say, the *polyascholi douleia*?"

"The busy work," I suggested.

"*Nai*, the busy work for no the reason but to make the job for someone the..." Vasilis threw his hands in the air, seemingly lost for the English word to complete his sentence. "To make the job for the *anipsios*."

"The niece," Takis translated.

"Nephew," I corrected, familiar with Greeks confusing their English genders. "Niece is *anipsia*."

"It is all the *nepotismos*." Vasilis insisted it was all nepotism. "I look forward to the retire and no more the bureaucracy to stamp on the neck so the nephew to make the easy job."

"What is the talk of the make the job stamp again?" The question was fired by an attractive middle-aged woman with exquisitely coiffed jet-black hair, her eyes dramatically outlined with kohl, her eyelashes weighed down with a heavy coating of black mascara. Carrying two coffees, she struck me as rather done-up for such an early hour.

Deflecting the question, Vasilis introduced the woman as his wife, Angeliki, telling her that I would be examining the kitchen to ensure it was clean enough for Takis to purchase. Before I could explain there was a tad more to my inspection than that, Angeliki rolled her eyes, scoffing, "All the years I to run the kitchen, never anyone official inspect him." Her response confirmed something I had long suspected; public health inspectors were extremely thin on the ground in rural Greece.

Noticing that I had pushed my coffee to one side, untouched, Angeliki asked if I would prefer a cup of mountain tea.

"Nothing, thank you. I make it a point to avoid beverages when I'm on duty."

"He to probably want to see how clean the kitchen is before he sample the anything from it," Vasilis jokingly said to his wife, unaware that he'd hit the nail on the head. "So, you to make the job of the inspect the taverna in the England?"

"Yes, indeed," I confirmed, not bothering to explain that Greek tavernas weren't really a thing back in Manchester.

"You have the uncle in the office?" Vasilis asked.

Thinking his question was a tad odd, I responded with a simple "No."

"You have no the family to get you the job..." Vasilis began.

His question was drowned out by Angeliki bluntly asking, "How much the job he to pay?"

Squirming under her direct gaze, I avoided answering by telling her that I was now retired. Although many Greeks seem to consider it perfectly normal to fire probing questions about the state of one's finances, it is something I have yet to adapt to and that I never feel comfortable answering. As much as I fancy the idea of turning a bit Greek to honour my adopted homeland, I retain my English reticence on such subjects. Still, it always amazes me when someone expects me to fess up about personal matters after mere minutes of acquaintance. To be fair, it tends to be a trait practised by the more elderly Greeks, the younger generation being a tad less inclined to subject practical strangers to the third degree. The gold medal for asking inappropriate questions of a personal nature would undoubtedly be bestowed on my next-door neighbour, Kyria Maria. Nothing is out of bounds as far as her nosy nature is concerned.

Changing the subject, I asked Angeliki if she was looking forward to retiring. I was relieved that she spoke such excellent English, thus sparing me the need to try out my Greek vocabulary on the subject.

"Yes, I cannot wait to get out of the kitchen. I want to retire the years ago but Vasilis want to hold on. He want to convince our daughter to take on the business but I tell him he stupid. Why she want to burden herself with working every hour of the day in the kitchen when she have the easy good government job? Vasilis stupid to think…"

"Why else I to work to build the good business if not to leave the fruit of my labour to the daughter?" Takis interrupted. "I hoped the Evangeline to see the sense and take over the family taverna."

"Take leave of her sense, you mean," Angeliki sneered. Turning to me, she said proudly, "Evangeline have the good job for the life in the Thessaloniki. She work in the customer service for the IKA. Vasilis, he think she should take over the taverna but he the crazy. Evangeline is paid the fourteen time every the year and the good pension when she retire."

Angeliki's words confirmed what I heard from my neighbours in Meli, that many public sector jobs paid an additional monthly wage at Christmas and Easter.

"Now she to learn to work the computer, she to get the extra six-day holiday on top of the summer break. I say to Vasilis, she be the crazy to give it up to slave in the kitchen here."

"But I wanted her to continue the family business..." Vasilis piped up.

"You are crazy. You want her to work the twenty hour every day, seven day all the summer..."

"But we not to work the winter..." Vasilis protested.

"Picking the olives to make the oil for the taverna is not the work?" Wincing as Angelika's fingers crept perilously close to my undrunk coffee, I cautiously edged my chair out of the firing range in case she chucked the cup at her husband. I didn't fancy my slacks becoming the victim to a deluge of coffee. Fortunately, Angeliki restrained herself, instead continuing her tirade. "My husband the delude. I am happy that the Evangeline have the good job that give her the free time. She not to be stuck in the kitchen from sun up to dark."

"Is your daughter married?" I asked, hoping to change the subject. It appeared that their daughter's reluctance to take over the family business was a bone of contention between the couple. I really was in no mood to start ducking if they started lobbing plates at one another.

"No, she to live with the boyfriend," Vasilis said.

"Ah, that's quite the modern approach over

here," I commented.

"I tell her not to the marry," Vasilis boomed. "I say to Evangeline, do not to marry. I tell her, if you not to marry, you can to keep to get the dead father's pension…"

"But you're not dead," I blurted out in confusion.

"The pension from the first father who is the dead. When I to marry the Angeliki, the Evangeline become my daughter," Vasilis clarified.

"Ah, so you're her step-father…"

"Vasilis is the good father, he take the Evangeline as his own daughter," Angeliki informed me. "Evangeline's first father was the officer in the army. Now that he dead, he get the very good army pension…"

"And the Evangeline entitle to the dead army pension if she not to marry. If she to marry, she would to burn the money," Vasilis continued, demonstrating his point by whipping a five euro note from his pocket and setting the corner alight with his lighter. Seemingly amazed that the flame had caught, Vasilis swore heartily before dunking the euro note in my coffee to douse the fire, tutting at the sight of the note's charred edge.

Attempting to get my head around the concept of a grown-up woman inheriting her deceased father's public service pension simply by virtue of remaining a spinster, whilst all the time having a well-paid public service position of her own, I queried aloud, "So your daughter is entitled to draw her dead father's army pension but only so long as she remains unmarried."

"Of course," Vasilis and Angeliki said in unison, the first time they had agreed upon anything.

"She is the entitle as long as she not to marry. She refuse to take over the business; the least she can do is to listen to me about the pension," Vasilis added.

"Vasilis not to care that I am the embarrass when people to ask if my daughter the marry or not..." Angeliki snapped. "Such the attractive girl and the people to think she cannot to get the husband."

"Better to have the security than the husband. She have the good job. If she to marry, she have no the dead father's pension and the husband may to spend all the day eating her wage..."

As the couple continued to snipe at one another, I reflected that Vasilis was encouraging his step-daughter to game the system. I had no clue how widespread such practices were or if they were considered akin to the infamous benefit fraud which the tabloid papers made out was so prevalent in England. It struck me that Evangeline was better off with a cushy government job than working all hours in the taverna, something I knew from personal experience was extremely hard graft. The apparently legal icing on the cake was the extra unearned income from her dead father's pension, though in order to continue to draw it she must make the personal sacrifice of not marrying her boyfriend.

I had it on the good authority of Spiros that positions in the public sector were considered jobs for life, even the most useless civil servants guaranteed life-course tenure and immunity from being fired, no matter how badly they performed on the job. The taverna regulars often railed against the nepotism within the public sector, a bloated sector of cronies with vested political interests resistant to change, employees lacking the motivation to do a good job since doing a lacklustre one had no detrimental effect on their prospects.

Moreover, I had heard that the additional benefits which Evangeline enjoyed by virtue of tapping her fingers across a keyboard had been won after much opposition to introducing computers. The staff, worried that they would end up being replaced by machines, had enjoyed the last laugh when they were awarded additional holiday days by reluctantly agreeing to get to get grips with computerisation. Going by my experience in the police station and the local KEP, there was no requirement for those that operated computers to have any particular skillset beyond the ability to stab the keyboard with one finger.

"Well, your daughter's loss in not taking over your business, is my gain," Takis interjected before the couple could come to blows. "Now, let me to just show the kitchen to the Victor and get his professional opinion. If all is well, we can to shake on the sale."

As Takis and I edged away from the table and headed towards the kitchen, Vasilis and his wife continued to bicker, seemingly oblivious to our departure. I shuddered to imagine how they would tolerate being retired off together; I supposed that they were well accustomed to being joined at the hip at the helm of the taverna. Perchance retirement would offer them the chance to develop separate interests and break the habit of throwing crockery at one another.

# Chapter 11

*Victor Dons his Hairnet Again*

**B**efore stepping into the kitchen, I replaced my jacket with my pristine white coat, covered my hair with my hairnet, and slipped my hands into a pair of disposable latex gloves. Brandishing a thermometer and a torch which would shine light into even the murkiest corners, I was ready to uncover and confront any gross hygiene violations. I must confess it felt inordinately satisfying to be back on the job, even though it wasn't in any official capacity.

At first glance, the kitchen struck me as a large well-organised space, certainly much cleaner than

Dina's kitchen in our local taverna. Stainless steel surfaces gleamed, the fryer was full of fresh oil, the grill sparkled with cleanliness, and the pans were so well-scrubbed that one could see one's reflection in their shiny finish. It struck me that perchance Angeliki kept everything so reflective in order to have substitute mirrors at hand when she trowelled on the eye makeup.

My guess that a few plates had been hurled with abandon earlier was confirmed when I spotted a pile of crockery shards neatly swept into one corner by a young Albanian woman wielding a broom. Shyly observing our entrance, she continued her work, scouring the already clean surfaces with a vengeance, giving Violet Burke a run for her money in her dedication to eradicating the merest hint of dirt.

"What are you to examine on your check?" Takis asked me.

"I follow a thorough checklist, the purpose of which is to ensure that the taverna complies with food safety law and that the food it produces is safe to consume. "

"So, you to check there is no the mouses?"

"Certainly. Any evidence of vermin would be totally unacceptable," I agreed.

"I think the cat will to keep the mouses away," Takis said, pointing to an overweight ginger tom curled up on a shelf beneath the work surface.

"That will have to go. It really isn't on to have cats in the kitchen," I told him, my voice lacking conviction.

"But surely it is good to have the cat for the no mouses…"

"Only if your customers are partial to picking cat hairs out of their food."

In my professional role as a public health inspector, I would have been horrified to discover a cat in the kitchen. However, I had grown so accustomed to having Marigold's imported felines cluttering up our kitchen in Meli that I no longer cringed at the sight of the odd domestic feline catching a nap in the vicinity of food preparation. Realising that I had allowed my standards to become somewhat lax, I squared my shoulders and adopted a more authoritative tone, instructing Takis to give the fat ginger its marching orders.

Although I had spotted other cats in the taverna, the dining area was outdoors, making it difficult to police. Most taverna owners faced a dilemma when it came to cats invading their premises: some diners abhorred felines having the run of the place, while others, particularly tourists, often encouraged them, considering cute Greek cats a quintessential part of their holiday experience. Often the taverna staff just couldn't win: cat lovers taking umbrage and labelling the staff nasty cat-haters if they shooed the unwanted visitors away, cat-haters cringing in annoyance at the sight of feline beggars demanding they share their food.

"What else you to check?" Takis quizzed me after he'd seen off the cat.

"Well, there's a whole list of things. I need to ensure that all the insectocutors are properly maintained..."

"Insector...?"

"The electrical devices that zap insects," I clarified.

"*Ilektrikos mygoktonos*," Takis helpfully translated.

"Some establishments allow them to get clogged up with dead flies, thus rendering them inefficient. Also, I must ensure that all food waste is stored correctly and that cleaning materials such as bleach are stored separately to food. Additionally, I will need to check the kitchen is adequately ventilated, that all equipment is maintained in a pristine condition and that all food supplies are rotated, dated, and labelled correctly," I continued. "The most relevant part of my inspection as it pertains to your purchase is the state of the appliances. You don't want to be shelling out for a deep freeze or dishwasher that are little better than antiquities that aren't up to the job, fit for nothing but scrap."

Climbing a step ladder, I shone my torch into a corner of the kitchen ceiling, whilst Takis thoughtfully footed the ladder to prevent it toppling over. "See, up there," I pointed out with a shudder. "It appears that there is blood splattered on the ceiling."

*"Yiati yparchei aima sto tavani?"* Takis called out to the Albanian kitchen assistant, asking her why there was blood on the ceiling.

*"Den einai aima. I Angeliki petaxe tis gemistes ntomates ston Vasili,"* she replied, saying it wasn't blood, explaining that Angeliki threw stuffed tomatoes at Vasilis.

"Angeliki's aim must be the terrible," Takis opined, immediately directing the young Albanian woman to take my place on the ladder and give the ceiling a good scrubbing.

After giving the kitchen a rigorous inspection, I was happy to give it my thumbs up, only noting a few minor violations: a freezer in urgent need of defrosting, a lack of paper towels next to the hand washing facilities, a growth of mould in the dishwasher that needed tackling urgently, and a commercial fridge that was so knackered it failed to record the requisite temperature for storing food. Advising Takis that said fridge would need replacing, he beamed with delight.

"Excellent, I can to batter the Vasilis down to a

lower price to compensate for the necessity of re-place the fridge."

"Barter," I automatically corrected, wondering if batter wasn't actually apt considering the state of the ceiling. I wasn't entirely convinced that dried blood wasn't mixed in with the splattered residue of stuffed tomatoes.

The other minor violations I noted were of no consequence to Takis' purchase since they simply reflected the lax standards of the current owners. Noticing a lack of adherence to the red/green bucket system, I suggested that Takis should implement said bucket system as a matter of priority if he took over the taverna. The system is foolproof if one al-ways uses a red bucket containing water and a cloth to wipe debris from kitchen surfaces, and a green bucket full of hot soapy water for sanitising the sur-faces, always ensuring no cross contamination be-tween the two buckets. Whilst it may be natural to assume that the red/green bucket method pertain-ing to commercial kitchen cleanliness is named in honour of V.D. Bucket, it is just a passing coinci-dence.

I called Takis' attention to a *moussaka* left un-covered in one of the fridges in flagrant disregard for covering cooked dishes. Takis was genuinely shocked by the sight of the uncovered dish, demon-strating that the culinary school he had attended had been hot on hygiene issues. Peering intently at the *moussaka*, Takis drew my attention to a rather suspect clump of black spots barely visible to the naked eye, adorning the top layer of baked bechamel sauce. Voicing his worry that the dish may be tainted with vermin droppings even though we had uncovered no evidence of any vermin life in the kitchen, he asked Angeliki and Vasilis to come into the kitchen to explain. We both visibly relaxed when, after staring at the *moussaka* as though she had never seen it before, Angeliki had a light-bulb moment. "It must to be my mascara. We were to running late this morning and I had to do my eyes in the kitchen. Luckily a bit the mascara never to give the customer the food poison."

"How many times I to tell you to not do the eyes in the kitchen?" Vasilis complained.

"Where else I to do when you keep me chain in the kitchen night and day," Angeliki fired back.

"Shall we to go to the table to talk the buying?" Takis suggested, steering Vasilis out of the kitchen before the argument could escalate into another frenzied bout of plate chucking. Taking my arm, Takis hissed, "You think it is the good buy?"

"Well, that must be your decision, Taki, but I am happy to give my seal of approval to the kitchen. It has been maintained at a very high standard and only has minor violations that can be easily fixed."

Despite the domestic acrimony between Vasilis and his wife, the kitchen was certainly up to scratch, largely I suspected due to the dedication of the young Albanian woman beavering away like a workhorse.

"I will to do it, Victor. I will to buy the taverna. My mind was to the almost made up but now I am the sure. Now I must to just, how to say, hobble the price?"

"Haggle," I corrected.

"I think to batter the Vasilis down by the five thousand evro…you see with your own eye before, the Vasilis have the money to burn. He can to go lower the price."

"Well, I wish you the best of luck in your negotiations," I said, slipping my hairnet back into my satchel and preparing to take my leave.

"You cannot to go yet. If we to shake on the price, you must to celebrate with the me…and we to talk the menu, yes."

"Why don't I leave you to negotiate a price for the purchase with Vasilis and pop back in a bit?" I suggested.

A walk along the seafront would provide a pleasant intermission whilst Takis concluded his business. It would also offer some respite from the now deafening elevator music which had been turned to maximum volume to drown out the sound of Vasilis and Angeliki engaging in another marital spat.

# Chapter 12

*Percy Bysshe Shelley Finds Victor's Leg Desirable*

Surreptitiously pocketing a handful of paper napkins as I left the taverna, I headed towards the almost deserted pebble beach, thinking the napkins would come in handy for drying my feet off if I fancied a paddle. I relished the idea of having the beach to myself: although the setting was one of great beauty, it wasn't too popular as a sunbathing destination. Whilst it tends to attract a few holidaymakers in the height of the season, so early in the summer it remains devoid of commercially for-hire sunbeds and umbrellas, giving it little allure as a tourist draw. Negotiating the stones and large pebbles underfoot can make access to the sea a tad challenging. Sun worshippers hailing from foreign parts invariably seem to prefer the feel of sand between their toes and the convenience of beachside cafes delivering exotic Greek beverages to their sun loungers.

I considered it a shame that Marigold was so set on the whole sand under our toes malarky for the upcoming renewal of our vows. When I had suggested this very beach as an ideal location for the ceremony, due to its absence of people, Marigold had dismissed my idea out of hand, insistent she absolutely must have sand. Since sand attracts beach goers en masse, I mused that Marigold would only have herself to blame if a bunch of Brits, kitted out in indecent budgie smugglers, photobomb the pictures that she has persuaded Adam to take.

Stepping under the canopy of tamarisk trees standing sentinel at the rear of the beach, I made my way onto the pebbles, taking a deep bracing breath of the fresh sea air. The sea looked inviting with a clear turquoise tint, small surface waves breaking onto the beach in a rush of foamy white froth. Heading towards the edge of the shore, I stepped over piles of driftwood, making a mental note to return with Marigold for a spot of kindling collecting; it was an activity we occasionally enjoyed together, combining exercise with boosting our stock of kindling for the winter.

In the distance, I noticed the lone figure of a woman taking her morning constitutional; as she came nearer, I spotted a large dog racing towards her. Instead of stopping when she called out to it, the dog soared right past her. As it bounded towards me, I was able to identify it as an enormous and over-enthusiastic Labrador. Clearly lacking any obedience training or sense of boundaries, the dog hurled itself at me, almost knocking me off my feet as it mounted my leg and started humping my thigh.

Refusing to unlatch itself from my limb, the Labrador appeared to be under the mistaken belief that my leg was an object of desire, even though I was clearly an unsuitable mating partner and my slacks had no convenient aperture for the dog to stick its rudely enlarged appendage in. As I fought to free myself from its ardent attention, the statuesque woman who clearly had no business being in charge of a dog, rushed towards me, shouting, "Percy Bysshe Shelley, get down at once. Heel. Percy Bysshe, stop humping the man at once."

Her repeated cries of "Heel" went ignored, the dog continuing to find my leg desirable. Making a move to grab the dog by the collar, the woman quipped, "Percy Bysshe, get a kennel." She was obviously barking mad if she imagined that the ghastly ordeal her pet was subjecting me to was in any way funny. I found nothing at all entertaining in her dog's mounting passion, my futile efforts to fight it off completely knocking the wind out of me.

"Get this thing off me," I demanded, my attempt to push the dog away only seeming to encourage it to latch on tighter. My annoyance grew as I felt the damp slobber of dog drool seeping through the fabric of my lightweight summer slacks. The dog owner was much better protected than I, her imposing form sensibly wrapped in a waterproof anorak.

Clipping the dog lead onto its collar, the woman yanked the frenzied dog off my leg, instructing it to sit. "Oh, dear, I'm sorry about that," the woman apologised, her tone blithely unapologetic. She made no effort to stifle her snort of amusement when she clocked the wet patch on my upper thigh; embarrassingly placed, the dog drool made it look as though I'd had an unfortunate accident.

"Have you been with a bitch?" she brayed in a plummy English accent. I bristled at her coarse language, belatedly realising she was referencing a female dog. "If he can smell one on you, then it's tantamount to you encouraging him."

"The only dog that may have possibly rubbed

up against these slacks since their last wash is Waffles, and he's a boy."

"Oh, well, Percy Bysshe isn't fussy, he'll hump anything that moves. Though in his defence, he usually limits himself to trying to mate with the sofa or that funny little Albanian fellow that delivers the garden manure."

"Guzim?"

"That's his name. You know the fellow? I can't understand why Percy Bysshe is so attracted to him. He always stinks of chickens and rabbits."

"The lingering aroma of dung is only to be expected since he dabbles in manure," I commented, tight-lipped, feeling personally slighted that she thought nothing of disparaging my gardener, a prerogative I preferred to keep to myself. Catching a noxious whiff of Labrador saliva emanating from my trousers, it struck me that I was smelling none too clean myself. Not only was the woman incapable of controlling her ridiculously named pet, she clearly neglected its oral hygiene. Reaching into my pocket, I used the paper napkins from the taverna to rub at the damp patch, flapping the woman's hand away when she snatched one of the napkins and moved a tad too close to my thigh.

"I can manage perfectly well," I snapped. "You really ought to keep your dog on a lead. The thing is a total menace. Imagine the damage it could have done if I'd been a frail pensioner; it would have had me over on the pebbles."

"You can't expect me to keep Percy Bysshe on a lead. He needs his exercise."

"Considering that you appear to have named your dog after the neurotic poet, Shelley, who met his end by drowning, it seems to be tempting fate to leave him unleashed so close to the sea," I retorted.

"Ah, you got the reference to his name. Not many people get it, you know. It seemed quite apt to name Percy Bysshe after the poet since Shelley was a fellow grecophile who penned the wonderful poem, Hellas. Did you know that's the name the ancients gave Greece?"

"Just because I am covered in dog drool, it doesn't mean that I am a total philistine," I snapped, edging away as Percy Bysshe strained against his lead, eyeing up my one remaining dry leg, its heated expression exaggerated by its tongue lolling out as it panted. "You really ought to consider taking Percy there to dog obedience classes."

"Well really, there's no need to take that tone. Percy Bysshe was only being playful. Dogs will be dogs."

"Dogs should be kept on a lead in public places," I reiterated.

"There's no sign saying that dogs must be leashed on the beach…" the woman argued, her sentence remaining incomplete as Percy Bysshe, spotting something a tad more desirable than my leg, practically yanked the woman off her feet as it took off after fresh prey. Keeping only a tenuous hold on the lead, the woman was dragged off at speed as the dog tried to keep pace with a cyclist pedalling along the road adjacent to the beach. His legs, pitifully exposed in a pair of short shorts, seemingly a more attractive proposition than my slack covered limbs.

"I will make a point of calling in at the *Dimarcheio* and make my feelings known on the matter. There should be laws for people like you with no control over their pets," I yelled out after her. Satisfied that I'd had the last word, I continued my stroll across the pebble beach, thankful there were no more canines to fight off.

Making my way to the water's edge, I slipped off my boat shoes and socks, rolling the hem of my slacks up. Marigold may well prefer sand on her beaches but I am quite partial to stepping on pebbles as I access the sea, finding their surfaces act as natural pumice stones, helping to slough the dead skin from the soles of my feet.

After enjoying a refreshing paddle in the shallows, I stepped back onto dry land, sticking my hands in my pockets to retrieve the paper napkins that I had filched from the taverna earlier to dry my feet. As my hands encountered nothing but a lump of soggy paper, I realised that said paper napkins were now covered in dog drool. With nothing else for it, I was forced to use my socks as a makeshift towel before pulling them over my still damp feet. The annoyance I felt only exacerbated my determination to kick up a stink at the *Dimarcheio*. I was quite prepared to bend the ears of some jobsworth about the need to ban unleashed dogs from the beach and enforce the edict with a prominent sign.

Returning to the taverna, I reddened as I felt Angeliki's eyes zoning in on my damp patch.

"I had an unfortunate encounter with a large Labrador," I said by way of explanation.

"The vinegar he will to sort it," Angeliki decided. Ignoring my efforts to fight off her ministrations, in no time at all she was clucking over me, vigorously rubbing a vinegar doused cloth over my slacks. Flushing with embarrassment at her close proximity to my nether regions, I stoically endured her rub-down, thinking at least the smell of vinegar was an improvement on the pungent scent of dog slobber.

Takis informed me that he and Vasilis had shaken on a price and would consult with a lawyer the next day regarding the change of ownership. Takis appeared very ebullient, delighted at the prospect of owning a taverna of his own in the near future.

"The red tape to start from the scratch would be the nightmare," Takis explained. "To buy the going concern is much the simpler way to be in the business."

"You must to both come to celebrate this evening," Vasilis invited, clearly satisfied with the offer that Takis had made. "Victor, you have the wife? You must to bring her too."

Reluctant though I was to spend the evening ducking out of the way of flying plates, I hadn't the heart to turn down Takis' invitation to join him, a request made all the more enticing when he said that he would value my opinion on the new menu he planned to create. I quite fancied the idea of being involved in the early stages of his business venture. If Takis found my advice indispensable, who knew what possibilities lay ahead; I could well end up with the glamorous title of restaurant consultant. Marigold would likely be chuffed to bits if such an eventuality came to pass. Since she has always hankered after being married to a restaurant critic rather than a public health inspector, a role as a restaurant consultant may well make her proud, appealing to her latent snobbery.

Still dithering over the prospect of returning to dine there that evening, I was won over by

Angeliki's ecstatic reaction to the news that Takis would be taking over the taverna, thus freeing her from a life of kitchen drudgery. Angeliki was so thrilled at the prospect of imminent retirement that I doubted we'd have to do much ducking that evening.

Bidding the threesome farewell, I promised to return that evening with Marigold. Once behind the wheel of the Punto, I concentrated on mentally translating my complaints about unleashed dogs being allowed on the beach, into Greek. It was only as I neared the *Dimarcheio* that I realised I would hardly make a good impression if I rolled up looking as though I'd wet myself and stinking of vinegar. Sighing in frustration, I decided I was in no mood to grapple with the necessary Greek vocabulary to explain away my soaked slacks. It would be better all-round if I returned another day and made my complaints in a pair of dry trousers that smelt of nothing more suspect than fabric freshener.

# Chapter 13

*Trotting Out Three Languages*

ood grief, Victor. What on earth is that appalling stench?" Entering the kitchen, Marigold scrunched her nose in disgust.

"I'm just knocking up a vat of curry. Thinking that some of our guests next week may fancy a home-cooked curry, I decided to cook one up in advance and bung it in the freezer."

"I can't imagine why you think they'd fancy one of your curries when they can get the real thing at the Curry Mile," Marigold said dismissively. Wandering over to peer in the pan, she opined, "It smells perfectly horrid. That chicken looks rather odd, not to mention unnaturally slimy."

"That's because it isn't chicken. I am experimenting with a prickly pear vindaloo…"

"That sounds dangerous. Did you peel them first?"

"I'm not an idiot, Marigold. Naturally, I peeled the pads. I would hardly risk our guests getting a mouthful of glochids."

"There are times when I seriously question your sanity, Victor," Marigold said, rolling her eyes dramatically. "In what part of your warped mind did you conjure up a recipe for prickly cacti curry? If you're that desperate to save money and too tight to splash out on a Lidl chicken, you should just wring the neck of one of those smelly creatures that you keep in the coop."

"How many more times, Marigold? I refuse to cook up one of my beloved pet chickens. You know I have a certain attachment to them. As for adding cacti pads to my cooking repertoire, it was your son's idea," I said.

"I notice that you call him my son when he comes up with some daft notion…"

"Benjamin assures me that eating cacti pads is all the rage in Mexico."

"But that is an impoverished country, Victor, they probably don't have much choice. I doubt they have a convenient Lidl on every corner."

I didn't bother to point out that our nearest Lidl involved a ninety-minute plus drive over a mountain though I found Marigold's attitude a tad contrary. Whilst my wife is forever harping on about eating my pet chickens, she is set against eating anything we could forage. Despite foraging being something of a local habit, she refuses to engage in such an activity, espousing the belief that it would send out the wrong image about the state of our finances.

Moreover, Marigold professes her dislike for wild asparagus and refuses to let me cook the very popular dish of *horta*, foraged wild greens, at home. I suppose that she does have a point when it comes to *horta*. The smell of boiled greens is unquestionably vile and lingers for days, so foul that it makes boiled cabbage smell almost good in comparison. Funnily enough, Marigold doesn't object to eating *horta* when I pay good money for it in a restaurant, even though it is clearly a rip-off to pay through the nose for something that grows with wild abandon in the fields.

Plunging a spoon into the depths of the simmering stew, Marigold taste tested the curry. Spitting it out in the kitchen sink, she pronounced it beyond disgusting.

"That is the vilest concoction that you have ever cooked up. Those cacti pads have the exact same texture as pan scrubbers…"

"They are renowned for being fibrous," I pointed out defensively, resisting the urge to quiz my wife on her hitherto undisclosed habit of snacking on balls of coiled stainless steel.

"Do get me some water, Victor," Marigold demanded between a bout of choking. "There's something abhorrently sticky in that curry. It's practically glued my tongue to my teeth…"

"I suppose the pear pads may be mucilaginous…"

"Oh, do speak English…I haven't mastered Greek words with so many syllables."

"I am speaking English. Mucilaginous refers to a typically viscous consistency. When you mentioned their gluey texture, it made me wonder if perchance cacti pads share the same glutinous tendency as okra."

"Any dish that uses anything remotely resembling okra is not fit for human consumption, Victor," Marigold pronounced, making no attempt to hide how much she despised the mallow vegetable. She had never understood my preference for an okra based bhindi bhaji when we had dined at the Bhilai Bhaji, our favourite Indian restaurant back in Manchester.

When I had snuck some okra in from the market to try out the Greek recipe of stewed okra with tomatoes, *bamies stifado me domates*, Marigold had flatly refused to even sample it. Still, the okra hadn't gone to waste. I had demonstrated preparing and cooking the dish in one of my cookery classes, though I must admit it didn't go down too well. Since the other expats in the village shared my wife's dislike of the innocuous vegetable, Milton's cats had been the only beneficiaries, eating extremely well that evening.

"You may as well just throw the contents of that pan in Guzim's direction."

"There's far too much curry here for one scrawny Albanian to put away," I pointed out.

"But Guzim isn't just any Albanian; ever since he downed his first mouthful of the stuff, he's had an insatiable curry addiction. I'm sure he's capable of polishing off that pan full of botched curry if he eats it for breakfast, lunch and dinner, though goodness knows what that gluey texture will do to his insides."

"He seems to have a pretty robust constitution," I said, thinking that I had been remiss in failing to taste test the curry before allowing Marigold to gum up her mouth.

"Speaking of Guzim," Marigold said. "We really should make a decision about whether we are going to invite him to our vow renewal service…"

"It's nothing to do with me. I have left the guest

list in your capable hands," I reminded her.

Marigold's reservations about inviting the Albanian shed dweller were a tad shallow. When the subject had come up previously, she had voiced her worries that he would stand out and ruin the photographs.

"I think perhaps we ought to invite him," Marigold dithered.

"He'll steal the show if he turns up in that cast-off Lycra..."

"Nonsense, he's got that button down of yours that he took off the scarecrow. You'll just have to have a word with him and make sure he understands that we expect a certain dress code."

"He's your Albanian..." I began to say before intercepting one of my wife's withering looks. "Yes, dear. I'll have a word."

"I forgot to ask. How did your health inspecting thingy go?"

"The kitchen passed muster and Takis has made an offer on the taverna which the owner has accepted. Takis has invited us to dine there with him this evening..."

"Which taverna is it?"

When I filled Marigold in on the details, she expressed her delight at the prospect of our dining there that evening. "I would have really enjoyed our last visit to that taverna if you hadn't ruined the evening by grumbling about your mediocre *moussaka*…"

"It turns out that I was right to grumble. Angeliki leaves her *moussaka* uncovered in the fridge, a deplorable practice that leaves it open to dripping condensation and cross-contamination…"

"It's not as though it gave you a dose of food poisoning…" Marigold interrupted before I had chance to tell her about Angeliki's mascara tainting the cheese topping.

"I was likely spared such a fate since I left most of it uneaten due to it being unappetising and dry…"

"You should have had the stuffed tomatoes, dear," Marigold reminded me. "They were excellent."

I didn't have the heart to tell Marigold that she may well have consumed a dish that had been scraped off the kitchen ceiling.

"I have to say that I really enjoyed the atmosphere in that taverna. It certainly made for a lively evening," Marigold said.

Indeed, I recalled that Marigold had delighted in shamelessly eavesdropping on the heated argument playing out in the kitchen. When I had pointed out that it was rude of her to listen in, she had retorted that she was taking the opportunity to recognise Greek vocabulary that she had studied in her classes but never had the opportunity to use.

"Well, I can't guarantee that the food will have improved since our last visit but I am expecting high standards once Takis takes over the kitchen. He trained professionally at a culinary school and would like to pick my brain about ideas for a new menu."

"Just don't go mentioning that vile smelling cacti curry…"

The shrill sound of the bell attached to the gate ringing out in the kitchen caused both of us to jump in alarm. Hardly anyone ever rang the bell. The ornate gate, being somewhat redundant since Harold had left the village, was left permanently unlocked to save us the annoyance of traipsing down to admit any callers.

"I wonder who that can be?" Marigold questioned. Peering out of the kitchen window, she announced, "There's a woman and a small boy at the gate. We don't see many children in the village."

"I'd clean forgotten that I promised Blat that I would tutor his son…"

"Blat?"

"Yes, a labourer who's working on the pointing."

"Well, the boy at the gate looks a bit young to be suffering one of your lectures on hygiene," Marigold observed.

"No, you've got the wrong end of the stick. Blat wants me to give Tonibler an English lesson…"

"Tony Blair? Have you lost the plot, Victor?"

"I'll fill you in later, darling. It's a long story. You might prefer to make yourself scarce unless you want to be dragged into something surreal."

"You've piqued my interest, now. I'll go down and let them in whilst you find somewhere to hide that pan of revolting curry until you can offload it on Guzim. Do find an air freshener and start spraying. We don't want to asphyxiate that poor child with the ghastly smell."

My wife scuttled down to admit our visitors, returning with a plump woman who appeared to be in her early thirties, her open smile indicating a pleasant demeanour. Her curly hair could have benefited from a session in Athena's kitchen to liven up what, I believe in hairdressing terms, is described as mousy colouring. I presumed that the bespectacled young boy with an unnaturally serious expression on his face for one of such tender years, was Tonibler.

For some bizarre reason, the child was wearing what appeared to be the sort of school uniform one associated with English public schools. His short, slight frame was dwarfed by a smart grey blazer emblazoned with red piping, the cuffs of the sleeves flapping loosely down to his knees. Only the hem of his matching grey shorts was visible below the bottom of the blazer, the smart effect totally ruined by his grey knee socks, held up by suspenders and paired with grubby plimsolls featuring a hole in one toe. Since the nearest Greek school has no uniform code, I was pretty certain that Tonibler's formal outfit would leave him open to being a figure of ridicule from his classmates.

The woman surprised me by introducing herself in hesitant English as Blerta, Blat's wife and the mother of Tonibler. Having expected Blat's wife to be barely out of her teens, I was taken aback by Blerta since she seemed to have a good fifteen years on her husband. Blat had given no indication that he was a toy boy.

Speaking in a convoluted mix of Greek and English, neither of which she was particularly proficient in, Blerta thanked me profusely for taking the time to school young Tonibler in perfect English.

"It is the Blat…*pos*… *oneiro* to live in the…*pos*… *Megali Vretania*," Blerta said, spicing up her English with a hesitant stuttering of *how* and the Greek words for *dream* and *Great Britain*. I must confess that it came as somewhat of a relief that she didn't babble away at me in rapid fire Greek. Her odd mix of the two languages, neither of which were her mother tongue, didn't put me at a disadvantage. I was touched when she pressed a small paper bag into my hands containing four perfectly formed eggs and a rather deformed looking carrot still covered in soil.

"So, your husband wants me to tutor young Tonibler here in English," I said after thanking her for the fresh fare.

"*Ti?*" Blerta replied, failing to understand my English.

Before I could repeat my words at a slower pace, Tonibler stepped up to the plate, translating for his mother by speaking in her native Albanian tongue before repeating his words in confident English. I liked his approach as it gave Blerta the opportunity to improve her English, hanging on the child's every word as she did. "Mr Bucket said we are here to learn my English."

Turning to me, Tonibler said, "Mama speak only a little Greek and little English." Intelligence beyond his years reflected in the boy's eyes as he spoke.

"*Bravo*, your English is very good already," I praised the sombre six-year-old child, hoping his mother had either enough English or Greek to understand simple ironing instructions. According to Guzim, the family spoke Gheg Albanian. The only Albanian words I was familiar with were the few expletives that I had picked up from my gardener and they were pronounced in the Tosk dialect, not that I had any intention of swearing at Blerta: perish the thought that I would conduct myself in such a crude manner. I had no desire to emulate Milton's appalling language.

Considering Tonibler appeared to be almost bilingual in English and Gheg Albanian, I asked him in Greek if he also spoke Greek. "*Milas kai esy Ellinika?*"

"*Nai, ta mathimata mou sto scholeio einai sta Ellinika.*" The boy replied in the affirmative, telling me his lessons at school were in Greek. Hearing his excellent pronunciation of grammatically correct Greek made me feel a tad inferior. I had been grappling with the Greek language for almost three years, yet my efforts came nowhere close. I was put to shame by someone barely taller than my knees who was capable of trotting out three languages proficiently.

"But I cannot read and write the English. You will to help me, please? I want to read the English good when we move to the Great Britain." The child was certainly eager. "I learn the alphabet but have no English book and not know how to put the letters together."

"I'll certainly be able to help you with that," I confirmed as Marigold took hold of the boy's sleeves and rolled them up neatly to expose his hands.

"What school uniform is that?" Marigold asked Tonibler.

"It is the uniform of the Tonibler school, the Dublin Chorister School," Tonibler answered.

"You go to school in Dublin?" Marigold queried in confusion.

"No, I go to the school in…" Tonibler replied, naming a village about forty minutes away on the coast. "I go on the bus in the morning."

"So, why do you wear a school uniform from a school you don't attend?" I asked.

"Because the great Tonibler wear this uniform at the great Chorister School," Tonibler explained in a measured tone, as though it was all perfectly rational instead of decidedly peculiar. As he spoke, he ran a hand through his greased back hair before adjusting his spectacles, leaving an oily sheen on the one lens that wasn't covered with a flesh-coloured medical adhesive plaster.

I recollected reading in one of the Sunday papers that, as a public schoolboy, the young Tony Blair had kept his unruly long hair in place with butter; it appeared that Blat was bringing Tonibler junior up to emulate his hero's style, though the sheen of the grease in young Tonibler's hair indicated he may have slicked it down with olive oil rather than butter.

Dragging me off to one side, Marigold hissed in my ear. "Why didn't you mention this before, Victor?"

"It clean slipped my mind," I admitted.

"And I suppose you expect me to entertain the young woman while you tutor her son?"

"Not at all. Blat offered his wife's services in return for my giving Tonibler an English lesson. Blerta is going to do the ironing. Just point her in the direction of the ironing board…"

"Oh, Victor, how thoughtful of you. You know that ironing is one task that I absolutely abhor. It's complete drudge work." As Marigold smiled in relief, I could see the cogs in her brain visibly turning. "It doesn't seem right though for me to hang around like lady muck while Blerta irons your Y-fronts; it will only embarrass her. I'll sort her out with the ironing pile and then make myself scarce. I'll drop in on Sherry and have a coffee with her."

I reflected that Marigold pulling a disappearing act was only to be expected. She always made a point of clearing off when Violet Burke slopped her mop around, as though her absence excused her idleness.

# Chapter 14

*Something of a Child Prodigy*

With Marigold out of the way and Blerta set up with a humongous pile of ironing in a corner of the grand salon, I turned my attention to my young charge.

"Your father didn't say you wanted to learn to read. I would have sorted out some suitable books if I'd known," I said, thinking I would borrow some of the books I had bought for Anastasia before our next lesson, my own reading material a tad too advanced for a six-year-old. "Still, you said you know the alphabet. Can you recite it for me?"

Tonibler impressed me no end by rattling off

the English alphabet at the speed of light. I declined his offer to also recite it backwards, not wanting to encourage the child to get a swollen head.

"Until I can sort out some children's books to help with your reading, we can practice sounding out letters and putting them together," I improvised. Grabbing Clawsome by the scruff of the neck, I held her aloft, asking Tonibler if he knew what it was in English.

"Cat," he replied.

"Exactly. Now if we put the letters C A T together, they spell cat," I explained, sounding out each letter phonetically with great emphasis. Tossing Clawsome aside, I wrote the letters down on a piece of paper for Tonibler to study.

Pulling Marigold's sunhat down from the hook by the door, I repeated the exercise, Tonibler correctly identifying the object as a hat and repeating the letters so that they formed the word. Pleased at Tonibler's progress, I held one of Marigold's scented candles aloft, sounding out the letters T A T.

"I learn the English word for that is candle," Tonibler corrected me.

"But it is a prime example of superfluous tat," I explained before twigging that my vocabulary was a tad too advanced for the now flummoxed child. Rushing to the front door, I returned with the door mat and repeated the exercise by sounding out the word M A T, relieved that Tonibler could follow the lesson if I stuck to simple words illustrated with household objects and pets. Running the A T combination through my mind, I realised that even if I could locate a gnat to hold aloft to demonstrate the word, it may prove a tad difficult for Tonibler to get to grips with the concept of a silent G. It was, after all, only his first lesson.

Instructing the child to copy the words cat, hat and mat on a piece of paper, it occurred to me that I was woefully ill-prepared to teach the lesson. I ought to have done my homework. It had been totally remiss of me to have such low expectations of the child's abilities; in my defence, Blat had given no indication that his offspring was something of a child prodigy. After meeting Tonibler, I could better understand why Blat harboured such lofty ambitions for his son and I determined to help the child if I could.

My initial idea had been to replace the A T sound combination with E T but I had neither a convenient net nor vet lying around the place to demonstrate their meaning. Changing tack, I told Tonibler that we would concentrate on improving his conversational English until I could get my hands on some age-appropriate books.

Realising that I had completely forgotten

Marigold's instruction to remove the curry from the hob, I pondered the possibility of salvaging the dish by spooning out the cacti pads and replacing them with chicken. Recalling how impressed I had been by the young contestants on 'Junior MasterChef,' even though watching the programme meant enduring the insufferable presentation of Lloyd Grossman with his ostentatious Mid-Atlantic accent, I realised that I could kill two birds with one stone by teaching Tonibler some useful culinary skills whilst we practised our conversational English.

Wrapping the child in Marigold's pinny, I was impressed when after correctly identifying a pan and the cooker, he used the term kitchen utensil to describe a slotted spoon. Whilst I was well up on the Greek word for cooker since it happens to be the same as the word for kitchen, *kouzina*, I was clueless as to the Greek for the slotted that preceded spoon. When Tonibler enlightened me that it was called a *trypiti koutali* in Greek, I realised that not only would our lessons help Tonibler improve his English, they would be handy for improving my Greek.

Kneeling up on a stool by the side of the cooker, the child eagerly accepted my invitation to spoon out the slimy looking pieces of cacti so that I could replace them with chicken. As he cautiously lowered the slotted spoon into the cavernous depths of the pan, I answered his questions about what type of typical English foods he might expect to encounter when he made it to England and tucked into school dinners. I wasn't sure if the information I imparted was terribly up to date since it was based on my own memories of school dinners.

"They used to be big on liver with mash, and cottage pie made from mince and gristle." Seeing the rather dubious expression on Tonibler's face, I assured him that whilst the main courses may sound stodgy and less than tempting, at least the puddings were worth queuing up for. "I expect they still serve jam roly poly with pink custard. It was always popular back in the day. Of course, they may have expanded their repertoire by now. It wouldn't surprise me to learn that curry is on the menu on these days."

"I hope not. It looks horrible," Tonibler said, a squeamish look on his young face. Depositing a cacti pad on a plate by the pan, he downed the slotted spoon whilst he adjusted his spectacles. Glancing over at the child, I immediately noticed that the medical adhesive plaster which had obscured one of the lenses of his spectacles, was no longer in place.

"What's happened to that plaster that was on your glasses?" I asked with a sinking feeling.

"I think it drop in the pan," Tonibler admitted.

"I do hope not. It will contaminate the curry," I groaned.

"What is contaminate?" Tonibler's question reminded me to curtail my use of vocabulary that was a tad too advanced for a child only just beginning to learn English.

"It means that your plaster may have polluted the curry..." Seeing the confusion on his face, I continued, "It may have made it unfit for human consumption...inedible, not fit to eat..."

"What's not fit to eat?" Violet Burke barked, striding into the kitchen without bothering with any of the niceties such as knocking.

"To what do I owe this unexpected pleasure, Mother?"

Ignoring my sarcasm laden question, Violet Burke continued her interrogation.

"Has your Marigold been cooking up some revolting French slop again for one of them dinner parties what she's so keen on?"

"No, Mother. I was preparing a vat of curry but the plaster has dropped off Tonibler's spectacles and may have landed in the curry, rendering it inedible through contamination."

"Tony Blair. Are you having a laugh, lad?" Violet Burke snorted, rushing forward as Tonibler's lips began to wobble and he burst into tears.

"I am sorry that I spoil the food," the child

stuttered.

"'Ere, wipe your eyes, lad," Violet Burke said, thrusting one of my pristine tea towels under Tonibler's now snotty nose. From the corner of my eye, I noticed that Blerta had downed the iron, a worried expression creasing her face.

"*To agori einai entaxei,*" I called across to Blerta, assuring her the boy was okay. Concerned that she may be alarmed by the sight of an officious looking harridan bursting into the kitchen and mopping up her son, I reassured Blerta by telling her it was my mother. "*Afti einai i mitera mou.*"

Visibly relaxing, Blerta resumed her ironing, applying a generous measure of spray starch to my Y-fronts. As my mother consoled the child, I muttered, "I always make a point of using blue detectable plasters in the kitchen in case of mishaps such as this."

"You said that the plaster came off the boy's glasses. It should be clean enough, it's not as though it will be smeared with any nasty puss that suppurated out of a wound," Violet Burke reasoned.

"That's hardly the point. It could present a choking hazard," I argued.

Violet Burke ignored me as she lifted Tonibler down from the stool. Settling him on his feet, she gave him a nudge. "Now, lad, is my Victor having a laugh or is your name really Tony Blair?"

"It is Tonibler," the child sniffed. "I am named after the great prime minister of the Great Britain."

"It could be worse," Vi snorted. "Imagine if you'd been named after that Margaret Thatcher."

Rolling my eyes at the absurdity of my mother's reasoning, I explained, "I am giving Tonibler an English lesson."

"Then you're a lucky lad. My Victor speaks right proper English," Vi said, clucking Tonibler under the chin. Noticing Blerta doing the ironing, Violet Burke cackled, "I see that Marigold has got someone in to do her ironing for her, the lazy mare. That wife of yours doesn't half live the life of Riley. She's got me to do the cleaning, you doing most of the cooking and now she can't even be bothered to press your undies."

"It is a simple exchange of labour. Tonibler's mother, Blerta, is doing the ironing in payment for my tutoring young Tonibler."

"And you've roped the poor little lad into doing your cooking..."

"No, we are practising conversational English and were just discussing the food in English schools."

Tonibler surprised us both by asking, "Will I eat the fish and chips at the school in the Great Britain?"

"Fancy you knowing about fish and chips," Vi

cooed.

"It is the favourite food of the great Tonibler," Tonibler enlightened us.

"I can't see the likes of him queueing up at the chippy for battered haddock and mushy peas," Vi sneered.

It was on the tip of my tongue to point out that my mother had hit the nail on the head since I re-called reading that the prime minister's fickle taste had exposed him as a hypocritical fraud. When pandering to the trendy Islington set, he avowed that his favourite food was fettuccine in a fancy sauce, but when playing up to his grassroot Labour supporters, he apparently loved nothing more than eating fish and chips from a newspaper. I decided to bite my tongue; it would be cruel to shatter Tonibler's adoration of his idol by pointing out that Tony Blair had feet of clay.

"If it's fish and chips that you're after, lad, I can cook you the best fish supper with mushy peas that you'll ever taste," Vi volunteered, having clearly taken to the child who appeared a little overawed by the invitation. Calling over to Tonibler's mother, Vi said, "Would you be all right with me having the lad over for his supper some night?"

"*Ti?*" Blerta replied, unable to make head or tail of my mother's words.

Spotting the confused expression on Blerta's

face, Violet Burke hissed in my ear, "Is she the full shilling?"

"I think so. Blerta hasn't scorched my socks yet," I hissed back.

"Blerta, what kind of name is that?" Vi demanded.

"A Kosovar Albanian one," I told her.

"In Albanian, Mama's name means blossom," Tonibler piped up.

"Never! Fancy that. My maiden name was Blossom," Violet Burke told the boy. "You could knock me down with a feather..."

Clearly confused by the idiom, Tonibler grabbed his backpack. Rummaging through the contents, he produced a feather which he handed to my mother with a shy expression, as though presenting her with a bouquet of flowers.

"Eh, thank you, lad. 'Appen this feather will look right smart in the hat what I'm planning to wear when my Victor gets married again. Tell your mother that before I was wed, I was a Blossom too."

A smile transformed Blerta's features when Tonibler duly translated my mother's words into Albanian.

Examining the pan of curry, I decided against replacing the cacti pads with chicken. With Tonibler's plaster lost in the sauce, I couldn't in all conscience risk serving it up to my imminent houseguests. I decided that I would simply bung the cacti pads back in the curry and follow my wife's advice of offering the pan of curried slop to Guzim. Of course, I would need to warn him to keep his eyes peeled for the missing plaster. Considering Guzim's appetite for curry seemed insatiable, most likely he would be prepared to risk it. As far as I could recall, the plaster in question had appeared to be of the standard polyethylene type, such plasters often having an absorbent pad treated with an antiseptic solution. Perchance the antiseptic would kill the odd germ that had latched onto the external layer membrane of the plaster.

As I removed the pan from the hob, Violet Burke opined that it smelt disgusting. "Are you planning on eating that curry muck tonight?" she asked.

"No, if I'm honest, the recipe was a bit of a flop. I'm going to palm it off on Guzim as he's addicted to curry and isn't too fussy what he stuffs in his gob." As I spoke, I imagined that the Albanian shed dweller would likely be ecstatic when I told him the curry wasn't even leftovers but freshly cooked. "I must warn him not to gobble it down but to chew every mouthful to avoid choking on the missing plaster."

"How's he going to go about chewing it when he's got nowt but toothless gums?"

"He's still got the odd tooth," I reminded her, thinking I would perhaps need to warn Guzim to suck the curry up carefully through his gums.

"If you're not eating that curry tonight, you could pop downstairs and I'll do you some nice bangers and mash," my mother invited.

"Actually, we're dining out tonight with young Takis who is buying the taverna where I inspected the kitchen this morning. Takis is quite keen for my advice on his menu. I suggested that he could introduce some British dishes that might appeal to expats over the winter."

"'Appen I'd best come with you, lad. I reckon my advice on British cooking would be a sight more useful than any of those fancy recipes that you experiment with. I didn't spend all them years working in chippies without knowing what tickles folks fancy."

"Really, there's no need," I protested. "I can't imagine that Takis will be up for concocting a winter menu of fried Spam, mucky fat toasties and mushy peas. It's not as though it would likely hold any appeal for expatriate grecophiles."

"But 'appen them coastal Brits will be queuing up for a decent Sunday dinner. You know what a dab hand I am at turning out my Yorkshire puds."

I had to admit that my mother had bested me in the argument since I had indeed suggested to Takis that roast dinners may well attract the British contingent.

"It's certainly true that no one turns out a Sunday roast with Yorkshire puddings as tasty as yours."

Accepting the compliment as her due, my mother changed tack.

"And this Takis fellow. Single, is he?"

"I believe so…"

"That's handy," Vi said enigmatically, not bothering to elaborate on why Takis' marital state was handy. "Right, that's settled then. You can pick me up after I'm done peeling the spuds for Dina's chips."

I winced at the thought of Marigold's reaction when she heard that we would be lumbered with Violet Burke for the evening. I couldn't imagine she would welcome my mother butting in on her conversation with Takis and stealing the limelight. Marigold has a tendency to revel in the attention of younger Greek men who are unfailingly polite to their elders. She had almost made a fool of herself more than once when Lefteris had flattered her with more compliments than he bestowed on his pampered pet poodle, Fufu.

"It looks as though Blerta has finished the ironing," I observed, noticing her putting the well starched clothes into neat piles. She'd certainly done an excellent job of accentuating the traveller's crease in my slacks, the collars of my button downs fairly standing to attention.

"Mr Bucket, can I to come again for another English lesson?" Tonibler pleaded.

"Certainly. I will sort out some suitable children's books before your next lesson and let your father know when it is convenient," I told him, pleased that he had not found my tuition lacking despite my being woefully unprepared. Turning to the child's mother, I thanked her profusely in Greek for making such an excellent job of the ironing and agreed to ask around amongst my friends and neighbours to see if any of them were in need of her services.

As a parting gesture, I told Tonibler to ask his mother if she'd like to take some of the curry home. In spite of his addiction to the stuff, I couldn't really see Guzim managing to guzzle his way through the full pot. As Tonibler repeated my generous offer in Albanian, I noticed the changing expressions flitting over Blerta's face. Her pleasant visage finally settled in a look of aghast revulsion that led me to believe my young pupil had done more than merely repeat my offer. I rather suspected that he had told his mother that I was trying to poison the family with contaminated curry.

As I shooed Tonibler and Blerta out of the

kitchen, the child beamed at my mother, reminding her, "'Appen I'll see you soon for fish and chips." He really was a remarkably quick study, picking up my mother's dropped H's as though born to them.

"You can't go round saying 'appen, lad," Violet Burke corrected him. "Victor would have my guts for garters if you start talking right common."

# Chapter 15

*A Pan Full of Misunderstandings*

O nce we were alone, I impatiently asked, "Did you pop up for anything in particular, Mother?"

"I did have something in mind, lad." Violet Burke paused for dramatic effect before coming out with a ludicrous suggestion that sounded ominously like a demand. "Seeing as how I missed out on your first wedding, I reckon I ought to walk you down the aisle to give you away?"

"There is no aisle, Mother, we're doing it on the beach. And you can't give me away because I already belong to Marigold."

"But…"

"No buts, Mother. In case it's slipped your mind, you weren't around for our wedding because you scarpered pretty sharpish after abandoning me in that bucket…"

"All right, keep your hair on, lad. There's no need to keep harping on about buckets, it was just an idea. You've got buckets on the brain."

Violet Burke's mention of the upcoming vow renewal service reminded me that I really ought to be getting on with penning some sentimental guff for the occasion. Marigold would have kittens if I didn't come out with some poetic masterpiece to recite on the beach. In truth, I was beginning to panic that I'd gone and left it to the last minute like I'd done with my best man's speech for Barry's wedding. Once the Bucket household was overrun with guests arriving from England, I doubted there would be any free time to get creative. Cognizant of the urgency to pen my vows, I ushered my mother out and headed to my office.

In my mind, this whole vow renewal business could be summed up with one succinct phrase: *I still do*. However, since I couldn't quite see those three simple words cutting muster with Marigold, I decided to trawl Google for inspiration, hoping there would be something not too soppy that I could copy and pass off as original. As I waited for the desktop to slowly come to life, my mind drifted back to our wedding day and the traditional vows we had exchanged in church.

Recollecting that Marigold had promised to love, cherish and obey, until death do us part, I chuckled. Marigold had been quite vocal about protesting the obeying part, claiming it was unfair that I, as a man, was not subject to such sexist drivel. Luckily, I am not the sort of man to bark marital commands, which is just as well since Marigold had no intention of complying with any such edicts even though she vowed that she would. I believe that these days the obeying bit is optional.

The preponderance of information offered up by Google pertained to writing one's wedding vows rather than renewing them, though I supposed if anything caught my eye, I could simply adapt it for the occasion. Trawling the internet, I hit upon a site rife with sickly suggestions about spouting eternal love. I found the vows way over the top for a reserved Brit such as myself to come out with. Wondering who came up with such gumpf, I realised the site was based in Charleston, the home of excessive Southern charm. Although it may well inspire Manolis if he ever got round to proposing marriage to the still married Doreen, I discounted the romantic drivel, instead navigating my way to a site that suggested keeping it light and humorous.

Pondering how Marigold would react to a promise of my loving her forever whilst trusting her with my credit card, I shuddered at the thought that she may well take it too literally.

A site filled with famous quotations about marriage led me to the conclusion that most of the contributors seemed to have a jaded view of the institution. After reading Robert Louis Stevenson's opinion that marriage is more comparable to a field of battle than a bed of roses, I gave up, deciding I would pen my own words and then bend Barry's ear on their suitability. Being close to his sister, he would steer me right if I came up with something too cringeworthy.

Recalling the dewy damp eyes of my blushing bride on our wedding day, I played around with adapting the same vows that we had exchanged thirty-eight years earlier. Marigold may well appreciate the sentiment of hearing that I still took her for better or worse, and that I still loved and cherished her. Adding a lovey-dovey flourish to our original vows, my thoughts were disturbed by the dulcet tone of my wife screeching my name, demanding to know why I hadn't got rid of the pan of disgusting curry. I chortled to myself, thinking although I hadn't promised to obey Marigold, she certainly expected me to jump to her commands.

"Sorry, darling, I was just composing my vows..."

"Oh, you old romantic," Marigold cooed. I stared at the floor, thinking the words that I'd penned really weren't going to cut it in Marigold's critical eyes. It wouldn't do for my wife to chide me with a 'could do better' remark mid-ceremony.

Hearing the familiar putter of Guzim's clapped out old moped pulling into my garden, I assured Marigold that I had been waiting for Guzim to come home so that I could waylay him with the curry on the way to his shed. I expected that the surly disposition he had demonstrated of late would morph into hyperbolic elation when I delivered Marigold's invitation to come along as a guest when we went through the whole rigmarole of renewing our nuptials. It is glaringly obvious why Guzim is rarely included in social events: in fact, it is fair to say that Guzim doesn't seem to have much of a social life beyond sharing the odd bottle of Amstel with one or other of his compatriots. This practice does nothing to endear them to the owners of any local hostelries, the owners tending to resent the way in which penny-pinching scruffy Albanian labourers often hog a table all evening whilst nursing one solitary beer between them.

Lugging the gargantuan pan of cacti curry down to the garden almost gave me a hernia. Fortunately, Guzim noticed the way I was struggling and rushed over to proffer his assistance. Too winded to speak, I indicated that we should carry the pan to the shed, only finding the energy to draw breath once we'd set the pan on the ground.

"*Eisai eleftheros tin epomeni Triti?*" I said, asking Guzim if he was free next Tuesday.

"*Sou eipa prin den doulevo dorean,*" he responded, immediately getting the wrong end of the stick as he reminded me that he had told me before that he didn't work for free. I hardly needed reminding since I was never remiss in paying his wages, a sum that had added up to quite an exorbitant amount over the last couple of years.

Realising that Guzim was confused, I racked my brain for the correct Greek wording to invite him to come along to the vow renewal service. What should have been a simple invitation inevitably became a minefield of misunderstandings when Guzim got it into his head that I was marrying the woman he had thought was already my wife.

I was taken aback to receive a decidedly smug lecture from my gardener extolling his superior morals because he had made an honest woman of Luljeta. He informed me that if he had known he was working for foreigners living in sin with loose morals, he would never have deigned to muck out my chickens. Shocked to be on the receiving end of my gardener's unexpected judgmental scorn, I interrupted him.

"*Eimaste pantremenoi trianta okto chronia,*" I said, telling him that we had been married for thirty-eight years.

"*Tote giati pantrevesai?*" Guzim asked, 'Then why are you getting married?'

I suppose that I ought to have expected nothing less than his total bewilderment at the strange foreign concept of the Buckets renewing our vows. Since it flummoxed most of the Greeks we'd invited, it was almost a given that the very idea would be beyond preposterous to a muddled Albanian. Following a prolonged explanation, Guzim still appeared somewhat confused as to why his presence was requested at the beach.

I was completely taken aback when Guzim spat out his loathing of beaches, explaining that his hitherto hidden phobia of the seaside stemmed from his first ever experience of such places: he'd had the misfortune of swimming in human waste due to lax Albanian regulations about pumping sewage into the sea. Nevertheless, after I had assured him that he would be under no obligation to go for a dip, he agreed to show up, most likely won round by the prospect of free food and drink being served at the taverna once the pesky business of Marigold and I trothing our love for a second time, was out of the way.

After warning Guzim that Mrs Bucket would

expect him to shower and dress in his best clothes, I told Guzim that the curry was for him. *"Afto to kary einai yia sena."*

*"Tossa polla ypoleimmata,"* Guzim gushed, saying, 'so many leftovers.' Removing the lid from the pan, a rapturous look transformed his face. He inhaled with such gusto that he practically snorted the stuff up through his nostrils. It struck me that imbibing the curry through his nose would be one way to avoid the risk of choking on Tonibler's missing plaster.

*"Den einai ypoleimmata. Einai freskomageiremeno,"* I said, assuring him that it wasn't leftovers but freshly cooked.

*"Ola yia mena?"* Asking if it was all for him, Guzim prostrated himself on the ground. Making his customary grab for my shins, he grovelled his heartfelt thanks for my amazingly generous gesture, declaring that a good Bucket curry was nothing short of ambrosia. Considering that Marigold had pronounced the contents of the pan to be inedible slop, I felt a tad embarrassed to think I may have misled Guzim into thinking the curry was up to my usual standards. Realising it may be best to come clean, I explained my altruistic largesse by telling him that I had cooked a giant pan of curry but unfortunately the new recipe I had tried out had failed to meet with Mrs Bucket's exacting standards.

Peering into the depths of the pan, Guzim sniffed suspiciously before declaring that the chicken didn't look like chicken. "*To kotopoulo den moiazei me kotopoulo.*"

"*Afto giati den einai kotopoulo,*" I said, telling him that's because it isn't chicken.

"*Ochi. Mageirepses to kouneli.*" Guzim's scream of no, followed by the ridiculous accusation that I had cooked a rabbit, practically blasted my ear drums. Turning puce with seemingly irrational anger, Guzim went off on some expletive laden Albanian tangent that made not an iota of sense. The only words that I could pick out of his enraged tirade were the names Sampaguita and Doruntina, the latter being his beloved pet rabbit.

"*Mila Ellinika.*" Since my grasp of Albanian is non-existent, I instructed Guzim to speak Greek.

"*Pame to spiti tou Spirou, tora,*" Guzim growled, his tone brooking no argument as he demanded that 'we go to the house of Spiros, now.'

Baffled by the sudden change in his temper, I found myself hurrying after Guzim as he marched out of my garden. His features contorted, he practically spat at the mouth as we made our way to the undertaker's house. Reaching our destination, Guzim used the full force of his clenched fists to bang on Spiros' door, completely ignoring my desperate plea that he calm down and get a grip on himself.

Still clueless as to the reason why my gardener was so riled up, I shuffled in embarrassment when Kyria Kompogiannopoulou thrust her head out of her upstairs window, demanding to know what all the racket was about and threatening to chuck a bucket of water over Guzim if he didn't pipe down. Fortunately, before Kyria Kompogiannopoulou could make good on her threat, a bleary-eyed Spiros appeared in his doorway clad in a pair of shorts and a grubby white undervest. I surmised from Spiros' scruffy appearance that Guzim had disturbed the undertaker's siesta.

Scratching his belly, Spiros yawned widely before demanding to know why Guzim was making such a din.

"*I xeni gynaika sou evale to moro kouneli sto kary,*" Guzim shouted. Shocked by his ludicrous claim that Spiros' foreign wife had put the baby rabbit in the curry, I seriously questioned my grasp of Greek and my translation skills.

"*Ti? Ti kary? I Sampaguita den echei kanei tipota. Einai sti douleia tis sto Nektar,*" Spiros said, insisting that Sampaguita hadn't done anything and that she was at work in Nektar.

Refusing to listen to Spiros, Guzim continued to rant, his words becoming ever more indecipherable as he upped both the speed and volume of his accusations.

"I can't make out anything he's saying," I told Spiros. "Can you translate?"

"The Guzim he, how you to say, barking? He accuse the Sampaguita of murdering the baby rabbit and putting it in the curry."

Scratching my head in confusion, I wondered if Guzim was ranting about the same baby rabbit that he had gifted to Sampaguita as a thank you present for taking care of Doruntina on his recent visit back to his Albanian homeland after the birth of Victor Mabel.

Switching to Greek, Spiros emphatically insisted that Sampaguita hadn't cooked any rabbits. Before he could even complete his sentence, Guzim demanded to know how the rabbit ended up in the curry if Sampaguita hadn't chucked it in the pot.

Whilst Spiros gaped at Guzim who had clearly lost the plot, I grabbed hold of the Albanian's arms and shook him, telling him that there was no baby rabbit in the curry, "*Den yparchei moro kouneli sto kary.*"

"The Guzim is the unhinging," Spiros observed, still half-asleep.

"Unhinged," I corrected.

"Is he to confusing that vile cat of the Cynthia's with the rabbit?"

Since Cynthia had named her cat Kouneli,

which is the Greek word for rabbit, I snorted at his wit before explaining. "I cooked the curry myself and can assure you that neither cat nor rabbit were part of the ingredients. I simply substituted the usual chicken with cacti."

"Cacti?" Spiros queried

"Prickly pear cacti," I clarified, before offering the Greek translation. "*Frankosyko.*"

"Why you to cook the *frankosyko*?" Spiros asked me, his tone as dismissive as though I had just announced I had converted to vegetarianism. "You have no the money to buy the rabbit?"

"It was an experiment. That's hardly the point though, Spiro. We need to make Guzim understand that no rabbits were sacrificed in the making of the curry," I said. Turning to Guzim, I reiterated that I did not put rabbit in the curry. "*Den evala kouneli sto kary.*"

"*Alla mou eipes oti den itan kotopoulo.*" As Guzim argued that I had told him it wasn't chicken, his fit of pique ran out of steam.

"*Den einai kotopoulo, einai frankosyko,*" I said, telling him it wasn't chicken, it was prickly pear. I was still at a complete loss as to why Guzim had jumped to the ridiculous conclusion that Sampaguita had had a hand in concocting the curry that emanated from my kitchen.

"Victor, if you want to cook the rabbit, you

should to buy from the Giannis," Spiros suggested. "Personally, I to enjoy the nicely cook rabbit but the Sampaguita refuse to cook him. When the Guzim give the rabbit to Sampaguita, I say to put in the oven with the tomato and rosemary but the Sampaguita say he is the cultural taboo in the Philippine to eat the rabbit. She want to keep it as the pet."

Fortunately, at that moment Sampaguita arrived home and Guzim was able to hear it from the horse's mouth that she hadn't thrown the gifted baby bunny into my curry. Sampaguita patiently explained that after the war, the Peace Corps introduced rabbits to the Philippines as a way of dealing with food shortages. However, the local population had baulked at the idea of eating rabbits, preferring to adopt them as pets, a trend that had soon caught on. Suitably shamed, Guzim launched into a grovelling apology, saying he didn't know what had come over him. I pointed out that he had acted completely irrationally, reminding him he was happy to breed Doruntina with Giannis' rabbits knowing full well that the Greek man sold the offspring for meat. Guzim's logic failed me when he stubbornly argued that was different before offering a suitably grovelling apology to Sampaguita for accusing her of murdering his gift. I have to say that Sampaguita demonstrated remarkable tolerance in yet again forgiving the Albanian shed dweller for his verbal nonsense.

Heading indoors to prepare their evening meal, Sampaguita quippingly asked Guzim if he had any objection to her cooking pork.

"*Prepei na fygo.*" Guzim abruptly announced that he had to go.

"*Pou pas?*" Spiros asked him where he was going.

"*Prepei na synantiso ton Alvano me to ena cheri.*" Guzim's grumbling response that he had to meet the one-handed Albanian left me baffled, his guttural explanation spewed at such speed that I failed to keep up with his train.

"Well, really. He hasn't even done his gardening duties yet. I need him to start weeding around the spinach," I complained as Guzim scampered off. "What was all that about?"

"The Guzim has been the rope in to help the one-handed *Alvanos.*"

"As in literally one-handed?"

"You not to know the one-handed *Alvanos?*" Spiros seemed surprised by my ignorance of such a person.

"I can't say I've come across any one-armed bandits locally."

"*Ti?*"

"Never mind," I replied, realising that yet another idiom had clearly gone over Spiros' head. I was in no mood for proffering an explanation, my head spinning from attempting to make head or tail of Guzim's nonsense.

"The one-handed *Alvanos* expect the help from the fellow *Alvanoi*. He claim that he cannot to work since he explode the hand."

"His hand exploded?" This was becoming more bizarre by the moment.

"When he to dynamite the fish," Spiros replied as though it was perfectly obvious.

"He dynamited the fish," I repeated sceptically.

"It is the illegal fishing method," Spiros explained. "You not to hear of the blast fishing?"

"I can't say that I have," I admitted. Mulling the concept of dynamiting fish over in my mind, I added, "It strikes me as a pretty stupid thing to do. Surely the fish will be blown to pieces, thus rather defeating the object."

"It not to blow the fish up, Victor." Spiros could barely contain his laughter at such a notion. "The dynamite to create the explosion in the water and the pressure to stun the fish. Only the idiot with no the boat, fish with the explosive. It is not only the illegal but the dangerous. None but the fool *Alvanos* do it here because everyone know how the old Panagiotis lose both the hand."

"Old Panagiotis?"

"I to bury him last year."

"I suppose the shock of having two hands blown off must have killed him," I said, thinking it odd that I hadn't heard of the incident.

"No, he lose the one hand thirty the year ago. It not to stop him to dynamite the fish and then he to lose the other. He only to stop the dynamite fishing when he to blow the nose off."

"He blew his nose off!" I exclaimed, realising I was beginning to sound like a parrot.

"When he have the no hands left, he try to throw the lit dynamite from the mouth. He light it with the cigarette but he not to spit it out the quick enough and it to blow the nose up. But the Panagiotis was not like the lazy *Alvanos*. Even with the no hand and the no nose, he still to work the hard. Every the winter, he to pick the olives with the stubs…"

"Stumps," I corrected as Spiros demonstrated his point by rubbing his wrists together.

"So, he died last year when he blew his nose off?" I clarified.

"No, he to die in the bed of the old age. But he show, the how to say, to put the other off from the fishing with the explosive?"

"He served as a cautionary tale."

"That is the it, Victor. The dynamiting the fish is the bad business. It can to ruin the net of the real fishermen and it to make the destruction in the sea."

"I can imagine," I said, my mind rife with images of exploding sea beds and mini tsunamis.

"You look in need of the *ouzo*," Spiros observed, steering me into his house.

"I really shouldn't," I objected as Spiros wielded the bottle. "I have to drive shortly.

"Let the Marigold to take the wheel. You look to have the weight of the world on your elbows…"

"Shoulders," I corrected before confiding in Spiros about my lack of progress in writing my vows.

"I can to help you. I have many the good romantic lines."

Although it may have been considered clutching at straws, I decided to accept my friend's help. If nothing else, his many years of making *kamaki* had made him something of an expert in coming out with romantic claptrap.

# Chapter 16

*Living in Greece for Sixteen Years*

Strolling home through the village, I reflected that the Albanian shed dweller's diverse set of peculiarities never failed to surprise me. His earlier nonsense had at least steered me in Spiros' direction, which had in turn resulted in some flowery lines that I could conceivably mould into vows to wow Marigold, if I got really desperate. Deep in thought, I walked slap-bang into a man hurrying out of one of the houses close to the village square.

"*Sygnomi, den se eida ekei,*" I said, telling him I was sorry, I didn't see him there. Despite my apology, I considered that he should be the one apologising since he had backed out of the house with total disregard for any random passerby being knocked off their feet.

"*Sygnomi, den koitaxa pou pigaini,*" he said, telling me he hadn't looked where he was going. The Greek words were pronounced with a distinctive west country accent that instantly gave him away as a fellow Brit.

"Ah, you're British," I said.

"Indeed, but we have lived in Greece for sixteen years," he said in a slightly miffed tone, before repeating his sentence in some semblance of mangled, grammatically incorrect Greek.

Perchance he was the type who became impatient when his attempts to converse in Greek were met with a response in English. I could sympathise with his frustration: often when I was out and about beyond the confines of the village, I would try out my Greek language on Greek shopkeepers, waiting staff, and office bureaucrats, only to have them reply in English. Of course, I recognised that they welcomed the opportunity to try out their own skills in a foreign language. However, I never engaged in conversations in Greek with fellow Brits, believing such an exercise to be the height of pretension.

"Ah, I…"

The stranger interrupted me before I could

continue my sentence. "I say, in all modesty, that when British people hear me speaking Greek, they often presume *eimai Ellinas*."

I found it hard to believe that anyone could mistake him for Greek when he paired his socks with sandals, a habit I had recently dispensed with when I realised it made me look like a tourist. Marigold liked to take credit for this change, assuming her repeated assertions that I was a walking fashion disaster had finally sunk in. The stranger's pronunciation of the words 'I am Greek' was a dead giveaway that he was a foreigner. Still, I supposed, people not familiar with the language may well assume he spoke it with some competence. Certainly, from the little he had said, I gauged that his Greek language skills were about on a par with my own; that is, sadly lacking but passable. There is no point in denying the fact that every time I open my mouth to speak Greek, I sound like an Englishman trying out a foreign tongue; it would be the height of delusion to imagine otherwise. In my defence, I haven't been living in Greece for sixteen years like this chap claimed.

"*Xereis afto to chorio*?" he said, before repeating his question in English when instead of replying, I snorted, unable to contain my bemusement at his lack of self-awareness. "Do you know this village?"

"Indeed, I do. I live in Meli," I replied once my

snorting was under control.

"Ah, I'm considering buying a property here. This house actually," he said, indicating the dwelling he had just exited. Extending his hand, he introduced himself. "The name's Macey, John Macey."

"Bucket. Victor Bucket," I said, shaking his slightly damp hand and wishing I'd had the foresight to bung a bottle of hand sanitiser in my pocket.

"The estate agent let me have the key for another look. I like the house well enough but I want to get a feel for the village before doing anything rash. I don't want to make the mistake of going in blind and then end up living check to jowl with a bunch of ignorant expats. No offence intended."

"None taken. Personally, I detest the term expat, preferring to refer to myself as a European citizen with Greek residency," I said modestly, thinking perchance I had run into someone sympatico who shared my aversion to the expat label.

"A pity more of the Brits over here don't think that way. We had a place in *Kriti* for sixteen years. The island is becoming overrun with the sort of British that want to turn the area into a carbon copy of little England in the sun. I don't know why they didn't just move to Margate and have done."

"Sixteen years is a long time..." I began to say, ruminating that something about sixteen years had a familiar ring. "What makes you want to make the move to the mainland?"

"Well, *Kriti* was fine to begin with but now I'm after somewhere Greek that is less of a tourist draw and not so overrun with Brits. Nothing worse than the locals assuming one is an expat."

"Quite. We've made it a point to integrate since we moved to the village…"

"I say in all modesty, that when we were in *Kriti*, we made every effort to demonstrate that we weren't the sort of Brits that the locals would mistake for tourists."

As Macey spoke, I took in his appearance, noting he was almost as tall as me and that he had kept himself trim. I gauged, from his grey hair, that he was probably a tad older than me, unless he hadn't yet discovered the advantages of a liberal application of Grecian 2000. Wide framed spectacles, rather too large for his face, concealed most of his eyebrows, brows which only revealed themselves when he raised them. When the eyebrows were raised, I was struck by how black they were in contrast to his hair, making me wonder if perchance he'd run out of Grecian 2000 after dyeing his upper facial hair. Moreover, his eyebrows appeared to have been waxed into shape, the edges adjacent to his nose pointing upwards as though he was in a state of constant surprise, gave him a slightly ludicrous air.

"I notice that you said we. Does that mean there's a Mrs Macey…or perchance a Mr?" I asked.

"Do I look gay?" John Macey sneered.

"There's no need to put a derogatory slant on it. My son is out and proud."

"We're not the kind of people who judge. I say that in all modesty, of course. If I may prevail upon you, Vic…"

"It's Victor," I interrupted. His constant reference to we made me assume there must indeed be a Mrs Macey, even if he avoided answering my question. Perchance they hadn't actually tied the knot.

"Ah, quite. Well, I'd appreciate your insight on the village."

"Meli is a marvellous place, off-the-tourist track but within easy access to the coast. A big plus is having a decent sized town just a ninety-minute drive away. We lucked out when we discovered the village. It's a fabulous place to live and the local Greeks couldn't have been more welcoming."

"And not too many Brits?" He managed to make the word Brits sound like an expletive.

"Let's see, there's my brother-in-law, Barry, and his wife, Cynthia. Barry is…"

About to tell him that Barry was in partnership with a Greek builder, I paused, the penny suddenly dropping when I recollected that Barry had told me about a prospective customer who was considering buying a house in the village, a Brit who had peppered his sentences with the unsolicited information that he had lived in Greece for sixteen years. Although Barry clearly hadn't taken to the fellow, I would form my own opinion, nothing about John Macey having rubbed me up the wrong way thus far in our very limited acquaintance. Admittedly, he sounded a tad dismissive of fellow Brits but I could understand his desire to live in a village that was quintessentially Greek rather than somewhere resembling an English housing estate. I had my own sorry experience of living cheek by jowl with the wrong sort of Brits when Harold and Joan had been resident in Meli. No doubt Macey had suffered from living in proximity to similarly uncouth neighbours and was in no rush to repeat the ordeal.

"And then there's the Hancocks; he writes…" I bit my tongue to stop myself blurting out that Milton wrote porn. It wouldn't do to give the impression that Milton was some kind of pervert. "And Doreen and Norman…"

I paused again, wondering if it was quite the done thing to mention the estranged couple in one breath. Considering it was a tad too soon to be spilling the beans on my neighbours' living arrangements, I continued, "There's the Stranges but the only strange thing about them is their name."

I left a suitable pause, expecting him to respond with a jocular laugh, but he failed to even crack a smile at my little quip. "And then there's Sherry. Oh, and my mother, of course. All very respectable sorts, rather dull but perfectly amiable."

I pondered if I was stretching the truth just a tad. Describing Violet Burke as respectable was a bit of a stretch, not to mention the way that Doreen was carrying on with Manolis had set a few curtains twitching. In fairness to the British residents of the village, they weren't the types one would particularly go out of one's way to avoid; Norman's obsession with traffic cones might be a bit of a bore fest but he was intrinsically harmless…and perhaps my mother was best served in small doses. Perchance if the Maceys happened to be in need of a char, Violet Burke was likely to become invaluable to them. The Stranges certainly proclaimed that they couldn't manage without her.

"So, just a handful of Brits. I expect I could cope with that as long as they aren't the sort to live in each other's pockets…"

"Well, we do tend to rally round in times of emergency," I admitted, thinking of how Marigold had offered up our spare bedroom when Doreen walked out on Norman and how I had stoically put up with the intruder, never once complaining.

Recalling how we'd all mucked in when Milton was in the hospital, I reflected it might be a good thing in the scheme of things to welcome another pair of Brits to the village. They could potentially lighten the rallying round load, not to mention extra numbers lessened the likelihood of my being seated next to the terminally dull Norman at the expat dinner parties. Admittedly Barry hadn't taken to this Macey fellow, but he'd never taken to Sherry and she wasn't such a bad old stick, as long as she wasn't trying to seduce me. She seemed to have calmed down a tad of late, her over-the-top jolliness having suffered a dent after Heinrich had used her as his punching bag.

"What about tourists? I don't fancy being stuck in a place overrun with holidaymakers," John Macey enquired.

"There's nowhere for them to stay in the village," I told him, omitting to mention that we were in the process of rectifying the lack of tourist accommodation by renovating a place we intended to turn into two apartments for rent.

"I had a nice chat with the local shopkeeper earlier, a very pleasant type…"

"The local shop is a wonderful place. Tina ensures it meets all the local needs," I told him, omitting to mention the outrageous prices.

"The charming shopkeeper I spoke to introduced

herself as Despina…"

"The shop serves as a coffee shop too…" I volunteered, almost choking on my words at the thought that anyone could describe the wart-faced busybody, Despina, as charming. It was a bit of a blow to hear that Tina's mother was back on the scene as I thought we'd seen the last of her. I made a mental note to avoid the local shop for the foreseeable.

"Ah, I wondered if there was anywhere local to eat?"

"There's a fabulous taverna serving the freshest of food," I told him, omitting to mention it was a bit spit and sawdust. There was no need to hark on the state of the place; after all, it had markedly improved in the cleanliness state since Violet Burke had started giving the taverna a good bottoming.

"You're certainly painting the village of Meli in a good light."

"Well, we like it."

"That's certainly encouraging to hear. I must say, ever since the estate agent showed me this house, I was rather taken with it," he said, gesticulating towards the house he had exited. "In fact, this little house spoke to me, it said 'I'm your new home.'

"Talking houses is a new one on me," I quipped, my joshing met with yet another deadpan look, only his unnatural eyebrows reacting by sliding out over the top of his spectacles like two manicured slugs.

"Of course, it's in desperate need of some work. The builders reckoned they could have it sorted inside a couple of months if I go ahead with the purchase."

"The local builders are excellent," I told him, omitting to mention that one half of the local duo was my aforementioned brother-in-law.

"I'd be interested in seeing some of their work for myself before committing."

"Well, you're welcome to pop round to mine for a look-see some time. They did a marvellous job. The house was a tad outdated when we purchased it; they fitted a new kitchen and bathroom. And then of course they completely renovated the *apothiki* and turned it into a separate living space for my mother."

"No time like the present," he said, surprising me by effectively inviting himself round right away.

"Wouldn't you rather wait until Mrs Macey is with you?" I said, considering him a tad pushy.

"No need for that. She won't be living here..."

"Oh, sorry if I went and put my foot in it...it was just the way you kept referring to 'we' that made me think..." My words tailed off. Whilst he had indeed continually referred to himself in the plural, he hadn't actually confirmed that there was a Mrs Macey.

"Force of habit. Hard to break when one has been married for nigh on a quarter of a century."

Since his tone made it sound like a prison sentence, I decided not to probe. As he had invited himself back to mine, Marigold would no doubt prise any pertinent information regarding his marital situation out of him, in short order. Marigold would be over the moon if it turned out that he was single; he would be new fodder for her eternal matchmaking.

"So, are you up for me taking a look at your place now whilst I'm in the village. I need to return the key to the house to the estate agent in the morning," John Macey pressed.

"It will have to be a very quick look, I'm afraid. My wife and I have a dinner date." Although Marigold might be a tad put out if I turned up with a strange fellow in tow just before we were due to head out for dinner, I knew she would swallow her annoyance once I explained his impromptu visit may be the deciding touch in securing a local building contract for her brother.

Macey fell into step beside me as I headed in the direction of home. I pondered the wisdom of mentioning that the Nordic estate agent he was dealing with was a bit of a shyster, the locals holding him in little regard since it was common knowledge that he greatly inflated the price of the houses on his books in order to pocket an obscene commission. Since John Macey gave the impression of being a bit of know-it-all, I decided to keep my own counsel that the agent was likely ripping him off. I got the distinct impression that John was someone who liked to know better and wouldn't welcome his judgement being questioned.

"It's certainly a lovely village," Macey observed. "The agent showed me a few properties in other mountain villages but they seemed a bit dead."

"Yes indeed, it's such a shame the way that many of the higher-up villages are becoming depopulated as the older generation dies off. Meli seems to be bucking the trend with the incoming population getting younger."

Although the average age of the villagers decidedly skewed to pensioned, a number of relative youngsters had settled here in the last couple of years. Kostis' wife, Eleni, was a mere girl in her thirties, as was the recent addition of Panos' granddaughter, Yiota. Giannis the bee man had returned from the city and even Barry liked to think of himself as a mere spring chicken now that he had sired a baby daughter. Additionally, with the exception of Violet Burke, the recent expats that had moved to the village were still on the right side of sixty.

Drawing level with the *apothiki*, I knocked, but there was no response. Noticing that my mother's bicycle wasn't there, I assumed that Violet Burke was still peeling her way through a mountain of spuds in the taverna.

"My mother isn't in so I won't be able to show you the builders' handiwork in there." I had learnt my lesson about barging into the *apothiki* with my key. "Come on up and I'll show you the work we had done in ours."

No sooner had I opened the door than the sound of Marigold's carping washed over us. "Really, Victor. All you had to do was take one pot of curry down to Guzim. I can't imagine why it took you over an hour. We're going to be late…"

Marigold, all done up in a floral frock, her Titian locks artfully coiffed, stopped mid-sentence, clearly flustered and taken off-guard when she realised that I wasn't alone.

"Darling, this is John Macey. He's thinking of buying a house in the village and I offered to let him look over the renovations we had done."

The glacial look in Marigold's eyes indicated she didn't appreciate my foisting a stranger on her when we were about to head out to dinner. Nevertheless, she attempted to hide her annoyance by shaking hands with my guest.

"May I?" John Macey nodded towards the kitchen, obviously keen to get a look at the builders' handiwork. As he strode into the kitchen, I noticed his nose crinkling as his olfactory senses were assaulted by the lingering pong of cacti curry.

Grabbing my arm, Marigold hissed in my ear. "Victor, what are you thinking? We have to meet your friend Takis in forty-five minutes and you haven't even changed yet."

"If he likes the work we had done, he may employ Barry and Vangelis to transform the village house he has his eye on…can you entertain him while I go and change?"

Without waiting for a reply, I rushed through to the bedroom to find some suitable attire for the evening. As I hurriedly changed, snippets of John Macey's attempts at conversation filtered through to the bedroom. I could hear him telling Marigold that "we have lived in Greece for sixteen years" and declaring "in all modesty", "we're not that kind of people," but Marigold's responses were too softly spoken to reach my ears. Chuckling to myself, I noticed John Macey's irritating tendency to speak in catch phrases, just as Milton continually peppered his sentences with 'old chap' and 'what?'

After hurriedly changing, I joined the two of them in the grand salon where Macey was holding court, talking at my wife. Spotting the glazed look in Marigold's eyes, I reflected it was most unlike her to be unable to get a word in edgeways.

"I hope that you've seen enough to give you an idea of the craftsmanship of the builders," I interrupted him.

"They've certainly done an excellent job," John Macey conceded. "I was just telling your lovely wife that when we lived in Crete…"

"An anecdote for another day," I interrupted. "As I mentioned earlier, we're running a tad late for a dinner engagement."

"In the village?" John Macey asked.

"No, further afield tonight," I said, mentioning the name of the village where we were dining.

"What an extraordinary coincidence. I've rented an apartment in that very village for three months whilst I house hunt," he said, clearly angling for an invitation to join us.

"Victor." Intercepting Marigold's icy glare, I interpreted it as *don't you dare invite him to join us* warning.

"I'd ask you to join us," I fibbed. "But I'm afraid that it is a business dinner with a colleague."

Steering John Macey out of the Bucket residence, I wished him luck with his purchase if he decided to go ahead.

"What were you thinking, bringing that

arrogant twit round here?" Marigold scolded. "You know what a low tolerance I have for pompous know-it-alls."

# Chapter 17

*An Uncomfortable Drive*

**H**ang on a sec, lad. I've just got to finish poncing myself up," Violet Burke declared when I knocked on at the *apothiki* to collect her for dinner.

"Well, don't be all day about it. Marigold's waiting outside in the Punto," I muttered impatiently. My wife wasn't exactly in the best of moods; having taken umbrage with me for foisting John Macey on her without warning, she had accused me of rolling home from Spiros' house under the influence. I considered the term rolling a tad over the top considering I wasn't even close to swaying.

However, I did feel just a smidgen of guilt that after I'd imbibed a couple of *ouzos* with the undertaker, Marigold was forced into the role of designated driver for the evening. If, as I rather suspected, I might never hear the end of it, I may be forced to bring up the subject of Marigold's own overly fond relationship with Mastic Tears.

Shuffling in annoyance, I watched as Violet Burke took her sweet time daubing some blue slap on her eyelids before pencilling in a couple of skew-whiff eyebrows with a heavy hand.

"I thought I'd make a bit of an effort, like," my mother said, smoothing the creases out of some lurid purple number struggling to contain her solidly podgy frame. Since we were already late, I kept my own counsel on the suitability of her winter outfit for such a balmy evening, simply making a mental note to sit downwind in case she got overly hot and sweaty. Slamming the door, Violet Burke claimed dibs on the passenger seat next to my wife, leaving me to climb in the back of the Punto. Marigold, engrossed with adjusting the mirrors and touching up her lipstick, barely acknowledged my mother.

"So, what's this Takis fella like?" my mother demanded. Rudely shoving the passenger seat backwards to better accommodate her bulk, she nearly cut off the circulation in my legs.

"Well," I replied, wincing in pain. "I've only

met him a couple of times but he seems perfectly pleasant. He has a very business-like approach to running the taverna."

"Aye, but is he a catch?" Vi persisted.

"Really, Mother, you've only just buried Panos," I spluttered. Perchance I had given my mother the wrong impression about Takis and she'd got it into her head that he could replace the welly wearing farmer in her affections. Struggling to recall if I'd happened to mention that Takis was barely past his thirtieth birthday, I spat it out. "Mother, Takis is far too young for you. You have a good fifty years on him."

"You daft apeth, fancy you thinking I'm after a fancy man. I'm asking for Yiota, you dipstick. The lass needs a fella of her own. That farm's too much for her to manage on her lonesome. If she can hook herself a husband, she can put him to work as free labour."

Although it was on the tip of my tongue to blurt out that my mother was getting as bad as Marigold with her matchmaking meddling, I restrained my-self. My wife was likely to explode if I compared her to Violet Burke.

"Shift your knee, Vi," Marigold instructed as she finally started the Punto, her tone barely con-cealing her annoyance at my mother's flab hovering over the gearstick.

"Don't forget to stop off at Panos' place. Though 'appen I should start calling it Yiota's place now since Panos is six feet under and won't be living there anymore," Violet Burke said, as pragmatic as ever.

"Why do you want to stop there?" I enquired. "We're already late."

"I asked the lass to join us…"

"Just because I let you bulldoze me into inviting yourself along for the evening, Mother, it doesn't give you carte blanche to go adding a plus one…"

Whilst I found Yiota delightful company and had no personal objection to her joining us, Takis had only included my wife in his invitation to dinner. I didn't know him well enough to gauge his reaction when I turned up with not only one, but two uninvited stragglers in tow.

"You're the one who said this Takis fellow was single…" my mother argued.

"I have high hopes for Giannis and Yiota getting together…" Marigold chimed in.

"I thought it would keep Giannis on his toes if he reckons he's got a bit of competition. It might give him a bit of a nudge, like," Violet Burke interrupted as Marigold pulled up outside the farmhouse.

Unlike my mother who had kept us waiting whilst she tarted herself up, Yiota was already outside. Judging from Yiota's casual attire and the way she had hastily styled her long hair in a messy upswept bun, it struck me that Violet Burke must have neglected to mention that she intended to dangle the younger woman in front of a potential beau.

As Yiota joined me in the back of the Punto, I cringed at Violet Burke's insensitivity in berating her for not making more of an effort with her appearance. "You could do with a bit of cleavage and some lippy, lass. I suppose it's a blessing you didn't turn up in your wellies."

"I barely had time to change," Yiota said, attempting to stifle a yawn. "The farm is so much work, but I do enjoy it. I dread the thought of going back to an office job if I can't make a go of the farm."

"Don't worry, lass. We'll sort it," Vi promised before turning her attention to Yiota's appearance. "At least pinch your cheeks to rouge them up a bit. Here, Victor, swap seats with me so I can try and sort out Yiota's hair before she meets that fella of yours."

"You didn't tell me we were meeting a man, Vi," Yiota sighed.

"We have to take every opportunity we can get to fix you up with a husband right sharpish," Vi retorted.

Swapping seats with my mother, I pointed out that she was being completely insensitive and that the way she was meddling in Yiota's private life was totally out of order.

"You have the wrong end of the twig," Yiota objected. "I asked Violet to keep her eye out for a suitable husband. The old boys in the village have been helping me out with the farm but it's not a permanent solution. Once their interest in helping me wanes, I will have to employ someone on the farm unless I can snare a likely husband."

"And apart from Giannis, there isn't a single eligible bachelor in Meli under pensionable age," Marigold butted in. "Yiota will have to throw her net wider if Giannis doesn't take the bait soon. Of course, with his smouldering good looks, Giannis would be the perfect catch. And it's what Panos wanted."

"Shove your seat forward, Victor. I can barely feel my knees. At this rate they'll end up as swollen as my feet," Violet Burke complained, thumping the back of the passenger seat. "Now, if Yiota here can catch the eye of this Takis fella, it might make Giannis jealous enough to speed up his courting. I reckon he's right half-hearted about it because he's still moping after that daft super model."

"Poppy wasn't daft. Studying bacteria is a very competitive field," I said.

"It hardly makes for riveting conversation though." I considered Marigold's remark tactless in the extreme since I often peppered my own conversation with references to bacteria. Patting her hair, my wife practically swooned as she stated, "Poppy must be dafter than she looks, putting bacteria above Giannis. He's practically a Greek god in the looks department."

"Is this Takis fella handsome?" Violet Burke quizzed me.

"He's perfectly passable," I said, realising that Takis would fade into the wallpaper if he was lined up next to Giannis in a masculine beauty competition. Still, looks aren't everything and he could perchance cook his way into Yiota's affections. "Anyway, I don't see how Giannis will get jealous of Takis, since he won't be there."

"You reckon we'll be able to keep it quiet in Meli, you pillock. Someone's sure to blab," Vi reasoned.

The peace that finally reigned in the car was short lived. Marigold started to complain to my mother about my dragging John Macey over to the house without so much as by her leave. Although my wife clearly hadn't taken to Macey, she had managed to ferret out some pertinent information about his marital situation, learning that despite his habit of dropping an unnecessary we into his every utterance, he was in fact recently divorced.

"I thought you would welcome a single man to

our social circle…" I began.

"I can see why his wife left him. Didn't you notice how insufferably smug he was, Victor? The way he kept harping on about having lived in Greece for sixteen years as though it gave him some superior knowledge, demonstrated a clear case of someone obsessed with one-upmanship. He's the sort who always knows better by virtue of having been out here longer than other Brits."

"But as he's single, think of the match making opportunities you can engage in," I pointed out.

"Single doesn't necessarily equate to eligible," Marigold snapped. "You're forgetting that Norman is likely to be single soon…"

"Fair point," I agreed. "Still, a single man is likely to be in need of a char which could mean another regular job for mother. Don't forget that Norman has replaced Vi with that young Jehovah's Witness."

"I have to say that I do prefer cleaning up after fellas," Vi said.

"But surely they're messier…" Marigold suggested.

"Aye, but they tend to leave me to get on with it without bending my ear with mindless chatter. That Sherry never stops bleating on. She never knows when to put a sock in it."

"Speaking of Sherry," I tentatively ventured.

"Perhaps John Macey might tickle her fancy."

"He's got to be an improvement on that smelly hippie," Vi agreed.

"Just leave the matchmaking to me. You two are clueless," Marigold said dismissively.

"You won't be saying that if Takis falls head over heels for Yiota," I said.

"You do like to have the last word," Marigold scoffed. "You sound like you're in training for a tedious round of one-upmanship with that Macey chap."

# Chapter 18

*Vi's Heinrich Manure*

Strolling into the taverna, the background music was just low enough to ensure the three ladies could hear my quiet warning. "Whatever you do, steer well clear of the *moussaka* this evening."

"That goes without saying, lad. You know that I can't be doing with them nasty aubergine things. Right slimy, they are." Making no attempt to lower her voice as she disparaged the national vegetable, Violet Burke immediately attracted the bemused attention of the other customers.

"Well, I'm quite partial to a nice plate of

*moussaka,*" Marigold said.

"Best avoided when it's garnished with mascara," I warned her as Vasilis bowled forward to greet me.

"Victor, I am the please you make it. I have the best table for you," Vasilis said. Taking my arm, he steered me towards a table overlooking the beach, a reserved sign adorning the table that had been laid for three. "Takis will to join you soonly. I let him to use the kitchen to prepare the special dish for you."

"Actually, there's four of us joining Takis," I said apologetically.

"The very next best the table," Vasilis hastily backtracked. Abruptly changing course, he led us towards a table at the back, sandwiched between the kitchen and the lavatory. Eyeing my three companions, he grabbed hold of Violet Burke's hand and kissed it. "You must be the Mrs Bucket."

"It's Burke, and there's no need to go slobbering all over my hand," my mother admonished him.

Seemingly taken aback by the reprimand, a glimmer of interest sparked in Vasilis' eyes, as though Violet Burke had thrown down the gauntlet for a challenge. "The hands of the hardworking woman," he cooed, receiving a daggers drawn look from his wife, hovering in the kitchen doorway.

"Mrs Burke is my mother and this is my wife,

Marigold, and our friend Yiota," I said, making the introductions.

Taking our seats, Yiota and Vasilis gabbled away together in Greek, allowing the rest of us to take stock of the taverna. Most of the other tables were occupied with tourists dressed up to the nines, enjoying leisurely holiday dining in the stunning setting with a spectacular sea view. The cat that Takis had chucked out of the kitchen that morning was the lucky recipient of some fresh anchovies. Gobbling up the small fish that a woman on a neighbouring table was sneaking it, the feline nevertheless kept its eyes peeled in search of a better offering from another gullible, cat-loving customer. I smiled in amusement when I overheard the woman telling her male companion that she would never have ordered the anchovy starter if she'd realised the fish would still be raw.

"Victor, you make it. Why the Vasilis sit you next to the toilet?" Takis said, bounding over to greet me with a genuine smile on his face. Casting his eyes over my three companions, he went on the sort of charm offensive which would stand him in excellent stead as an owner/chef.

I have observed that customers do love to be flattered and fussed over by taverna owners. I find that tourists are particularly susceptible to being fawned over by charming Greeks, often returning to the same establishment more than once during their annual holiday if they feel a personal connection has been forged. The best in the business manage to lure a captive audience back for the full duration of their holiday. I once chatted to a couple of tourists who visited the area twice a year and who chose to eat breakfast, lunch and dinner in the same taverna every day for a fortnight. Considering the owner to be a personal friend simply through frequenting his establishment, they even invited him and his wife to holiday at their home in England when the taverna was closed over the winter.

"There wasn't enough room for the five of us at the reserved table," I said. "I do hope that my turning up mob-handed won't mess up the menu you've planned for this evening."

"I am the chef. I can cook for the three or the thirty-three," Takis declared. Brushing off my apology, his gaze settled on Yiota. I considered by the way he sucked in his paunch and ruefully rubbed his stubble as though wishing he'd made the effort to shave, that the young woman had caught his attention.

"I hadn't realised you'd be in the kitchen tonight. It was good of you to go to so much trouble," I said.

"I want to repay your kindness of the morning by cooking for you and your lovely wife. The

Angeliki was happy to let me to work in the kitchen; between you and me, she is the jaded. I will to join you the now and the Angeliki will to serve the *mezethes* I prepared," Takis said, pointedly grabbing a chair and squeezing in next to Yiota.

"Tell me he didn't just say that he's gone and cooked up that mess stuff?" Violet Burke grumbled.

"It's not mess, it's *meze*. Just be grateful you're getting a free meal," I snapped at my mother.

Before Takis had the chance to turn the charm on Yiota, Marigold commanded his attention, congratulating him on his imminent ownership of the taverna. Whilst the two of them chatted, Angeliki appeared, carrying the selection of choice *mezethes* prepared by Takis. Considering the amount of mascara weighing her lashes down, I doubted there would have been any specks left in the tube to garnish our food; nevertheless, I intended to observe it closely for any tell-tale black specks. Noting the amount of hairspray holding Angeliki's back-combed hair in place, I imagined she would find Athena a kindred spirit.

Practically flinging the dishes on the table, Angeliki left no opportunity for me to introduce her to my companions. The moment her hands were free, she trotted back to the kitchen, a murderous expression on her face as she bellowed her husband's name. The volume of the background music noticeably went up a notch, no doubt a deliberate ploy to drown out the sound of any breaking plates emanating from the kitchen.

Takis immediately turned his focus to the food, proudly describing each dish in turn. "I have to cook the selection of Greek *mezethes* for you. He is the *melitzanosalata*, a smoky aubergine dip…"

"Them slimy aubergines are bad enough when they're hidden in that *moussaka* slop without you going round pulverising them until they resemble baby food," Violet Burke complained ungraciously.

Clearly clueless to the meaning of pulverised, Takis ignored my mother. "He is the *chtapodi se xydi*…"

"What's that when it's at home?" Vi barked, making no attempt to disguise her disgust at the sight of the cold appetiser of marinated octopus in vinegar. I doubt she had ever served that up in the chippy. "Ah, something I recognise that's actually edible, though I have to say it's a bit odd serving up honeyed doughnuts as part of the starters."

As Violet Burke speared what she assumed was a sweet *loukoumada*, Takis piped up to disillusion her. "The dish is *patatokefthedes*, fried balls of the mash potato with *kefalotyri* cheese…"

"They're not half bad," Vi praised, shovelling the fried potato balls into her mouth. Fortunately, a mouthful of *patatokefthedes* prevented her from passing her opinion on the next dish of *marathokefte-des* which Takis described as fried fennel fritters, a popular dish originating from the Island of Tinos. I presumed it went without saying that Violet Burke would consider anything made of fennel as too unspeakably vile to sample.

As the five of us tucked into the delicious food, I couldn't fail to notice that Takis seemed quite taken with Yiota even though Marigold was distracting him by flattering his culinary skills. A sharp elbow in my ribs drew my attention back to Violet Burke.

"He won't do for Yiota," she hissed in my ear.

"Why ever not? He seems quite smitten."

"'Appen because he's only seen her sitting down," my mother elaborated. "When she stands up, that little short arse won't even come up to her shoulder. She needs a proper man, not a midget. You didn't do right well there with your matchmaking, Victor."

The notion that I had anything to do with attempting to fix Yiota up with Takis, left me gobsmacked. Any matchmaking that had gone on was down to Violet Burke; even my meddling wife hadn't had a hand in it, only jumping on the fixing up bandwagon when she heard about Vi's intentions.

"He's a perfectly respectable height. It's just

that Yiota is exceptionally tall…" I defended.

"No woman wants a man she'd have to look down on that much. If they tried to have a chat standing up, he'd end up conversing with her bosom."

"You were a head taller than Panos," I reminded her.

"Aye, but you can't be too fussy when you get to my age. Yiota's young and still has her looks."

Having no desire to spend the evening discussing suitable candidates for Yiota's affection, I was relieved when Takis turned his attention to me.

"So, Victor, I have given much the thought to your the suggestion of catering to the British immigrants in the winter. I am the thinking it is the excellent idea to cook up a taste of their home. I must to pick your the brain because I am not the well up with the English cooking," Takis said.

"I think that familiar comfort food would go down a treat in the winter," I said. "Dishes like shepherd's pie are always popular…"

"You put the shepherd in the pie?" With his mouth gaping, Takis was the picture of confusion

"Aye, lad," Violet Burke wound him up. "Course you have to give the shepherd a good shearing first…."

"Take no notice of my mother, she is pulling your leg…" I began

"'Appen toad-in-the-hole would be right popular..." Vi interrupted.

"The English to eat the toad?" Takis was becoming more flummoxed by the minute. "I think it would be the difficult to find the toad in the market..."

"'Appen that Cynthia could give you some from that slimy looking ecological pond of hers," Vi suggested. "She's plenty to spare. The croaking buggers breed like rabbits."

"Mother, we are attempting to have a serious discussion about Takis' winter menu. Please keep your ridiculous suggestions to yourself," I urged.

"Pardon me for breathing..."

"I think a traditional Sunday roast would most appeal to the British," I advised. "Roast beef, roast potatoes, Yorkshire pudding and vegetables... or roast pork with apple sauce and roasted veggies."

"You don't want to be taking cooking advice from my Victor..." Vi blurted.

Bristling at her put down, I climbed on my high horse. "I think that I have established my expert credentials as a food aficionado by leading the very popular and successful gastronomic tours..."

"What's that got to do with British grub?" Vi interrupted. "Victor's cooked nowt but Greek muck since he moved over here."

"I made a curry only today," I argued.

"And even that scrawny mite, Tony Blair, turned up his nose up at it."

"It's Tonibler," I snapped, annoyed that Violet Burke had drawn attention to my culinary mishap in front of a professionally trained chef.

"Speaking of that rancid curry you were cooking up earlier. It only nearly went and finished off that gormless gardener of yours," Vi said with a chuckle.

"Guzim?"

"How many gormless gardeners do you have, lad?"

Ignoring her rhetorical question, I waited for her to elaborate on Guzim's supposed near death experience. Violet Burke remained tight lipped, perhaps just as well since she'd just shovelled another *patatokeftheda* into her mouth. Making an elaborate show of chewing her food, she finally swallowed. My mother certainly knows how to work a room; everyone at the table was waiting with bated breath for her to finish spilling the beans. I just hoped that I hadn't inadvertently given Guzim a nasty dose of food poisoning. As a retired public health inspector, I would never live that one down.

"I'd just got back from peeling Dina's spuds when that Guzim came running and nearly had me off my bicycle. The fella was choking, all red in the face with his eyes bugging out and his lips a horrible blue. There was nowt else for it. I had to give him the Heinrich Manure."

"I think you mean the Heimlich Manoeuvre, Mother. You appear to be confusing your life-saving techniques and your smelly hippies," I said sceptically, certain she must be exaggerating the incident for dramatic effect.

"Hemlock, Heimlick, Heinz. Do you have to be so pedantic, lad? Anyway, Guzim gobbed out a plaster that was stuck in his throat. I reckon it must be the same one that Tony Blair boy dropped in the pan."

"How many more times? It's Tonibler, Mother," I said, grasping at any diversion to mask my horror at the thought of Guzim almost choking to death on my plaster contaminated cooking. I recalled with shame that I'd completely forgotten to warn Guzim to suck up the curry and to keep a sharp eye out for foreign objects. I had fully intended to warn him about the pesky plaster, but with all his wittering about rabbits, it had clean slipped my mind.

"If I hadn't got a right tight grip on his ribs, 'appen he might have croaked it," Vi boasted before adding with a cackle, "Croaking by choking."

"I'm sure that you are exaggerating any danger Guzim was in…" I began.

"Where did you learn to do the Heimlich

Manoeuvre, Vi?" Marigold interrupted, clearly impressed by my mother's life-saving skills.

"It was something I used in the chippy, lass. It came in right handy when that Edna Billings got a huge piece of fried haddock stuck in her gullet…the greedy cow started scoffing the haddock before she was even out of the chippy. Not that the ungrateful mare appreciated the effort I went to. She did nowt but complain that I'd broken her rib. I can tell you that a broken rib is nothing more than summat and nowt. I told her straight, I never made out that I'd done some fancy first aid course where I learnt to finesse my technique; it was just something I picked up off the telly."

I made a mental note to go out of my way to avoid Guzim in the coming days. I would never hear the end of it if he discovered that I knew the curry contained a choking hazard.

"I not to put curry on the winter menu," Takis decided after hearing the tale.

"I can show you what proper English food is, Takis," Vi volunteered. "I've no time for any of that foreign stuff."

As Violet Burke launched a laundry list of British dishes, bending Takis' ear about her mastery with Yorkshire puddings and suet dumplings, I got the distinct impression that Takis was keen to hear more of her ideas. I realised I would need to put a stop to it or Violet Burke may well end up ousting me and claiming the coveted title of restaurant advisor.

"And of course, the English like to finish off with a nice pudding," Vi continued.

"The Yorkshire one?" Takis queried.

"You can't put jam in a Yorkshire pud, lad. I'm thinking more along the lines of a nice roly poly or a spotted dick…"

"Or one of Marigold's trifles," I suggested with just a hint of sarcasm.

At the sound of her name, Marigold zoned in on the conversation. "Are you taking my trifles in vain, Victor?"

"Perish the thought."

Ascertaining that we were discussing possible desserts that may attract local Brits to the taverna in winter, Marigold came up with an outrageous suggestion. "Taki, you really should consider serving Norman's patisserie delights."

"Norman?" Takis queried.

"A fellow Brit who lives in Meli. He's become rather obsessed with creating fancy cakes. They really are quite scrumptious." Naturally Norman's offerings appeal to Marigold's sweet tooth.

"Delectable they may be, but Takis can't just go around serving desserts that are prepared in a domestic setting. Norman's kitchen would never pass a food hygiene inspection in a month of Sundays. Anyway, there are laws about that kind of thing. He would need to establish himself as a business and comply with HACCP requirements relating to food safety management."

"What's that when it's at home?" Vi demanded.

"Hazard Analysis Critical Control Point," I schooled my mother. "Surely you must be familiar with it from your time at the chippy?"

"I didn't see you having our kitchen inspected before you took your lemon drizzle to serve up at Nikos' taverna," Marigold said accusingly. "Don't tell me you flouted health and safety requirements?"

"There's no need to pick hairs. Anyway, you know our kitchen would pass muster…"

"I'm just pointing out your double standards, dear…"

Grabbing Takis' arm, Violet Burke volunteered, "I could come down and give you a hand, show you what's what."

"Don't be ridiculous, Mother. You'd never make it all the way here on your bicycle."

"Victor, I was to thinking perhaps you could help in the kitchen in the winter," Takis suggested. "You tell me you have the experience of cooking in your local taverna."

"I could perhaps supervise the preparation of

English Sunday lunches." Whilst I quite fancied the idea of becoming involved in an advisory capacity, I didn't fancy driving all the way down to the coast for any evening shifts. At least when I had toiled in Nikos' kitchen, it had only been a short walk from home.

"I could come with you, lad," my mother said, determined to get in on the act and steal my thunder.

Much as I wished she'd keep her beak out of my business, I was forced to admit to Takis, "My mother is a dab hand at peeling potatoes."

"And frying chips," Vi boasted, before hissing in my ear, "Now, this fella just coming in is more of a match for Yiota, height wise at least."

Turning to follow Violet's gaze, a frown crossed Marigold's brow as she exclaimed, "I don't believe it! That's all we need."

About to shift in my seat to see what had caught their attention, Marigold instructed me, "Whatever you do, don't turn around, Victor. I don't want you encouraging him."

Marigold's warning was too late. Naturally I had already turned around; I am only human and defy anyone not to turn when someone directs them not to. My heart sank and I wished that I had heeded my wife when I spotted Vasilis leading John Macey to a nearby table. Considering that he had already angled none too subtly for an invitation to join us and just happened to know where we were dining, it wasn't too much of a stretch to presume he had deliberately turned up in the same venue, like some kind of desperate stalker. Hoping that the back of my and Marigold's heads weren't too recognisable, I attempted to make myself inconspicuous, no easy task when in the company of my mother. I have no doubt that Violet Burke could make a vulgar exhibition of herself on a deserted island.

"Who's that then?" Vi demanded.

"Shush, don't be so obvious. It's someone I ran into in the village earlier who is thinking of buying a house in Meli," I whispered, adding, "Marigold didn't take to him and I don't want to ruin her evening by encouraging him."

From the corner of my eye, I watched as Angeliki fluffed her immovable hair before approaching John Macey's table to take his order.

"*Echete fresko chortofagiko mousakas*?" Since John Macey's voice had a tendency to carry, I could hear him asking Angeliki if she had any fresh vegetarian moussaka.

Angeliki replied, of course, "*Fysika*," before brazenly adding that it had meat in it. "*Alla echei kreas mesa.*"

"*Afto den tha kanei katholou.*" John retorted that

it wouldn't do at all before adding in a boastful tone that he was a vegetarian. *"Eimai chortogafos."* I was only surprised that he didn't add how many years he had practised his meat free lifestyle. He certainly struck me as the type who would want everyone to hear he was morally superior by eschewing the eating of meat.

*"Ti? Den katalavaino."* Rolling her dramatically made-up eyes, Angeliki told him that she didn't understand.

I presumed Macey's ego would suffer a dent at this linguistic hurdle. Since John Macey's Greek had been perfectly comprehensible to my ears, I must confess that I felt for him. It is always embarrassing to come out with what one presumes is a perfect Greek sentence, only to be met with wide-eyed incomprehension.

Resorting to English, John Macey's slug-like eyebrows slimed their way up his forehead as he spluttered, "You don't understand my Greek? I suppose that must be down to my Cretan dialect..."

"We speak the proper Greek in the Mani," Angeliki schooled him.

Rushing over at the sound of his wife's raised voice, Vasilis apologetically interjected. "The vegetarian is no the problem. My wife can to pick the meat out of the *moussaka* for you, yes."

"No. No self-respecting vegetarian would eat

*moussaka* that has been contaminated with meat," John insisted.

*Not to mention mascara*, I thought to myself. On balance, if I was a vegetarian, I might consider meat the lesser of two evils. At least it was liable to be fresh whilst the mascara could have been lurking in a mucky contaminated tube for years.

"We have no the vegetarian *moussaka* but we have many other the food…" Vasilis began.

"Fresh today?" John interrupted him.

"What you cook the fresh today?" Vasilis asked his wife.

"*The kleftiko*…"

"That has lamb in it," John objected.

"And the *stifado*…you eat the beef, yes?"

"No, I'm a vegetarian." It struck me that Macey's patience was wearing thin.

"I cook much the *marathokeftedes, patatokefthedes and melitzanosalata*, all the vegetarian dish," Takis chimed in. I cringed inwardly at his intervention, realising it would naturally draw Macey's attention to our table. However, despite John Macey's constant boasting that he had lived in Greece for sixteen years and liked to consider himself fluent in the language, he was clueless what the dishes were until Takis went into detail. I reflected that although I had lived in Greece for less time than John Macey, only one of the three aforementioned dishes, *marathokeftedes*, had stumped me. In my defence, I have never ventured to the Island of Tinos where the fennel delicacy originated.

Intercepting a warning look from Marigold, I turned my back on Macey and started a new line of conversation, thinking he was less likely to interrupt us if we appeared otherwise engaged. Whilst I had made a point earlier of telling him that we had a business dinner, I suppose that our little gathering didn't appear very business-like.

"Tell me, Yiota, what will you be selling on the market tomorrow?"

"Garlic, aubergines, peppers and cucumber. And *vlita*…"

"*Vlita*, that's Victor's department. He helped your grandfather sell that on the market," Marigold said.

"Kyrios Stavropoulos promised to come at first light to help me load the pickup. He will help with the animals when I am at the market," Yiota said.

"How are you coping with Apollo?" I asked, referencing Panos' vicious guard dog.

"He still miss my *pappous* very much," Yiota said.

The mood lightened and Yiota giggled in amusement when Marigold regaled us with the tale of Apollo's close call with the Punto and how the dog that we had presumed was dead had been hidden in Guzim's shed, only to rise from the dead and take a bite out of the Albanian's bottom when he returned home. I added to the tale by recollecting how Panos and I had loaded Guzim into the tractor to take him to the clinic to have his buttock stitched up. Whilst Guzim was having his medical needs attended to, I had joined Panos in the *kafenion* where he had ordered fresh sardines. The others all laughed when I recounted how I had been looking forward to tucking into the fresh sardines, only to be thwarted in my desire when Panos fed them to his fiendish dog.

As we chatted, I noticed that despite the height difference between Yiota and Takis that my mother had perceived as a romantic obstacle, the two Greeks were getting along remarkably well. It was only when Yiota stood up and excused herself to visit the bathroom that Takis' face fell. He hadn't realised until that moment that the attractive young woman he had been flirting with was a veritable Amazonian who towered over him.

# Chapter 19

*The Dog Dilemma*

Leaping to its feet, the overweight ginger tom which had been slumbering under a table after overindulging on anchovies, meowed in alarm, arched its back and charged past our table, its tail bristling in fear. Glancing around to see what provoked the cat to suddenly sprint into the kitchen, I tutted in annoyance at the sight of Percy Bysshe Shelley dragging its owner across the taverna in hot pursuit of the feline.

"Heel. Heel, Percy Bysshe," the woman screeched in desperation as the Labrador created a disturbance, brushing against the diners. Desperately hoping the dog would continue to pursue the cat rather than be distracted by my irresistibly desirable leg, I spotted John Macey jumping up and grabbing hold of Percy's collar with a firm hand. To my amazement, the disobedient Labrador immediately obeyed Macey's authoritative command to sit before it could resume its amorous relationship with my leg.

"You have to show him that you're in control," John told the English woman whom I recognised from the beach that morning. Considering she was still sporting the same shapeless waterproof anorak that she'd been wearing earlier, I presumed that Percy must have dragged her into the taverna against her will; she clearly had no idea how to control the mutt. I doubted that she had intended to come out for a meal considering that she hadn't made any effort with her appearance. Marigold would never dream of venturing out to dinner without brushing her hair.

"I try my best but he won't listen to me," the woman brayed in her plummy English accent. Flattering John Macey, she added, "I do admire the way you seem to have the knack with Percy Bysshe."

"Well, I say in all modesty that I have some experience with Labs. We used to have one before we moved to Greece sixteen years ago."

Catching my eye, Marigold raised her eyebrows in amusement. Like me, she had caught on that John couldn't resist boasting about his extended sojourn in Greece in a self-important manner, using any excuse to let everyone know he was neither a tourist or a recent import.

As the woman chatted with Macey, both of them ignored the by now restless Labrador. Taking advantage of their disinterest, Percy Bysshe made its move, rushing over to me, seemingly unable to resist the temptation to hump my leg again. As Percy latched on to my trousers, John Macey noticed my predicament and dashed over, yanking the besotted creature off my leg.

"Victor? I didn't see you there. What a coincidence us both dining in the same taverna." *Coincidence, my foot*, I thought. He'd known all along we'd been there but had clearly been biding his time, waiting for an opportunity to attempt to insert himself into our little group.

"Don't encourage him, dear," Marigold hissed in my ear, before plastering a fake smile on her face and saying to Macey, "Fancy seeing you here."

"Indeed, what a coincidence," John Macey replied.

Before Marigold could come up with a scathing retort, I felt a hand on my thigh.

"I see that you managed to remove the damp patch from your trousers," Percy's owner said loudly, making no move to unhand me.

Marigold fired a contemptuous look at the woman. Although my wife isn't generally the jealous type, naturally she had every right to be suspicious of another woman, especially when said woman was clearly not a total stranger to me and had the audacity to brazenly fondle my thigh in an overly familiar fashion, right under her nose. Marigold was manifestly put out.

"A had an unfortunate encounter with this woman's dog this morning on the beach, dear," I hastened to explain, swatting the unwelcome hand away.

Intercepting Marigold's glacial stare, the woman laughed. "Oh, I hope you didn't get the wrong idea. It was Percy Bysshe that found this man so alluring, not me. In fact," she added, turning to me, "You were very rude to me as I recall."

"You left your unruly hound to roam free and take liberties with my leg," I retorted. "You ought to have kept it on a lead since it is apparent that you have no control over the slobbering creature. I had a terrible job getting the dog drool out of my slacks."

Rushing over, Vasilis greeted the dog owner enthusiastically, addressing her as Penny before asking, "Is everything here the okay?" It appeared that our little contretemps was attracting the attention of the other customers.

"It will be once that disorderly dog is removed from the taverna," I told him.

"But the Percy is with the Penny," Vasilis said. "You are eating, yes, Penny?"

"I was planning to but I don't see a vacant table," Penny said.

"You're more than welcome to join me. I'm on my own," John Macey invited. "I could give you some dog training tips."

"Oh fab, that's awfully decent of you," she trilled.

I sighed in relief, thinking Macey's offer would keep the pair of them at a distance. It was obvious that Marigold hadn't taken to either of them. As John led the Labrador over to his table, Violet Burke grasped the woman's arm.

"Hang on a sec, I reckon I know you. Penny, that's it. I knew that I knew you from somewhere…"

"I don't think so," the woman said, firing a disdainful look at my mother.

"You were at the expat book club last month," Vi said.

"What on earth were you doing at the book club, Vi? I wouldn't have thought it was your cup of tea," Marigold chimed in.

"I'd need my head examining if it was. That book club's nowt but an excuse for a load of bored housewives to sit around nattering and knocking back wine."

"So, what were you doing there?" Marigold persisted

"I cadged a lift down with that Sherry. She was off to the book club and I wanted a few cheap bits from the supermarket and a bit of a dip. The prices at the village shop are something shocking…anyhow, I had to go and round Sherry up when I'd done with getting my bits and bobs…"

"I remember you now. I didn't recognise you without that floral swim cap and that rather quaint skirted bathing costume," Penny exclaimed, breaking into a broad smile. "You laid into Bessie and gave her what for…you certainly put her in her place. It was quite something to see. I think a few of us wished we'd had your courage in standing up to Bessie."

"You laid into Smug Bessie?" Surprised that my mother hadn't mentioned it to me, I wished that I could have been a fly on the wall and witnessed Smug Bessie being taken down a peg or two. I find the woman unspeakably loathsome.

"Well, I recognised her right off the bat as that miserable cow what tried to get me and my old mucker Captain Vasos chucked out of that place at the harbour…"

"I remember it well," I said, bridling at the

distant memory.

"That Bessie was talking down to that Sherry something shocking, she was. Just because she hadn't read the book…"

"To be honest, none of us had," Penny said.

"Sherry might be a mithering nuisance, but I wasn't going to keep my mouth shut when that Bessie was having a go…a right little bully, that one. She had Sherry close to tears."

"Bessie had picked some dreadfully pretentious literary tome that bored the pants off us…quite impossible to get past the first page," Penny piped up. "She never seems to grasp that selecting grandiose literature with highfalutin prose leaves the rest of us cold. She seems to think her choice of book will impress us with how well-read she is, but most of us are after nothing more than a jolly good beach read."

Penny's words surprised me. Considering she'd named her dog after an acclaimed romantic poet, I expected her to be another literary snob.

"Sherry just goes along for the company…" Vi began.

"Well, if I'm honest, so do I," Penny interrupted. "Percy Bysshe is a great companion but he's not much of a one for meaningful conversation."

"Well, what do you expect? He's a dog, you daft lummox." Violet Burke rolled her eyes. "Sherry said that Bessie harangued her something dreadful when she suggested they read summat by that Jilly Cooper…"

"Now that's more my style. Lots of horses in her bonkbusters. One can't go wrong with anything equestrian. Well, nice to see you again Mrs…"

"Burke. Violet Burke…"

"Well, if you ever fancy joining us at the book club, you'd be most welcome," Penny invited before scampering off to join John Macey, presumably hoping he was more of a conversationalist than Percy Bysshe. From the corner of my eye, I watched as she shrugged her shapeless anorak off to reveal the sort of outdated Tweed number that wouldn't have looked out of place in Violet Burke's wardrobe.

"Your face wasn't half a picture, Marigold, when that Penny had her hands all over your Victor's leg," Vi chortled.

"Nonsense. I know that Victor would never look at another woman…"

"Of course, I wouldn't," I said. "You know that you are the only woman for me."

"Aye, she must be or you wouldn't be going through with all that getting married again nonsense next week," Vi said. "You'd never have got me saying 'I do' for a second time to any of them useless fellas I tied the knot with."

"How many times? We aren't getting married again, we are simply renewing our vows," I reminded her.

"Speaking of our vow renewal ceremony," Marigold said. "We'd love it if you could come along, Yiota."

"I'd like to, Marigold, but I'm not sure I can spare the time from the farm. I'm still on a sharp learning curve..."

"But Giannis is coming," Marigold said, dangling the bait. It was certainly news to me. I wondered how many others Marigold had invited without mentioning it to me. As far as I was concerned, if I was going to make a fool of myself by parading barefoot on the sand in my suit, the smaller the audience, the better.

"Perhaps I could persuade Kyrios Stavropoulos to look after the farm," Yiota said, her cheeks reddening.

"And you must come along too, Taki," Marigold invited before telling him all about the upcoming ceremony on the beach.

As Marigold droned on to Takis about all her plans for our imminent vow renewal and the arrival of our guests from England, I noticed that the chef was a tad distracted, visibly straining to hear what the customers on a neighbouring table were complaining about to Vasilis. As Vasilis headed back to the kitchen, Takis called him over.

"Vasili, I am listen that some the customers to complain about the dog in the taverna," he said, a worried expression on his face.

"Always it is the tightrope to walk with the animal," Vasilis admitted, throwing his hands in the air. "Some the customers think it the insanitary to have the dog in the taverna…"

"But all the tables are outside tonight so technologically the dog is outside…" Takis ruminated.

"Technically," I corrected.

"Exactly," Vasilis continued. But some the customer still not to like it but others to be the dog lover. If I to tell the dog to leave, I offend the Penny and lose her the custom and maybe the other dog lover. Penny live in the village and come in often. It is the always the same with the cats hanging about, some the customer want to rid, others encourage them by giving them food."

"What are your professional thoughts on the matter, Victor? Is it the insanitary? What they do in the England?" Takis asked.

"Well, speaking as a retired public health inspector, obviously animals must always be kept out of the kitchen. In England there is no specific health and safety requirement that precludes dogs from restaurants or other establishments where food is served. It is a matter that is left to the discretion of each individual business if they choose to allow dogs to enter. Of course, in England, cats aren't really an issue as the place isn't overrun with strays like Greece."

"So, if this was your the taverna, how would you to handle the Percy?" Takis persisted.

"Well…" I dithered. As far as Percy Bysshe was concerned, I would ban the drooling hound simply to spare myself the risk of becoming the target of any more of its vulgar humping. However, I had found it most convenient when Gordon brought along Waffles, the Goldendoodle, when the two of us had ventured out for lunch together over the winter. The taverna we had chosen was not only cold but the food was stale. Waffles had doubled up as both a handy foot warmer and a canine garbage disposal unit, sparing me the embarrassment of explaining a plate of leftovers to the rather officious, and frankly frightening, woman who ran the place. "On balance, I would only welcome well-behaved dogs that don't create a disturbance."

"'Appen that Percy dog would be a sight less trouble than that manky cat of Cynthia's," Vi observed.

"Whilst I'm inclined to agree, Mother, it's a bit of a moot point. Cynthia never attempts to take Kouneli out to eat."

Takis rubbed his hands together in glee,

announcing that Angeliki was bringing us our main course of chicken *souvlaki* that he had prepared earlier, leaving Angeliki to grill it. Fortunately, the skewered meat met with my mother's approval, particularly as it was served with a side of chips. With the food on the table, Takis invited Angeliki to join us, telling her about his plans to remain open during the winter and introduce English food that might appeal to British expats. Angeliki wasted no time slating Takis' plans, telling him he must want his head examining if he planned to open the taverna all year round.

"But I love to be in the kitchen. It is my calling," Takis explained.

"Me, I cannot wait to get out of the kitchen," Angeliki said. Reiterating her sentiments of that morning, she told the others that her husband had wanted their daughter to take over the taverna but Evangeline had more sense and had no intention of giving up her cushy job for life at IKA. When Yiota told Angeliki that she was giving up her job for life at KEP to follow her dream of running her grandfather's farm, Angeliki pronounced her quite mad.

"You give up the good government job with the pension for farm work?" Angeliki was even more astounded when Yiota confirmed that she too was entitled to an extra six days annual holiday for mastering nothing more strenuous than tapping a keyboard.

"The farm is the hard work but every day I will enjoy being outside in the fresh air rather than being stuck in a stuffy office…" Yiota argued.

"But think of the perks you give up. The coffee deliver to your desk, the good pension and early retire, and the finish every the day at lunchtime," Angeliki persisted.

When Yiota and Angeliki reverted to talking in Greek, I tuned out. Glancing around, I noticed that John Macey and Penny seemed to have plenty to say to one another. Nudging Violet Burke, I hissed, "Have you seen the way those two are flirting with each other? All without the benefit of any meddling matchmakers."

"Have you ever flirted, lad?" Vi asked sarcastically as though the idea was utterly preposterous. "That Penny's not flirting at all. She's like that Sherry, she's just desperate for some company. Now if you want to see flirting, look at the way your Marigold is fluttering her eyelashes at Takis."

Marigold's ears pricked up at Vi's words. Sending a scathing look at my mother and me, Marigold retorted, "I wasn't the one with a strange woman's hand fondling my thigh. And as for you, Vi, that old chap Vasilis has been flirting with you from the moment we walked in."

An icy silence descended as Angeliki absorbed

Marigold's words. As she stalked off to the kitchen, I swear I could see smoke coming out of her nostrils.

"Why on earth did you blurt that out in front of Angeliki?" I asked, my question drowned out by the distinctive sound of smashing plates.

With the customers' interest piqued, chatter across the taverna ceased and the lone voice of John Macey speaking to Penny reached me. "I must say I do love a spot of traditional plate throwing. There was a taverna in Crete where we lived for sixteen years that had a regular evening of plate smashing…ouch."

I couldn't refrain from laughing when the plate that Angeliki lobbed at her husband, missed its target and bounced off John Macey's forehead.

# Chapter 20

*A Stereotypical Greek Breakfast*

**D**eliberately dressing down for the part of a market trader in casual clothes, I slung my repping uniform into my satchel for later: it wouldn't do to be seen wearing the company logo whilst I was helping Yiota out on the stall. The small matter of where I could change before meeting the tourists signed up for the Greek Gastronomic Tour crossed my mind, presenting a conundrum. Since there were no convenient telephone booths at the market for me to slip into and emulate Clark Kent's quick change into his Superman costume, I resigned myself to the nasty business of stripping down in the unsavoury lavatories at the market.

Although it was still dark outside as I enjoyed my coffee, I wanted to make an early start. It struck me that it would be the gentlemanly thing to do to call in on Yiota to offer my reassurance before driving up to town. I knew that despite her attempts to hide it, Yiota was more than a tad jittery about her first time at the market. I could certainly empathise with her worries that flogging vegetables would be a far cry from dealing with paperwork at KEP; I had experienced the same fears. However, since retiring from my illustrious career as a public health inspector, I had worn a variety of job hats, whilst this would be Yiota's first time dealing with the public without the might of a petty bureaucracy machine behind her.

Leaving the house, I tripped over an unseen obstacle outside the front door. Whatever it was clattered over with a resounding clang. Pausing to identify the pesky obstruction by torch light, I cursed Guzim under my breath. The ungrateful wretch had dumped the panful of cacti curry back on my doorstep. Presuming the substandard meal hadn't been to his taste, I dismissed my mother's claim that he had choked on the food as stuff and nonsense. I reflected that Guzim appeared to getting complacently lazy, having made not the slightest effort to dispose of the curry and scrub out the pan. I made a mental note that in future I would refuse to cater to Guzim's curry addiction. It was only when the smell of curry hit me once I was in the Punto, that I realised some of it must have slopped over my shoes.

Keen not to disturb the ferocious guard dog, Apollo, I stealthily made my way through Panos' yard towards the house. Fortunately, as there was no sign of the dog, I relaxed. Spotting movement on the other side of the yard, I changed course, guessing that Yiota was already busy loading the pickup. Retracing my steps, Apollo appeared out of nowhere, its bark menacing as it strained against its chain, its slobbering tongue actually touching the toes of my shoes. Jumping back in alarm, I realised the dog was thrusting its lumbering great body at me in a desperate attempt to feed off my curry splotched shoes. Presumably it wasn't too fussy what it ate.

"*Poios einai ekei?*" Yiota called out, asking, 'Who's there?'

"It's me, Victor," I called back, my voice noticeably quivering in high-pitched fear.

"*Apollo. Kathiste.*" Yiota's command for the dog to sit was instantly heeded, sparing my shoes from being ripped to shreds. I tentatively moved towards the pickup, anxious not to further provoke Apollo.

Still baring its fang-like teeth, the guard dog began to whine miserably. I considered that if Marigold hadn't disposed of the pan of curry by the time I returned home, I could bring it over for Yiota to feed to the mutt. It may well earn me brownie points with Apollo, which could be useful if it ever broke free of its shackles again. I had seen its sharp gnashers in action when it tore a strip out of Guzim's buttock and I had no desire to be on the receiving end.

"Victor, what are you doing here?" Yiota asked as I joined her. Kyrios Stavropoulos, the communistic pensioner, stepped out of the shadows, struggling under the weight of a hefty box piled high with aubergines.

"I thought you may appreciate some moral support before you head off to the market."

"That's so thoughtful of you. I am a little apprehensive but also a little excited," Yiota said.

"If I wasn't committed to the Gastronomic Tour later, I would have driven up with you to help calm your nerves."

"Kyria Kompogiannopoulou offered to come up with me but I told her there was no need as you are meeting me there."

I was surprised to hear of the older woman's offer considering her bladder; perchance she wasn't familiar with the dismal and insanitary state of the market lavatories. Still, Sophia's offer demonstrated that the villagers were taking Panos' granddaughter under their wings, eager for her to make a success of the farm and settle permanently in Meli.

"*Afto einai to teleftaio.*" Saying 'that's the last of it,' Kyrios Stavropoulos wiped the sweat from his brow with a grubby handkerchief before emitting a weary sigh. Helping out on the farm was an exerting change from spending his mornings sitting outside the shop, knocking back coffee and playing *tavli* with his old cronies.

Inviting Kyrios Stavropoulos to come inside for a quick breakfast before she left, Yiota kindly included me in the invitation. Recollecting how Panos had also invited me in for breakfast before we ventured up to the market together, I experienced a feeling of déjà vu and gladly accepted. I remembered that Panos had taken me by surprise by serving up fried eggs; for some bizarre reason, I had expected his idea of food to be what I had perceived as the stereotypical, cardiac arrest inducing Greek breakfast of a strong black coffee, a cigarette and a tumbler of *raki*.

A cold shiver ran down my spine as I hovered in the farmhouse doorway, strangely reluctant to enter. My hesitation about going indoors was obvious: I hadn't been inside the farmhouse since the traumatic moment when I had discovered Panos, cold on the floor.

Gazing around the kitchen, I realised that the room had undergone significant changes for the better since my last visit. As an aside, it goes without saying that the removal of Panos' corpse was a definite improvement. Bracing myself, I stepped over the threshold and entered the room. The kitchen table had been moved to the other side of the room, a newly acquired rug tossed over the spot where the body had lain. Vibrant cushions atop a new throw added a feminine touch to Panos' old sofa, nestled next to the open fire. There was something strikingly familiar about the cushions; they appeared to have been fashioned from some old curtains that we'd had in Manchester when we were first married.

"The place looks different," I observed.

"Marigold's friend, Doreen, came in yesterday to give the place a bit of a lift. My *pappous* didn't have much sense of style. I left Doreen to it because I was busy harvesting the vegetables for today. It was a pleasant surprise when I returned."

"It's certainly cosier," I agreed, wondering if Doreen had snuck over with Manolis since neither of them had anywhere they could meet in private.

Yiota's next action prevented my thoughts from straying any further down the path of Doreen and Manolis' love life. To my amazement, she poured three coffees from the *briki* before producing a bottle of *raki* and an ashtray. Refusing the early morning smoke and snifter, I watched as Yiota and Kyrios Stavropoulos both lit up and knocked back the *raki*, confirming the preconceived stereotype I'd had when Panos offered me breakfast.

"I hope the *raki* will calm my nerves," Yiota said. "I am not used to dealing with crowds or selling things."

"You'll be fine," I assured her. "I helped your grandfather out a couple of times on the market and have to admit to quite enjoying it. I'm sorry I won't be able to stay past eleven but I'm sure that Panos' friends...Aristotle and Socrates, will be happy to lend a hand. Very interesting chaps with a surprisingly philosophical bent."

"Yes, my *pappous* spoke of them often."

I was relieved when Kyrios Stavropoulos announced he was off to tend to Yiota's animals. I had a rather delicate subject I wished to broach with Yiota, but felt self-conscious speaking in English in front of the non-English speaking pensioner.

"Yiota, I really feel the need to apologise for my mother's meddling behaviour yesterday evening. It was terribly insensitive of her to keep going on about finding you a husband."

Yiota wasted no time in disillusioning me of the notion that Violet Burke was either insensitive or a meddling embarrassment.

"I'm over thirty now and must find a husband soon. I asked Violet to help me find someone solid and reliable to help me to make a success of the farm. It is too much for me to tackle alone. My *pappous* had years of experience but it is all new to me and I am overwhelmed."

"But springing Takis on you like that…"

"He is a possible. At least he is young." Blushing furiously, Yiota confided, "I must confess that I find Giannis very attractive but I'm not sure if I can trust a man with such good looks. He may be a playboy who is just after a good time."

"On the contrary," I reassured her. "Despite what Marigold refers to as Giannis' Greek-godlike looks, he is solid and dependable. He fled the bright lights of the city to be at one with nature. I admire the way that he's made a real go of things with his honey and rabbits, not to mention his motorbike repair side-line."

"I don't think he is interested in me romantically," Yiota sighed. "I heard that his last girlfriend was both brainy and beautiful…"

"But she was clueless in the kitchen." I felt as though I was betraying Poppy when I stated this point. I liked Poppy very much and was full of respect for the way she had put her studies before romance, recognising that her budding career in streptococcus pathology would preclude her from settling down in a remote Greek mountain village.

"Perhaps you could give me a few pointers. I have heard that you give lessons in Greek cooking." Yiota's words surprised me. It seemed that the younger generation of Greeks had neglected to pick their grannies' brains in the kitchen. "Thanks to Violet, I can now cook perfect chips."

"Wouldn't you rather have Takis teach you? He seemed quite taken with you."

"I think he would not have time to help on the farm when he is running the taverna." It seemed Yiota was ruling Takis out as a prospective husband because of the demands of his own career.

"At least you wouldn't starve with Takis," I quipped.

"But I would be happy to live on honey," she chortled with a knowing wink.

# Chapter 21

*Fresh from the Nets*

Considering I had left Meli before her, Yiota must have burnt rubber to arrive at the market before me. Having located the stall allocated to Panos, she was already busy carting her produce from the pickup, under the curious glances of her fellow traders. Whilst keen to school Yiota in the art of selling, I was less inclined to hump large boxes of veggies, ever mindful of my budding hernia. Fortunately, Yiota appeared to have the lugging well under control; she is after all what Violet Burke would describe as a strapping young lass, not afraid to get her hands dirty.

# V.D. BUCKET

Although I wasn't much use when it came to the physical task of hauling the produce, I was delighted to be able to introduce Yiota to the neighbouring stall holders, Socrates and Aristotle. I was, by now, on quite good terms with the philosophically named pair: in addition to always stopping by for a chinwag when shopping at the market, I always made a point of steering my tourist charges on the Gastronomic Tour towards their stalls and singing the praises of their fresh fruit and veg. Enthusiastically extolling the virtue of purchasing locally grown produce helped to put the odd extra euro in their pockets.

The two farmers were thrilled to make the acquaintance of Panos' granddaughter whom they had heard so much about, assuring her they would be happy to give her pointers on running her stall. In turn, Yiota astutely checked out their produce, noting the competition of Aristotle's plump aubergines, sighing in relief when she spotted that Socrates' stall was piled high with uncompetitive fruit.

Volunteering to get the coffees in, I wandered around the market admiring the tempting displays of ripe seasonal fruit; luscious peaches and nectarines with temptingly silky skins, shiny sour cherries, pears, watermelons and cantaloupes. Although the full morning rush hadn't started yet, there were plenty of early birds making their selection. Taking a detour through the fish market, I regretted that I couldn't take advantage of the early catch; any fish I snapped up would be rank before I got them home, guaranteed to turn in the heat. Receiving nods of recognition from some of the fishmongers, I reflected that my Greek language skills had improved enough to understand a smattering of their prosaic banter.

Returning to Yiota's stall with the coffees, I was pleased to see the first customers eyeing her produce. Thinking to give Yiota a few tips on selling, I decided to replicate some of the bantering lines that I had picked up from the fish sellers.

"I find it boosts interest if you call out to attract attention to your produce," I told Yiota.

"I feel a bit shy to do that…"

"Don't worry, there's nothing to it. Just follow my lead," I assured her. Channelling my inner Del Boy and switching to Greek, I boldly called out to the passing shoppers, "*Ela kai pare. Farma fresko apo ta dichtya.*"

Potential customers stopped in their tracks, making no attempt to hide their laughter. It was not quite the reaction I'd been hoping for.

"Victor, why are you shouting out, 'Come and get farm fresh from the nets?'"

Blushing furiously, I realised that the sales pitch I had heard in the fish market must have stuck in my head and I'd inadvertently slipped in the Greek word for nets rather than fields. "Well, you get my drift. The main thing is to draw attention to your produce and I've certainly accomplished that."

As Yiota rushed to serve the eager customers, I realised I was the butt of their jokes, overhearing joshing remarks such as 'Did the Englishman fish for these peppers this morning?' and 'What bait did he use to get the onions to bite?'

Swallowing my pride, I hissed to Yiota, "See, my unusual line of blather has brought the customers in," hoping to convince her my linguistic error had been deliberate. Humouring me, Yiota called out to the next potential customers, her Greek spiel so rapid that I couldn't comprehend her words.

"What did you say?" I asked her.

"I told them to come and check the fresh produce plucked from the aubergine and onion trees," she said, winking at me.

"Well, it seems to be working," I said, rushing forward to help serve the bemused customers.

I weighed and bagged up the produce whilst Yiota sweet-talked the customers and took their money. Considering the number of customers attracted to the stall, I was delighted to see that my young charge was a natural market trader, demonstrating the gift of the gab. At this rate, I suspected she would soon usurp my title as the Del Boy of Meli.

As we worked alongside one another, I noticed Yiota suddenly coming over all flustered, blushing furiously as she finger-combed her hair and smoothed her clothes. Glancing around, I saw the source of her distraction: Giannis, the handsome bee man from Meli. I watched with interest as he approached the stall, a distinct twinkle in his eyes when he told Yiota that he had come to lend her a hand. It didn't take a lot of imagination to realise that his presence was much more welcome than mine. There was certainly a spark of electricity between the pair, despite Yiota having voiced her worry that Giannis wasn't interested in her. He certainly looked keen enough to me.

Catching only snippets of their private conversation as I dealt with the customers, I heard Yiota tell Giannis that he should have brought his honey to sell on her stall. He replied that he hadn't liked to take advantage. I thought it sweet when they agreed to share a stall next time and merge their products. Rather than lending a hand as he'd said, Giannis appeared to be more interested in flirting with Yiota. Realising it would make Marigold's day if I could report that the pair of them looked well on their way to becoming a couple, I left them to make eyes at one another, the bulk of the work falling on my shoulders.

As the morning wore on, I welcomed a lull in the crowds. Recognising a customer approaching the stall as someone familiar, it took me a moment to place him. Pondering where I knew him from, it dawned on me that he was the owner of a popular taverna in a coastal village where we often stopped for a swim and a bite to eat.

"Victor, my friend. *Eisai kala*?" The personable man shouted my name, asking if I was well as he rushed forward to embrace me.

"George. *Kalos, kai esy*?" His name came to me in the nick of time, thus sparing my embarrassment. The Greek man, Georgios, oozed practised charm and always insisted that all of his English customers use the Anglicised version of his name. His name ought to have been on the tip of my tongue as soon as I'd spotted him, since I had been thinking about him only the previous evening, associating him with the taverna where a pair of repeat English tourists dined for three meals a day throughout their fortnightly Greek holidays. I recalled chatting with the English couple the previous autumn and them telling me that they had invited George and his wife, Voula, to stay with them at their home in England during the off-season when the taverna was closed. Curious if he had taken them up on his offer, I asked him about his holiday.

"I go the England to stay in the home of the taverna friends," George told me, an enormous smile plastered on his face. From what I had heard on the grapevine, he regularly took advantage of invitations from his customers to holiday in their homes, thus saving himself the expense of splashing out on a hotel. Each winter, after the olives had been collected, he would spring a holiday surprise on his long-suffering wife to reward her for slaving away in the taverna kitchen seven days a week and for lugging sacks of olives around on her back. The poor woman had no say in their destination, any dreams of being whisked off to a five-star hotel shattered.

During one of our chats, Voula confided in me that she struggled with the inevitable break in whichever part of England her husband's friendly customers hailed from, since she spoke only a few words of rudimentary English. I imagined it must be quite a challenge for her to adapt to the well-meaning hospitality of her hosts, when she could barely understand them.

"Whereabouts in England did you holiday?" I asked George.

"The Lake District," he revealed.

"A beautiful area. And how did you find it?"

"It was not the problem to find. My friends to collect us from the Manchester airport," he replied, taking my question a tad too literally.

"And did you enjoy your stay in the Lakes?"

"We not to stay in the lake, it was full of the water. Our friends have the big dry house in the Ambleback." George appeared determined to answer all my queries literally even though he seemed to be confusing his back and his side when it came to Lake District villages.

"And did Voula enjoy the break?"

George stared at me with a puzzled expression before replying, "She not to break it, it was just the sprain; she not to enjoy the pain. Luckily it is the mend well enough for her to cook again in the taverna. How you to know she slip on the ice path and hurt the wrist?"

"I'd no idea she had. I was asking if she enjoyed the holiday?"

"*Etsi kai etsi*." George used the common Greek term for so-so, before elaborating. "She much dislike the big fry breakfast but she too the polite to tell them it greasy. She tell them is good. After that, they cook it every the morning for her. It no the wonder so many the English the fat if they eat the fry sausage and black cake every the morning."

"Black pudding," I corrected whilst suppressing a burst of involuntary laughter at George's words. With the way his expanding paunch hung over his belt, he could hardly boast a svelte figure himself, though he appeared completely oblivious that his middle-age spread was on the spread.

"To put the pudding with the bacon is the disgusting English habit, yes? Anyway, I not so polite as the Voula. I tell to them, even on the holiday, I like the good Greek breakfast…"

"Yoghurt and honey?"

"No, the black coffee and the cigarette," he said, confirming the convention that I had earlier dismissed as a cliché-ridden stereotype.

Remembering that I was at the market with a mission to flog vegetables rather than just engage in friendly banter, I encouraged George to cast his eyes over Yiota's selection. Rather than simply casting his eyes, George got a bit full-on with his hands, fondling the aubergines a tad too fondly before pronouncing them perfect for Voula's popular appetiser of *melitzanes tiganites*, fried aubergines. After declaring he would take all the *melitzanes* we had, we resumed our conversation whilst Yiota bagged up the veggies and weighed them, mouthing 'thank you' to me.

George informed me that the lack of olive trees in the Lake District had given him the idea of inviting English people to make a holiday of picking his olives.

"I've read about that type of working holiday becoming quite popular," I told him.

"No, you misunderstand. The olive pick is not the work. It will be the holiday for them. After pick, they can to eat in my taverna. I can to pay them with Voula's cooking instead of the evro."

I couldn't help wondering if he planned to send them off to the olive groves with their stomachs replete from a great British fry up or with just a black coffee and a cigarette to sustain them.

Tearing herself away from Giannis, Yiota pointed out that time was getting on, reminding me that I needed to meet the tourists signed up for the Greek Gastronomic Tour. Confident that Yiota had found her feet and that Giannis was there to offer moral support, I squirmed at the thought of dashing off to the market lavatories that were nothing more than dismal and insanitary holes in the floor, to change into my repping uniform. Noticing my reluctance, Giannis proved himself an utter gent by offering me the privacy afforded by the back of his van to change in. Thinking the offer of the van far superior to Clark Kent's telephone box, I could have kissed the handsome bee man. Naturally I resisted, though it crossed my mind that it wouldn't be too long before Yiota and Giannis were on kissing terms. Marigold would be over the moon.

# Chapter 22

*Heaping Smug Accolades*

T he delightful shop in the old quarter of town, specialising in Greek wine and liqueurs, was the final stop on my Greek Gastronomic walking tour. Gathering my tourist charges around me, I treated them to some interesting well-rehearsed spiel about the wines of the area before finishing off with some newly added material about Marigold's now favourite tipple, *mastika*.

"For a change from the usual *Metaxa*, I can heartily recommend *Chios Mastiha*. It is a sweet Greek liqueur made from the *mastika* resin that is unique to the mastic trees on the Island of Chios.

The liqueur has a long history; first referenced by Hippocrates more than 2,500 years ago, it is considered the oldest superfood in the world. Not only is it rich in antioxidants, it is also renowned for its antifungal and antibacterial properties. Hippocrates recommended *mastiha* for digestive problems and as a breath freshener."

I chose my words with careful deliberation, considering breath freshener sounded more enticing than the cure for halitosis that Spiros had referenced when he gifted a bottle of Mastic Tears to Marigold. Clearly impressed by my line of knowledgeable patter, the tourists eagerly snapped up bottles of the liqueur to add to their other purchases, staggering out of the shop laden down with local honey *meli*, dried figs *xera syka*, local olives *elies*, small jars of olive paste *pasta elaioladou*, and bottles of extra virgin olive oil *elaiolado*.

Stratis, the owner of the shop, called out to me as I joined my charges on the pavement, asking if he could have a quick word in private. Leaving the tourists to window shop in the neighbouring stores, I stepped back inside.

"Victor, your tours are the highlight of my week," Stratis flattered me. "Before your the Greek Gastronomic walking tour recommence for the season, I barely shift the three bottle of the *mastika* all the winter. Now, just today, I to sell eight the bottle because you to speak of it with such the persuasive eloquence. I must to pay you the commission, yes?"

"No, I couldn't possibly accept a commission, Strati. It would be unethical. I can speak of your wonderful Greek products with confidence because I have personally sampled them."

"In that case, please to accept the bottle of the *mastika* from me as the gift, not the commission," Stratis urged.

"I rather fear that would still be stretching the ethical boundary…" I objected.

"But if the gift was not for you but for your lovely wife…"

Hemming and hawing, I prevaricated, recalling that I had called in the shop over the winter with Marigold and treated her to a bottle of her favourite tipple. Clearly my wife had left an impression on Stratis.

"Well, I suppose that if it's for Marigold, then it's nothing to do with me and it can't really be considered a breach of ethics," I agreed as Stratis pressed a bottle of Mastic Tears into my hand. Nevertheless, I made a mental note to secrete the bottle of sweet liqueur in the boot of the Punto before calling into the tourist office with the customer satisfaction surveys.

The tour had been a resounding success. After enjoying a pleasant late lunch, sampling Greek delicacies with the gastronomic tourists, I returned to the office in a remarkably good mood, only to come down to earth with a nasty thud when I discovered an unwelcome visitor contaminating the chair facing Cynthia's desk. Ducking behind the filing cabinets to avoid being seen by Smug Bessie, I shamelessly eavesdropped as Bessie harangued poor Cynthia on why she was the perfect candidate for the repping vacancy that the tour company was suddenly desperate to fill. The position had come up unexpectedly: Cynthia had been forced to give the latest recruit, the inebriated Dennis, his marching orders. She was left with no choice after he fell into the lap of a teetotal American tourist woman when he turned up for work so plastered that he was unable to stand upright on the coach. It has to be said that the entitled tone adopted by Smug Bessie as she lectured my sister-in-law on her eminent suitability for a repping job was stunningly tone-deaf.

"My friend Judith told me that you desperately need someone to fill the vacancy. I'm far more qualified for the job than Judith and you took her on, I really can't imagine why. I've lived in Greece much longer than Judith has. She can't possibly understand local culture after living here less than a year...and I know all about the area. I carry quite some weight among the expats, you know, I started the expat book club…it would be very short-sighted of you not to hire me, it's quite clear that you employ some reps that are woefully inexperienced and undisciplined…"

As Bessie droned on, heaping smug accolades on herself and unashamedly doing the dirty on her supposed book club friend, Cynthia's efforts to hide her disdain for the pushy wannabe rep were fast coming unravelled. I reflected that Bessie was really quite ruthless in her efforts to depose and replace Judith from her repping position, putting me in mind of Guzim's attitude towards Blat. It seems that jealousy of one's own compatriots was a universal trend.

Not wishing to be overly rude, Cynthia chickened out of telling Smug Bessie to sling her hook by simply asserting, "We have no vacancies."

"But Judith said there was a position going…" Bessie argued.

"The position has been filled already," Cynthia fibbed.

Lurking behind the filing cabinet, my cover was blown when I dropped my folder of customer satisfaction surveys, the papers spilling out across the floor. Swivelling around in her seat, Smug Bessie looked at me with contempt before suggesting to Cynthia, "You ought to give serious consideration to replacing some of your existing staff. I would be much more suitable than some of the staff you currently employ. I could certainly knock this office into shape."

Not only was Smug Bessie clearly angling for my job if she couldn't usurp the newly hired Judith or step into the inebriated shoes of Dennis, she had now resorted to questioning Cynthia's competence as a manager. Oblivious to Cynthia's nostrils flaring and her cheeks turning an angry red, Bessie added, "It's quite obvious that you need help disciplining your staff."

Bessie's conceited speech was interrupted when Judith marched into the office. Each of the women looked equally taken aback to see the other there.

Reddening, Bessie addressed Judith in an accusatory tone. "I thought you weren't working today."

"I'm not. I was in town and just wanted to drop an anonymous care package off for Captain Vasos...what are you doing here, Bessie?"

"I popped in to apply for a job," Bessie replied. Turning back to Cynthia, she added, "Judith will be able to vouch for me. She knows how the other expats consider me invaluable at the book club. I was the founding member and the others do look up to me as an authority."

Instead of vouching for Bessie, Judith turned

her back and rolled her eyes.

"As I've said, there are no current vacancies. If you like, you can fill in an application form and I'll keep it on file," Cynthia offered in a desperate attempt to rid the office of Bessie. I know my sister-in-law well enough to know that the only place the application form would be filed was in the waste paper bin.

"I'll fill it in now," Bessie said, prolonging her unwanted stay. Ignoring her, I addressed Judith. "I'm quite intrigued by the idea of a care package for Captain Yannis. Do elaborate."

Looking extremely relieved to join me behind the filing cabinet and remove herself from Bessie's immediate vicinity, Judith broke into a wide smile. "I threw together a package with a couple of new tee-shirts, some carbolic soap and a sponge, a deodorant and a razor. I've taken over some of Dennis' trips on Pegasus and the good Captain doesn't half pong."

"My mother bought him some Old Spice anti-perspirant but Vasos mistook it for aftershave..."

"Oh, I know. I've seen the way he insists on blasting his nether regions with it without bothering to soap himself down first..."

Judith's words tailed off as the door was thrust open and Captain Vasos walked in, immediately sullying the air with ripely pungent body odour that he had cunningly attempted to disguise with a surfeit of Old Spice.

"Cynthia, I love you, mucky fat," he shouted, blowing kisses in her direction.

Cynthia responded with a lacklustre wave, clearly worn down by Bessie. Zoning in on me, Captain Vasos bellowed, "O Victor, *o filos mou, pos eisai* dumpling?"

"*Eimai kala*." 'I'm well' I responded to his question asking how I was.

Slapping me on the shoulder, he moved towards Cynthia's desk, depositing a grubby, oil-stained hand on Smug Bessie's shoulder, a lecherous look on his face.

"Get your hands off me, you horrible little oik," Bessie screeched.

"*Ti*? Beautiful towel," Vasos replied, massaging Bessie's shoulder, clueless that she had just hurled an insult at him.

"I've seen this smelly tramp somewhere before," Bessie snapped, waving a handkerchief in front of her nose, clearly racking her brain as she tried to remember where she'd encountered Vasos. "I know, he's that terribly common man who was knocking back vulgar cocktails at that place in the harbour with that awful old woman from Manchester."

"I rather fear that she's insulting my mother," I

whispered to Judith.

Turning to Cynthia, Bessie continued, "Can't you tell this vulgar person to leave. I wouldn't tolerate his presence if I worked here."

A genuine smile transformed Cynthia's weary expression. "You might as well bin that application form if you choose to look down your nose at the good Captain here. He's very popular with our clientele who go on his boat trips."

"You mean...surely not..." Belatedly realising she had scuppered any chance of gaining employment with the tour company by recklessly insulting the biggest draw on the books, Bessie flounced out, neglecting to apologise.

"I thought I'd never come across anyone with the hide of a rhinoceros like your mother, Victor, but that infuriating woman takes the biscuit. She just wouldn't take no for an answer. Can you imagine the reaction of the tourists if they had to put up with her on Pegasus?"

"There would be universal cries of man-overboard as they jump in the sea to escape her," I snickered.

"And can you imagine the cutting comments on the customer satisfaction surveys if I gave Bessie the chance to lecture our trippers?" Cynthia continued.

"At least mine would shine gloriously beside hers," I quipped.

"Judith, why on earth did you have to tell that insufferable woman that we have a vacancy to fill?" Cynthia demanded.

"I do wish I'd kept quiet. All I did was mention that Dennis had lost his job for turning up drunk…I never thought for one moment that Bessie would want the repping position for herself. I'd rather got the impression that Bessie looked down on those of us who work in the tourist industry."

"Despite her being so short, she looks down on everyone," I said.

"Oh well, hopefully we've seen the last of her," Cynthia said hopefully. "I'm glad you've popped in, Judith. I just want to confirm that you're still okay covering for Victor next week."

"No problem at all," Judith agreed.

"Sorry, I'd have invited you along to our vow renewal service if you weren't covering my shifts," I told her.

"*Ti? Ti?*" Captain Vasos demanded to know what was being said.

Staring at the bedraggled Captain, I pondered whether I should invite him along, but hesitated. Marigold was all for keeping the occasion select and upmarket. I supposed that if I invited Captain Vasos to join us, it would lower the tone and I could well end up in the doghouse.

# Chapter 23

*An Absurd Accusation*

A fter a long, exhausting day in town, I was relieved to pull into Meli, looking forward to nothing more strenuous than a quiet evening at home with my lovely wife. The second I alighted from the Punto, I was accosted on the street by an irate Guzim, stamping his feet and yelling, "*I mitera sou mou epitethike. Prepei na kaleso tin astynomia gia tin treli gynaika.*"

Needless to say, I was gobsmacked to hear that my mother had attacked Guzim and that he was considering calling the police on 'the mad woman.'

Presuming that I had misunderstood Guzim's

guttural Greek hysterical outburst, I told him to repeat himself slowly. Uncertain what inroads the Albanian had made in legalising his previously illegal status in Greece, I somehow doubted that he would want to do anything to attract the attention of any representatives of local law enforcement. Drawing a deep breath, Guzim peevishly repeated his ridiculous assertion that my mother had attacked him, churlishly demanding to know what I intended to do about it. In his warped pin-sized brain, the deluded Albanian seemed to believe that I was somehow responsible for Violet Burke's actions.

Knowing how Guzim is prone to engage in gross hyperbole, I responded incredulously, "*Sas epitethike mia odgontachroni gynaika*?" Though I say it myself, I was quite impressed that I managed to give the Greek words a sarcastic edge when I sniggered, 'You were attacked by an eighty-year-old woman?' Surely it would be unmanly of Guzim to admit that an old-age pensioner, and a woman to boot, had bested him in a street brawl.

"*Echete dei to megethos tis*?" I presumed Guzim's retort of 'Have you seen the size of her?' was rhetorical. Although admittedly, he made a valid point regarding my mother's substantial bulk, I highly doubted he was doing anything other than spouting nonsense. Violet Burke had never displayed any violent tendencies; surely if she was that way inclined, she would elect to flatten any adversary simply by sitting on them.

Whilst I argued that Guzim was the one that was mad and that I didn't appreciate him insulting my mother, he lifted his grubby shirt to display his scrawny torso. I jumped back in horror at the stench of his rancid body odour, equally horrified by the sight of some nasty coloured bruising on his ribs, the discoloured contusion standing out in stark contrast against the ingrained dirt on his body.

"*Einai spasmena ta plevra sou*?" I enquired if his ribs were broken.

"*Ochi spasmeno, apla poly pono,*" Guzim replied, grudgingly admitting, 'Not broken, just much pain.'

Still refusing to accept that my mother had inflicted such damage on him, I demanded to know when it supposedly occurred.

His reply of "*Chthes to vrady,*" meaning yesterday evening, led me to believe that Guzim was losing the plot. Violet Burke had a perfect alibi for the evening in question since she had been with Marigold and me at the coastal taverna. As I pointed this out to Guzim, I suddenly recalled Violet Burke's claim that she had saved Guzim's life by giving him the Heimlich Manoeuvre, or the Heinrich Manure as she'd put it. I recollected that Vi had said she encountered a red faced Guzim, choking on Tonibler's plaster, which he'd slurped up in the curry I'd cooked. I supposed that if Violet Burke had thrown her solid arms around Guzim's ribs with the full force of her weight, she may well have inflicted some accidental damage. Still, if she really had saved his life, the ungrateful wretch ought to be grovelling his gratitude instead of whining about the odd bruise. As per usual, Guzim loved nothing more than making a mountain out of molehill.

*"Kyria Burke sou esose ti zoi,"* I said, pointing out that Mrs Burke had saved his life and adding that he should be thanking her. *"Tha eprepe na tin efcharisteis."*

I will spare any readers the convoluted and confusing trilingual exchange that followed, with Guzim throwing in a number of Albanian expletives, and summarise the exchange in English. Appearing none too impressed with my reasoning, Guzim gawped at me, looking increasingly shifty. Racking my brain for the necessary Greek words, I explained to my nincompoop of a gardener that the plaster which he'd been choking on had been obstructing his airway and could have killed him if my mother hadn't jumped in with her life-saving skills. The fact that she may have been a tad rough was surely beside the point if she had indeed prevented him from croaking.

Expecting to see the penny drop and Guzim to

fall to his knees in his customary grovelling manner, I was taken aback when he changed tack. Giving me the evil eye, Guzim threw a farcical accusation at me, claiming that I had tried to kill him with the curry.

"Why on earth would I want to kill you? I need you to muck out the chickens," I told him bluntly. He must think that I deliberately planted the plaster in the curry.

Playing to an unimpressed and unsympathetic audience of one, namely me, Guzim made a song and dance of clutching his ribs and moaning in agony. When Guzim protested that he couldn't possibly fulfil his gardening duties with his bruised ribs, I asked him if he'd been skiving all day. Admitting that his injuries hadn't prevented him from doing a day's labouring down on the coast, Guzim threw out the ridiculous argument that his employer down there hadn't tried to murder him by sneaking adhesive plasters into his food.

"Plaster singular," I retorted whilst cursing under my breath because my Greek vocabulary didn't encompass the necessary words to accuse Guzim of being a fair-weather, hypochondriac malingerer. I reluctantly told him that he could have the evening off and I would personally muck out the chickens. However, I refused to accede to his outrageous demand for sick pay.

Announcing he intended to take to his bed, the Albanian flounced off in a strop. Relieved to be free of Guzim and his myriad grumbles, I groaned at the prospect of having to muck out the hen house and put the chickens to bed, not to mention splashing the hosepipe around the garden. The Albanian shed dweller really did pick the most inconvenient moment to skive off his gardening duties. Entering the house, a solution occurred to me.

"Marigold, have you got any of those old sheets left that you've been hanging onto?" I called out.

"That's a fine way to greet me when I haven't seen you all day," Marigold chastised. As I walked into the kitchen, I cringed when I noticed Doreen making herself at home. Together with my wife, she appeared to be making substantial inroads into a bottle of Lidl wine. I hoped it was just a flying visit. I really would be forced to put my foot down if she had ideas about moving into the Bucket household again. I didn't care how intolerable she found it sharing a house with Norman; I found it equally intolerable sharing my living space with the exasperating woman.

"I do have some old sheets lying around as it happens. Doreen and I have been using them to make some curtains for Yiota's place."

"Why didn't you just hang some actual old curtains? You seem to have an endless supply of the things?" I asked.

"Just leave Yiota's interior décor to us, we know what we're doing. Anyway, what do you want with old sheets?"

"Guzim's swinging the lead and trying to get out of his gardening duties. He accused my mother of trying to kill him…"

"How bizarre. What put such an absurd notion in his head?"

"He got a tad bruised when she gave him the Heimlich Manoeuvre…he'll be as right as rain if you could just bandage his ribs up with some old sheets."

"Bandage Guzim's ribs. I'm having nothing to do with it," Marigold protested, convulsing with laughter at my outrageous suggestion. Turning to Doreen, she complained, "I think Victor must have taken leave of his senses if he expects me to get up close and personal with Guzim's ribs."

"I don't mind doing it," Doreen volunteered. "I did a first aid course once where we practised bandaging a dummy, so I know what's what. I might be a bit rusty at it but I think I could even manage the kiss of life at a pinch."

"Rather you than me. Guzim isn't renowned for his cleanliness," Marigold warned her friend. "He has a very loose relationship with soap and water."

"I'll rub a bit of Vicks under my nose before I

start. That should put paid to any bad smells. I'll just finish this glass of wine and then I'll get right on it," Doreen said between hiccups.

"Thank you, Doreen." I was genuinely appreciative of her offer, though I imagined she might not have volunteered if she hadn't been noticeably tipsy. "I suppose I'd better come down with you and let Guzim know what you'll be doing. Otherwise, he's liable to get the wrong end of the stick if you ask him to remove his shirt…I wouldn't put it past him to be deluded enough to accuse you of being after his body."

"Well, I was a bit desperate for male attention when I was stuck in that miserable marriage with Norman…of course that was before I met Manolis *mou*…Marigold, did I tell you…"

"What? That you considered Guzim as a potential partner?" Marigold joshed.

"No, don't be absurd," Doreen protested, her blush belying her words. "Did I tell you that Manolis paid me a compliment which he insisted is the highest praise a Greek man can pay a woman?"

"Noooo." Marigold elongated the word in a remarkable impression of Sybil Fawlty. "What did he say?"

"He said that I was the most useful woman he'd ever met."

"I wouldn't consider that exactly a compliment,"

Marigold scoffed. "In fact, I'd take it the other way. It's a bit of an odd thing to come out with…just because he's twigged that you're a natural at stuffing cushions, it isn't exactly the sort of compliment a woman wants to hear. Do you suppose something got lost in translation?"

Though I kept my own counsel, I could only imagine my wife's reaction if I flattered her that she was useful and insisted it was a compliment of the highest order.

"I did tell Manolis that I thought it was a strange compliment since it's hardly romantic, but he says it is…he says it's the most romantic thing he's ever said to a woman."

"It's the sort of thing I'd expect a man might say to his char rather than his girlfriend," Marigold said. "I'm sure it was a language mix-up. After all, Greeks are always saying things that are a bit peculiar when they use English."

"How so?" Doreen asked.

"Well, I noticed when Spiros stayed here that whenever he went to get changed, he always said he was going to put his dress on."

"Oh, I never knew that he was one of those men that like to dress in women's clothing?" Doreen said, her excited tone implying she'd just uncovered some juicy gossip.

"He isn't. You're missing Marigold's point," I

said. "Spiros used the English word dress incorrectly. When he said he was going to put on the dress, he actually meant clothes. Most likely Manolis called you useful because he's angling to get you over there to do his ironing."

"No. I mean I would. I'd be happy to do Manolis' ironing but Christos is always hanging around."

"So, what exactly did Manolis mean by it?" Marigold pressed.

"Well, he says that because I hated him smoking, he gave it up for me, which means he'll live longer. So, I am the most useful woman he ever met as I have extended his life."

"I still can't imagine why he thought it was a romantic thing to say. I'd be mortified if Victor professed in his vows next week that he is committing to me for the rest of his life because I'm useful."

"Darling, no one could ever accuse you of that," I quipped. When it came to practical matters, the term useful could never be applied to my wife. "Well, idle chatter isn't getting Guzim's ribs wrapped up."

"I'll grab the old sheets," Marigold offered, slipping into the grand salon and rummaging through a mound of material. Holding up a pile of floral brushed nylon, she asked, "Do you remember these, Victor?"

"I'm hardly likely to forget them. They had so

much static that my hair was invariably standing on end by the morning. Haven't you got some cotton sheets that you can cut up instead? We'll never hear the end of it if Guzim's bandages end up shocking him with static."

"I've got those Thomas the Tank Engine sheets that Benjamin had on his bed when he was toddler."

"What on earth possessed you to cart them all the way to Greece?"

"One never knows when one can repurpose old fabric. They'll do for Guzim's ribs," Marigold said, grabbing her dressmaking shears and making speedy progress of cutting the cotton sheets into strips. "I'll come down with you, it ought to be entertaining if nothing else."

Rapping on the door of Guzim's shed elicited no response.

"Perhaps he's gone out," Marigold suggested.

"So much for being on his deathbed," I said. "I suspected all along that Guzim was playing hookey."

Pressing her ear against the shed door, Doreen said, "No, there's definitely someone in there. I can hear something shuffling around."

"It's probably that rabbit of his," I guessed.

"Perhaps he's tidying up," Marigold said just as

Guzim finally threw the door open. Squinting over his shoulder, she peered inside the pink palace of love. "Or perhaps not."

Despite the warmth of the early evening, Guzim was wrapped up in one of Barry's seasonal gifts to me that I had passed on, a brightly knitted Christmas pullover featuring the slogan 'Jingle', complete with immodestly placed bells. Sounding half asleep, Guzim rubbed his eyes as he asked what we wanted, telling us he'd been sleeping. "*Ti theleis? Koimomoun.*"

A torrent of unrepeatable Greek expletives followed as his pet rabbit, Doruntina, took advantage of the open door and escaped into my garden. The swearing only ceased when I promised him that I would round up the rabbit and return it to the shed when we'd finished providing medical aid to his bruised body. Since the exchange that followed was once again a convoluted nightmare of linguistic misunderstandings, I will parse the dialogue in English.

"Doreen has volunteered to bandage up your bruised ribs," I told him.

"Is she a doctor?"

"No, but she once bandaged up a…a plastic man on a first aid course," I told him, unable to conjure up the Greek word for dummy even though Guzim looked very dummy like at that moment.

"A plastic man," Marigold translated for Doreen's benefit. "Is that really the best Greek you could come up with, Victor? Tell him that she bandaged a *koukla*."

"A doll?"

"Well, it sounds better than a plastic man."

"Why not just tell him that I've come to wrap up his ribs?" Doreen suggested.

Since the Greek for 'wrap up' eluded me, I grabbed the improvised bandages from Marigold and demonstrated what Doreen intended to do by wrapping the sheets around my rib area. Fortunately, Guzim caught my drift. Holding his arms out to the side, he indicated that he was ready to be trussed up.

"Tell him that he'll have to take off his jumper before I get started," Doreen hiccupped.

Naturally Guzim made a song and dance of removing the pullover, laying on the groans with a trowel as he struggled out of the gaudy woolly to the accompaniment of jingling bells, before indicating Doreen could commence bandaging him up.

"Is he stupid? Victor, you'll have to tell him to strip his shirt off too," Doreen instructed.

"No way. I'm not taking my top off in front of foreign women," Guzim argued when I told him the shirt had to go.

"Is he seriously coming over all prudish?"

Marigold asked in disbelief. "His modesty seems misguided since he never cares who is watching when he strips down to his grubby underpants for one of his irregular showers. I remember how shocked Geraldine was the first time she caught an eyeful of Guzim under the hosepipe."

"Look, Guzim, Doreen can't very well bandage you up over the top of your shirt," I pointed out in exasperation.

Acting affronted, Guzim reminded me that he was a married man and it wasn't right expecting him to bare his torso in the presence of women he wasn't related to.

"Have you got religion or something?" I snapped.

"Can't you do the bandaging?" Guzim's tone took on a familiar grovelling tone.

"Do I look like a nurse? Doreen has done a first aid course…"

I was relieved that Doreen couldn't understand our exchange when Guzim pronounced that he couldn't trust Doreen near his naked chest because she was a loose floozy who was carrying on with that Texan even though they weren't married. Whilst I've always had Guzim down as a chauvinist, he was only now revealing his curious Puritanical streak.

"Oh, for goodness' sake, do as you're told and

let Doreen get to work," Marigold instructed.

Intercepting my wife's scathing glare, Guzim took on a cowed expression and visibly shrank before our eyes. Not daring to resist my wife, he reluctantly removed his shirt to reveal the mess of bruises, his embarrassment evident when he pathetically placed two fingers over his manly nipples.

Recoiling from the stench of Guzim's ripe body odour, Doreen proposed, "Perhaps you could hose him down first, Victor."

# Chapter 24

*A Cracking Manoeuvre*

Scouring the vegetable patch for the elusive escaped rabbit, I mused that with Guzim's ribs finally wrapped up securely in old sheets, he resembled a Mummy more than a dummy or plastic doll. With no sign of Doruntina, I gave the garden a good drenching with the hose-pipe before venturing into the chicken coop. Five of the current clutch of six chickens were grubbing around in the dirt, pecking for worms. I reflected that Mythos and Raki were getting a tad long in the tooth; although Raki still earned her keep by pro-ducing eggs, Mythos had stubbornly stopped laying. Striding past Fix, Dionysus and Baileys, I looked around in vain for any sign of the latest addition, Mastic. She ought to be easy to spot since she stood out from the rest of my brood by dint of her distinctive appearance; the only splash of colour on her plump white body being a bright red lobed wattle dangling well below her beak.

The strong odour of ammonia hit me as I entered the hen house where I discovered Mastic, hogging the nesting box, seemingly impervious to the acrid stench. Mastic was the most stubborn hen I had ever encountered, invariably spending the best part of the daylight hours perched on the box, straining to produce an egg. Bizarrely, Doruntina was sitting by Mastic's claws, seemingly fascinated by the bird, perchance mentally egging her on to lay.

"Daylight is fading fast. You might as well scoot outside as you won't lay an egg in the dark," I said to the hen. Even though they never respond verbally, I am a great believer in chatting to my chickens though I draw the line at starting a conversation with my plants.

Unsurprisingly the chicken didn't reply, simply staring at me with rheumy, unblinking eyes. As I reached over to grab Mastic in order to turf her out and change the straw, her claw swiped my arm, resulting in a gruesome splash of spilled claret. "Just for that, you can put up with the stench of rancid straw," I snapped, my impatience worn thin.

Scooping Doruntina up, I marched back to Guzim's shed. Yanking the door open, I deposited the rabbit inside, relieved that the sound of Guzim's snoring offered an excuse to avoid another nonsensical exchange. Returning to the chicken coop, I rounded up the five stragglers and watched as they jumped on their perches before locking them in for the night, feeling just a smidgeon of guilt that they would need to sleep in a hut with soiled straw.

On my return to the house, Marigold wrinkled her nose at the lingering stench of chicken coop wafting from my repping uniform, before suggesting, "You jump in the shower, dear, and I'll heat up some soup for dinner."

Considering I'd been out and about since the crack of dawn, I thought it wouldn't have killed Marigold to have made more of an effort on the food front. There again, she had downed more than the odd glass of wine whilst nattering with Doreen, so perhaps it was best if she avoided using any sharp kitchen implements.

"I could do with an early night. You don't mind if I don my pyjamas for dinner?" I asked, scuttling off to the shower before Marigold could voice her objections about my dining in such casual attire.

After revelling in a long, indulgent hot shower

and plastering up my chicken inflicted wound, I retired to the balcony in my jim-jams. Marigold delivered a welcome cup of Earl Grey accompanied by a
tender kiss, perchance wine induced, before popping down to the garden for some fresh herbs to
garnish the homemade roasted red pepper soup
she'd retrieved from the freezer. Needless to say,
the soup was my own creation, made from a glut of
glorious peppers I'd grown in the garden.

Catastrophe almost had the tea over when she
jumped on my lap. Stroking her fur as she purred
in rapture, I felt grateful that Marigold had decided
to purchase felines rather than canines to accompany us to Greece; there would have been no
chance of relaxing and admiring the exquisite sunset if there were dogs to be walked. At least Marigold's pampered domestics demanded nothing
more taxing than feeding, stroking, and the occa-
sional round of de-fleaing: not that they actually
have fleas, perish the thought, but one must take the
necessary precautions.

The peace of the evening was disturbed by the
sound of Violet Burke whistling tunelessly as she
cycled home. Clutching Catastrophe to my chest, I
leant over the balcony and shouted down to my
mother that I wanted a quick word.

"Well, pop down then. Those stairs of yours fair
knock the wind out of me and my feet are about to

explode."

"Just come up, Mother. I'm not showing my face on the street in my pyjamas," I retorted.

I considered it best to address Guzim's accusation that Violet Burke had attacked him before she got wind of it from the village gossips. If she found out what the ungrateful wretch was saying, she might well end up making mincemeat of him for real.

Violet Burke preceded Marigold onto the balcony. Clutching the freshly picked herbs, my wife sent me a withering look over her mother-in-law's shoulder. No doubt she had anticipated a Violet Burke free evening for a change.

"What's up, lad? I'm fair knackered and not in the mood for owt more than collapsing in front of a bit of Corrie." On hearing Vi's words, Marigold visibly exhaled in relief.

"I thought you ought to know that Guzim is going around accusing you of attacking him," I revealed.

"Attacking that gormless twit. I've better things to be doing with my time," Vi chortled.

"Guzim does have some rather nasty bruising on his ribs…" Marigold interjected.

My mother looked blank. "From the Heimlich Manoeuvre you administered when he was choking," I clarified.

"Cor, the cheek of some people, there's thanks for you. I should have left the ungrateful blighter to choke to death. That would have learned him."

"Is it possible you were a bit forceful with him, Vi?" Marigold asked.

Shaking her head at the absurdity of such a notion, Vi said, "'Appen it's possible that I don't know my own strength. There's no denying that Albanian of yours is pretty weedy. A puff of wind would have him over."

Grabbing my arm, my mother instructed me to stand up so that she could demonstrate the life-saving technique she had used, assuring me it was, "Nowt but a hearty hug."

Reluctantly dropping the cat, I allowed my mother to throw her arms around my chest. I must confess it made me feel a tad uncomfortable. Although I had grown used to having my mother around, we were not exactly on the sort of terms where we engaged in smothering embraces.

"So, I did nowt more than this," Vi said. Demonstrating a shoddy imitation of the Heimlich Manoeuvre, she rocked me forwards in a thrusting movement, pressing all the air out of my lungs with the full force of her not inconsiderable bulk. An audible crack filled the silence, followed by an agonising spasm in my rib area. "Did you hear that strange crack? Guzim's ribs never make that noise when I did that to him."

# Chapter 25

*Delivering the Patient by Hearse*

V i, what on earth have you done to Victor? Look how pale he's gone," Marigold cried.

"I think she's broken my ribs," I gasped between shallow breaths, sinking into the chair to avoid collapsing on the floor with indescribable pain.

"'Appen I really don't know my own strength," Vi said in a quiet voice, clearly shocked that she inflicted such an injury on me.

It is no exaggeration to say that Marigold was distraught at my predicament. Dissolving into tears, she threw her arms around me, triggering another stab of pain.

"I'll get some brandy for the shock," Vi said.

"I'm not sure that's a good idea with the state he's in," Marigold said.

"It's for me. I'm the one in shock," Vi asserted. "I just can't believe I've done this to my Victor. That Albanian of yours did nowt but yelp a bit after he coughed up that plaster. He never turned that right funny colour."

"But Victor wasn't choking on anything," Marigold reasoned. "Perhaps the Heimlich Manoeuvre is more dangerous when it's done on someone who's airway isn't obstructed."

Whilst Vi disappeared to rummage through the cupboards in search of a bottle of *Metaxa*, Marigold kneaded my hand tenderly, her face a picture of loving concern. When my mother returned to the balcony carrying two glasses of brandy, it was evident that she'd already indulged in a sneaky snifter or two in the kitchen.

"I'm worried that you've broken Victor's ribs, Vi," Marigold said, snatching one of the glasses and knocking the brandy back.

"Even if Victor does have a broken rib, it's summat and nowt. There's no point in him carrying on like a big girl's blouse." Emboldened by the brandy, my mother had soon changed her tune. "There was this window cleaner that used to come in the chippy. He fell off his ladder and broke every rib in his ribcage but he still dragged himself in for cod, chips and mushy peas twice a week without complaining."

"I really think I need medical attention," I whimpered.

"I'll give Doreen a call and get her to come back and bandage you up," Marigold said.

"Doreen isn't medically qualified. She's only ever bandaged up a dummy," I objected.

"She's just bandaged up Guzim."

"Exactly. Need I say more?"

"I'd rather you took charge of any bandaging," I told Marigold. If Doreen reappeared, we might never get shut of her for the evening.

"I'm afraid of hurting you…" Marigold prevaricated.

"Fetch me the bandages, lass, and I'll sort him out," Vi ordered. "There can't be owt to it."

Marigold dashed off to collect some strips of old sheets. Since all the good cotton sheets had been used up on Guzim, there was only static brushed nylon left to wind around my ribs.

"There's not much elastic in these," Vi scoffed as Marigold helped me to divest myself of my pyjama jacket. No one could accuse Violet Burke of having a bedside manner as she roughly wound the ripped bedding around my torso, provoking more pain and drawing blood when she accidentally skewered me with the safety pin.

"I'm in agony," I groaned. "I really think that I need medical attention."

"Don't be such a drama queen," Vi tutted. "It's summat and nowt."

"I don't know. I think Victor's right. We really should get him checked out. I'll give Barry a ring and get him to drive Victor to the clinic once you've finished bandaging him up," Marigold said. "I've had too much wine to drive the Punto."

A sudden look of alarm washed over my wife's features and she gasped; her initial show of sympathy replaced with panic. "What about our vow renewals? What if Victor's ribs are broken and he can't manage to stand up for the vow renewal service?"

"Get a grip, lass. I did nowt but hug him a bit hard. He'll be as right as rain by the morning." Vi sounded as though she was trying to convince herself.

"He'd better not try using this as an excuse to get out of the ceremony," Marigold chuntered under her breath as though I wasn't even there.

"Marigold, you know that nothing will stop me from going through with the ceremony and reaffirming my commitment to you," I muttered through gritted teeth. It was obvious to me that if I dared to use my injury as an excuse to get out of the whole rigmarole, I could count on being in the dog-house for the rest of the year.

"I really think you need to get me to the clinic," I urged again.

"I'll ring Barry now...I expect it's just a tiny crack that will heal on its own if you don't do any-thing too strenuous, but it's best to be on the safe side."

"Victor's hardly one for putting his back into anything strenuous..." Vi mocked the very notion.

Marigold was thwarted in her attempts to get hold of Barry, Cynthia reporting that he was still tackling the pointing over at the renovation project. "Try Spiros," I urged.

Fortunately, Spiros happened to be free. In two shakes of a cat's tail, he rolled up in the hearse. Spi-ros could always be relied upon to drop everything in an emergency and I considered myself lucky to count him as a friend. Since I was in too much pain to attempt to change into more suitable attire, it was decided it would be easier to bundle me down to the clinic in my pyjamas, thus compounding my in-dignity. As the three of them helped me slowly down the outside stairs and into Spiros' vehicle, I couldn't help but wonder what the reaction of the medics might be when they spotted a patient rolling up in a hearse.

"There is only the room for the one of you and the Victor," Spiros insisted.

Marigold and Violet Burke almost came to blows as they fought over which of them would accompany me to the clinic. From the way they bickered, anyone would think they were vying as to which of them would be lucky enough to go on some fun evening out.

"I'll go with the lad. 'Appen Marigold wouldn't make a good impression. She's been on the wine," Vi insisted, oblivious that she was breathing out brandy fumes.

"Only the Lidl stuff," Marigold countered.

"Don't worry, lass, I'll see he's right. When all's said and done, I am his mother," Vi said, even though she had demonstrated very little mothering up to now.

After helping to sandwich me in between Spiros and my mother, Marigold called out as the hearse pulled away, "Just make sure they give him the all clear for Tuesday." Clearly her anxiety about the ceremony being cancelled far exceeded any worries she may have about my painful condition.

Since there wasn't a body in the back of the hearse to worry about, Spiros put his foot down, taking the corners with no regard to the fact that with every twist and turn of the mountain road,

Violet Burke's elbow collided painfully with my ribs.

"I was to thinking about your the vows to say to the Marigold," Spiros said, reminding me that I had confided in him the need to come up with some romantic guff. "Because you like much the Greek culture, you could to recite some the words from the Ancient Greek Wedding Song."

"I've barely mastered Modern Greek, Spiro. Ancient Greek is a bit beyond me," I pointed out. "Anyway, Marigold wouldn't be able to make head nor tail of it if I started spouting Ancient Greek on the beach. She'd think I'd lost my marbles."

"You can to say in the English translate, yes. I think the Marigold would to find it romantic."

"Perhaps it would appeal to her if it translates romantically without being overly slushy. I will look up the Greek Wedding Song in one of my books. Does it have a name?"

"It is called the Hymen."

"The hymn. Victor's not one for anything religious," Vi butted in.

"No, not the hymn, he is the *ymnos*. I speak of the Hymen, how we to say, the *ymenas*." Since the two words sounded almost identical to my ears, it reminded me of all the ridiculous confusion between Tony Blair and Tonibler.

"The Hymen he is the Greek god of the

wedding," Spiros said. Swerving erratically to avoid an animal in the road, Spiros steered the hearse through a pothole, jarring my ribs. All thoughts of my vows fled my mind as my ribs once again collided with my mother's elbow and I groaned aloud.

"You are much in the pain?" Spiros enquired.

"Agony," I confirmed.

"The doctor will to make you the good. The medical he is invented in the *Hellas*."

"Hippocrates," I added.

"'Appen he did a wedding song too," Vi chuckled, nudging me in the ribs for good measure.

In truth I was a tad apprehensive about my trip to the clinic. It would be my first experience of dealing first hand with the Greek health system, though Marigold and I had both visited a Greek dentist. Being in robust health, the Buckets had been lucky until now. Moreover, much as my mother complained about her swollen feet, they continued to function without exploding and without the need to be doctored. Of course, I had experienced the Greek healthcare system second-hand, visiting both Litsa and Milton in the hospital, and delivering Guzim to the clinic to have his buttock stitched up.

"We are the here," Spiros announced, drawing the hearse up at the clinic. A wail escaped my lips as Spiros and Violet Burke assisted me in alighting from the hearse, the move from sitting to standing being a particular painful one.

As we entered the clinic, the nurse behind reception made a witty sally that she was relieved the undertaker wasn't delivering a corpse. Telling us that the doctor on duty was in with another patient, she directed us to wait on the plastic chairs lining the corridor.

"You are the lucky no one else to wait and that the Violet break your the rib in the evening. You should be seen the quick," Spiros observed. "If the Violet had to break your the rib in the morning, you could to wait for many the hour."

"Don't keep harping on about my breaking his rib. I reckon it's summat and nowt. Victor's likely just a bit delicate with having one of them white collar jobs all them years. If he'd had the sort of job where he was used to getting his hands mucky, 'appen he wouldn't make such a fuss," Violet Burke said.

"I wouldn't have got far as a health inspector with dirty hands," I pointed out. "Anyway, do stop trying to wriggle out of your responsibility, Mother. You caused my injury and must own up to it..."

My words were drowned out by the sound of an agonised scream emanating from an examination room. A cold shiver ran down my spine.

"At least you're not in such a bad way as that

poor bugger," Violet Burke cackled.

After waiting another ten minutes, a young doctor exited the examination room containing the screamer and consulted with the nurse at reception.

"Surely that's not the doctor. She's still wet behind the ears," Violet Burke pronounced. "It's one thing for policemen to start getting younger but that lass looks like she should still be playing hospitals."

After conferring with the nurse, the doctor approached us, asking in English, "What is the problem?" No doubt the nurse had warned her the patient was foreign. Much as I do enjoy practising my Greek, I was relieved to hear the doctor speak English since I hadn't had any time to brush up on my rusty medical Greek. One wrong word might result in some medical mishap; before I knew it, I could be on the operating table having my appendix needlessly whipped out.

"I think my ribs are broken," I told the doctor.

"I had to bandage him up," my mother revealed.

"I wouldn't have needed bandaging up in the first place if you hadn't caused my injury," I pointed out.

"Are you saying this woman attacked you?" the doctor asked incredulously.

"Did I heck, I'm his mother. I was just demonstrating that Heinz Manure on him..."

"She means the Heimlich Manoeuvre," I explained.

"You have choke on the foreign object?" the doctor enquired.

"No...my mother was simply showing me what she'd done to my gardener."

I surmised from the horrified expression on the doctor's face that she was torn between either requesting a psyche consultation for Violet Burke or calling the police on her, since my mother had painted herself as some kind of manic assailant.

"*Ela*, I will examine you," the doctor said, opening the door to a consultation room. Despite her youth, the doctor was surprisingly firm, putting Violet Burke in her place by refusing to allow her to accompany me inside.

Spiros released my elbow, hissing, "I will go to the outside." No doubt he was in need of a cigarette.

"No, you come in to help," the doctor barked at Spiros.

"I not to have any the medical training," Spiros objected.

"You can to translate if need…"

"I'll come in and help the lad out of his jim-jams," Violet Burke insisted, pushing her way past Spiros.

"There's no need for that, Mother. I've been undressing myself for years now."

"Wait outside," the doctor barked at my mother, demonstrating a formidable will equal to that of Violet Burke. Having been firmly put in her place, my mother simply gaped as Spiros slammed the door in her face.

The doctor fired a series of incomprehensible questions in Greek at Spiros. I was at a loss to make sense of them, her accent beyond me.

"You must to take off the blouse so the doctor can to examine you," Spiros said when the doctor finally paused for breath.

After cautiously slipping my pyjama jacket off to avoid aggravating my injury, my improvised bandages were met with disdain by the doctor who pronounced they would have to go too. Spiros stepped forward to unwind the old sheets, leaving my rapidly bruising torso on display.

"Why you to put the old rags?" the doctor enquired. "It is, how to say, the old bride tale to bandage the broken rib. You must to leave them free, not to compress. The bandage to squeeze the rib together, is not good for the breathing. Too much the squeeze and you to risk the pneumonia."

After slipping her hands into latex gloves, the doctor approached and started prodding my torso none too gently. As an aside, I was very relieved that I'd showered in advance of my injury.

"Are my ribs broken?" I asked.

"I not to think so but how to tell? There is no the X-ray machine in the clinic. I can to write you to go the hospital for the X-ray…"

"I can to drive you." Although Spiros volunteered, his tone was hardly enthusiastic. No doubt he would prefer to spend the evening snuggled up with Sampaguita rather than escorting me up to the hospital.

"I'd rather not unless it's absolutely necessary," I said. "The journey here was agonising enough without suffering another couple of hours in the hearse."

"Is it the necessary, Doctor?" Spiros asked.

"I would not to bother," she replied. "Broke or not the broke, it make no the difference to the treatment. I give you the strong pain kill but he to make you the drowsy, so not to drive or operate the big machine. There is nothing to do but to ice the area and to make the bedrest. Put the plenty of ice and avoid to play the sport."

"That's easily done, I'm not sporty," I said. "How many days of bedrest would you recommend?"

"A couple of day the bedrest but not to sleep the lie down. You must to sit up to sleep. Make the deep breathe and have the good coffee every two the hour."

"Ah, the *Ellinikos kafes* cure the everything,"

Spiros said proudly.

"No, not the Greek coffee," the doctor corrected herself. "I mean to say the good *vichas* every the two hour."

"A good cough," Spiros translated.

"After the bed, take it the slowly and not to lift anything the heavy. The rib will to heal the self," the doctor concluded. "I would to guess not the broke, maybe the tiny crack."

"So, I can be out of bed by Tuesday?"

"Yes, if you rest and ice for the next days. It will do good to be on the move by the Tuesday," the doctor confirmed, slipping off the latex and scrubbing her hands with a thoroughness that impressed me, before leaving the examination room.

As Spiros helped me back into my pyjama jacket, he said, "The Marigold will be the happy that you can be back on the feet for the remarry, yes."

"Thank goodness. Marigold would have had kittens if I had to give the vow renewal service a miss," I sighed. Recollecting that the doctor had advised against bandaging up injured ribs, I told Spiros that Doreen had wrapped Guzim up. I could only imagine Marigold's reaction when I told her she would need to pop down to the shed and unravel her Albanian. "He's not going to be a happy bunny. He hated having his ribs wrapped up in the first place. Can you believe that he came over all prudish when Doreen needed him to remove his shirt? Mind you, it wasn't a pretty sight…and as for the smell."

"But the Doreen is getting the reputation. Perhaps the Guzim to think she is the man mad."

"Barking more like," I chortled, immediately wishing I hadn't. Laughter in any form only aggravated the pain in my ribs which may or may not be broken. Whilst medical attention hadn't provided any definitive answers, at least I knew that my ribs would heal more quickly without being wrapped up in old sheets. The prospect of lying abed for a couple of days was intensely frustrating though as our guests from England were due to arrive the day after tomorrow.

Back in the hearse, I balled up the old sheets to create a protective cushion to ward off the blows from Violet Burke's elbow. The exertion of getting to the clinic had worn me out and I thankfully dozed all the way back to Meli. Marigold dashed down to the street the moment Spiros parked the hearse, demanding to know, "Can you still go through with the vow renewal service?"

"He be the right if he rest in the bed for the next few day," Spiros confirmed. "He need the sit up, the breathe and the lots of ice."

"Oh, thank goodness for that. I was quite

distraught thinking we would have to cancel." Belatedly realising that she was demonstrating more concern about the vow renewal service going ahead than my health, Marigold asked, "Are your ribs broken, dear?"

"Who knows? There was no X-ray machine at the clinic and I couldn't face the drive up the hospital. The doctor guessed a tiny crack and said my ribs should heal on their own. Bandaging them up was a bad move; apparently it squeezes the ribs together and hinders breathing. Someone needs to go down and unbandage Guzim; I'm in no fit state to do it."

"Don't look at me, I'm not having anything to do with it," Marigold protested. "Besides, I need to look after you, darling. I will telephone Doreen and ask her to pop over to the shed to sort Guzim out."

"Don't bother, I'll do it," my mother volunteered, adding, "If you fancy soaking them ribs of yours in a nice warm bath, lad, pop down to mine."

With that my mother stalked off across the garden to the shed, leaving Spiros and Marigold to assist me up the stairs. I could only imagine the Albanian's reaction when Violet Burke pounded on the door of the pink palace of love after dark, barged in and ripped off his sheets.

"Perhaps you'd be more comfortable if I sleep in the guest bedroom," Marigold suggested after Spiros had filled her in on the doctor's orders. I rather suspected that now my wife was assured that I wasn't at death's door and would be fit to recite my vows, she was perhaps selfishly worried that if I had a good cough every two hours as the doctor had recommended, it would disturb her beauty sleep.

# Chapter 26

*Victor's List of Undesirables*

Having never been one to malinger and take to my bed through illness, the prospect of lying abed for three days was certainly not one that I relished. Marigold was adamant that I must follow the doctor's orders to the letter, her overriding concern being that I would be upright on the beach and capable of reciting my vows by Tuesday.

After I'd suffered a fitful night's sleep sitting propped up in bed, Marigold expressed concern that the bags under my eyes would stand out in the celebration photos and she might need to give me a touch up with makeup on the big day. The idea struck me as ridiculous since any makeup she applied was sure to run down my face when I started to sweat in the heat. Needless to say, Marigold looked deliciously refreshed after spending an untroubled night in the guest bedroom. Deprived of my wife, I discovered that the cats made a surprisingly good substitute, though I thought it best not to mention that to Marigold. Having never imagined that I would be grateful for the cats' company, I was amazed that they seemed to sense that I was in need of comfort and duly provided it, cuddling in close and cushioning my ribs with their warm bodies.

Marigold kept me dosed up on painkillers that made me drowsy; even the strong coffee that I washed them down with did little to counter the somniferous effect of the pills.

As word of my injury got round the village, naturally exaggerated in every re-telling, the Bucket household soon began to resemble Piccadilly Station, with well-wishers dropping by in droves. I left strict instructions with Marigold that she must refuse admittance to any nuisance callers, namely Doreen, Norman, Edna, Guzim, and Kyria Maria. I was especially adamant that Milton must be kept at bay since I had horrors of him barging in and attempting to entertain me by reading aloud his latest porn to a captive audience.

I was delighted when Marigold reported that Guzim had made a remarkable recovery and was back to mucking out the chickens, confirming my opinion that he'd most definitely been swinging the lead all along. Marigold was of the opinion that Guzim was only out and about again because he was terrified of Violet Burke paying another nocturnal visit to his shed. Apparently, the unravelling of his bandages had left him a gibbering wreck. My mother can have that effect.

Naturally Barry was the first to rush to my bedside, bringing the children's books that I'd requested to help Tonibler with his English. Barry was full of concern for my plight. Observing that I was propped up on wet sheets, Barry got the wrong end of the stick. "Surely Marigold could have supported you when you needed the bathroom. I can't believe she's left you to lie in soaking wet sheets. You only need to holler for me if it embarrasses you to have Marigold assist you to the lav."

"I'm actually lying in a puddle of melted ice," I assured him. "The doctor recommended ice for my ribs. Marigold filled a Lidl carrier bag with ice but it's leaking, courtesy of Catastrophe's claws."

"Lean on me. I'll help you to the chair and strip the sheets," Barry said, yelling for Marigold to come and help him remake the bed.

"I can't believe all the extra work Victor is creating by lying around all day," Marigold complained, covering the mattress with plastic bags before spreading the sheet atop. "I've been run ragged all morning attending to his every need and whim. There isn't a solitary ice-cube left in the freezer. Here, Victor, hold this Tupperware bowl of frozen curry against your ribs. It's the best I can do."

"I could give Spiros a call and ask if he's got any dry ice hanging around in his funeral parlour. I'm pretty sure undertakers use it, bodies on ice and all that," Barry posited.

"Well, make sure it's not already been used. I don't want Victor picking up something nasty from ice that's been cooling a corpse," Marigold said, visibly cringing at the thought.

"Or you could just pop downstairs and raid some ice from my mother's freezer," I suggested.

"I don't know when I'm supposed to find time to get everything ready for our guests with all this running around after you, Victor. They arrive from England tomorrow," she reminded me for the umpteenth time before scooting off in search of ice.

"Whilst Marigold's out of the way, I need you to help me, Barry. She's going to have my guts for garters unless I get those blasted vows completed by Tuesday…"

"I'm really not one for spouting romantic

lines…"

"I don't need you to compose anything. Spiros gave me an idea about using something from the Ancient Greek Wedding Song. If you pop in my office, there should be a couple of solid tomes on Ancient Greek customs on my desk. Hopefully, one of them details the words of the Wedding Song and I can find something inspirational to borrow."

"Rightio," Barry chirped, keen to be of some practical use. Returning with the hefty tomes, he offered to flick through them in search of the Wedding Song, opining that the weight of the books may exacerbate the pain of my cracked rib.

"You do realise that the song you're after is called 'the Hymen.' I can't see Marigold taking it too well if you start spouting about hymens in front of your guests. You can hardly make out she's all virginal with Benjamin there."

"Hymen is the Greek god of marriage," I enlightened my unscholarly brother-in-law. "Just flick through it and see if there's anything that sounds likely."

"I don't know. I don't think Marigold's going to be too impressed with this…"

"Just read it out," I urged.

"'Come wife, to the fields'…blah blah…then something about her seeking your beauty…oh this is priceless…'enliven my nights, O Hymen!'"

"Give it here," I demanded, nearly doing my ribs another injury as I leant forward to snatch the book. "I think this could be right up Marigold's street… the Wedding Song is absolutely littered with exclamation marks."

"Careful, Victor, you'll crack another rib if that book slips," Barry said, grabbing the book and scrutinising the pages. "You'd have to be careful here. It could sound like you were blowing your own trumpet rather than flattering your wife."

"How so?"

Holding his sides as he guffawed, Barry quoted, "'The bridegroom's fig is great and thick.'"

"With a double entendre like that, it sounds like Milton's cheesy porn," I said, thinking I really would have expected something a bit more upmarket from the Ancient Greeks, rather than tawdry erotica. Barry's laughter was contagious and I laughed along with him until the pain in my ribs reminded me that jollity was banned for the foreseeable.

"I reckon it's a bit bawdy for Marigold's taste. I think you need a rethink, Victor."

"Back to the drawing board," I admitted, realising I only had two-and-a-half days left to write some honeyed words that Marigold would treasure.

"It sounds like you've got more visitors,

Victor," Barry said. "I'd best be off anyway. I'll let them in on my way out and pop back later."

"Be sure to vet them," I called out after Barry, hoping that Marigold had clued him in on my list of undesirables who were banned from gaining admittance. It would be just my luck if Norman sneaked past Barry or if Guzim wandered in to compare bruises.

"Victor, my friend." I relaxed at the sound of my good friend Nikos approaching the bedroom, delighted to greet him and Dina. "I cannot to believe you take to the bed with the rib."

"Doctor's orders to rest up for two or three days," I told him, warding off a hug from the lovely Dina since it was sure to hurt.

"You foreign to make the fuss over the nothing. The soft Englishman not to have the constitution of the Greek. I remember the time I to break four the rib when I to fall off the olive ladder. I still to finish the harvest and pick all the olive," Nikos boasted, before repeating his words in Greek for Dina's benefit.

"*Se epiasa xaplomeno kato apo ta dentra na klais apo ton pono,*" Dina retorted, saying she had caught him lying down under the trees crying in pain. In spite of knowing that I must avoid laughing, I couldn't resist releasing a hearty chuckle at her words. It seemed that Nikos' boasting was little more than hot air and he was just as much of a big girl's blouse as I'd been labelled by Violet Burke. My laughter triggered another sharp stab of pain in my ribs. Dina immediately started fussing over me, fluffing my pillows and moving the Tupperware bowl of frozen curry so it rested against a different rib. Dina delighted me by saying that she had brought me a hearty *saliggaria stifado*, snail stew. Nikos interrupted his wife to tell me that Dina had collected the snails herself, traipsing through the dew drenched olive groves at first light.

Marigold returned bearing ice-cubes that she had raided from Violet Burke's freezer.

"Marigold, I have the news that will make you the happy to burst," Nikos told her. "Last the evening, the Giannis bring the Yiota to the taverna to eat."

Throwing a hand over her heart, Marigold gasped. "You mean that the two of them were on a date?"

"They only to have the eye for the other," Nikos said with a wink. "They to make the handsome couple, I think."

"Don't go buying a new hat just yet. It's early days," I warned my wife. It certainly sounded as though there had been some interesting developments on the romantic front since I left the pair on the market stall.

The bedroom might as well have been fitted with a revolving doorway. No sooner had Marigold shown Nikos and Dina out, than Vangelis and Athena arrived. I told them it was surprising to see Greek couples visiting together during the day but Vangelis reminded me it was Saturday afternoon and they'd knocked off work for the day. Vangelis immediately started reminiscing about the time he had fallen off some scaffolding and broken a couple of ribs. Naturally, it didn't deter him from completing the building work. Since he didn't bother translating his words into Greek for Athena's benefit, I was deprived of hearing her version of events, though I was certain they wouldn't align with his. No doubt he had been much like Nikos, a snivelling wreck in reality but heroically stoic in the re-telling.

Before they took their leave, Athena told me that she'd brought me along a nice *chtapodi kokkinisto*, octopus in tomato sauce, which she'd cooked herself. Thanking her profusely, I felt like a hypocrite. I had no intention of tucking into Athena's likely hair ridden dish. I had never trusted her with a frozen octopus since our very first meeting when she had planned to refreeze the octopus that had defrosted in the back of Vangelis' van. I could never overlook such a flagrant hygiene violation. Still, I was sure the *chtapodi kokkinisto* would make a lovely treat for the cats. Over time, I had noted that Marigold's imported felines had developed remarkably strong stomachs.

As the afternoon progressed, I dozed between visitors, most of the Greek ladies in the village stopping by to deliver some choice home cooked fare from their kitchens. It reminded me of the time they'd operated a veritable meals on wheels service when I had been left to my own devices as a seemingly helpless male, whilst Marigold visited Geraldine in Manchester.

"Litsa and Kyria Kompogiannopoulou brought you some delicious dishes but insisted that they didn't want to disturb you," Marigold said as she breezed in.

"I expect they were worried about their good reputations. It may not reflect well on them if word got round that they were visiting a foreign man in his bedroom," I said.

"Perhaps. The only Greek women to set foot in the bedroom have been accompanied by their husbands." Lowering her voice, Marigold hissed, "Sherry's called round to visit you. She wasn't on your banned list but I wasn't sure that you'd want to encourage her when you're lounging about in your pyjamas."

"Tell her I'm sleeping and add her to my list of undesirables," I said. Even though I doubted that Sherry would try to seduce me again with Marigold in the house, there was no point in tempting fate now that Sherry was single again.

No sooner had Marigold sent Sherry packing, than she returned to tell me that Tonibler was here. "If you could entertain him for a while, his mother has offered to do some ironing."

"Send the boy through. I'm ready for him. Barry dropped those Doctor Suess books round earlier that I bought for Anastasia."

"You'll be pleased to hear that I got rid of Kyria Maria from next door, though it wasn't easy. She didn't appear to have any qualms about popping into a foreign man's bedroom. She's remarkably pushy for an old dear. She brought you a platter of freshly fried *loukoumades* drizzled with honey and topped with cinnamon," Marigold added.

"Oh, do bring some through. I'm sure Tonibler will enjoy them and I can never say no to one of Maria's honeyed doughnuts."

"Anything else your lordship needs?" Marigold asked impatiently.

"You can drop the sarcasm. Don't forget that you're getting out of the ironing. Not to mention that you won't need to cook for a month of Sundays with all those delicious Greek dishes piling up in the kitchen."

"Do you think I can pass them off as my own cooking if I serve them up to our English visitors when they arrive tomorrow? And I can freeze the rest for the days when you don't feel like cooking after work."

"Just be sure to bin Athena's octopus. I don't want my mother doing the Heimlich Manoeuvre on some poor innocent that is choking on a throatful of hair."

"I'll go and get the boy. Don't let him wear you out though, you need to rest those ribs," Marigold said, surprisingly solicitous.

Although it was Saturday afternoon, Tonibler was once again dressed in his formal school uniform, his spectacles sporting a new sticking plaster to replace the one which had fallen into the inedible cacti curry, setting off the unfortunate chain of events which ultimately resulted in my current predicament. Still, I didn't hold the child in any way responsible; if anything, it was my own neglect in failing to fish the plaster out of the curry before offering it to Guzim, that was to blame.

"I have some children's books we can read together…"

Tonibler clapped his hands in delight, clearly thrilled as I showed him the illustrated copy of 'Green Eggs and Ham.' Encouraging him to read out the words he could manage, Tonibler made an excellent job of it until his confusion got the better of him. He had a tendency to take things a tad literally.

"Do they really eat green eggs and ham in the Great Britain?" he asked, a puzzled expression on his face.

"Certainly not, but the author, Dr Suess, was an American."

"They eat the green eggs and ham in America?"

"One would hope not. Any food that isn't meant to be green is best avoided if it actually turns that colour. Egg yolks can sometimes present with a green ring if they have been boiled for too long but you should definitely avoid any meat that has turned green..."

Reflecting that explaining the process of oxidation that might result in a greenish hue on ham was a tad too advanced for my young charge, I suggested we switch books and read from 'The Cat in the Hat' instead. It proved to be the perfect choice since it featured many of the words which we had covered in our first lesson; indeed, I considered I had missed a trick by not putting Clawsome in Marigold's sunhat during our earlier get together. Such a move would have perfectly illustrated the title of the book.

Our reading was interrupted when Marigold arrived bearing Kyria Maria's *loukoumades*. To my amazement, Tonibler was not familiar with the sweet Greek treat, but we soon put that to rights.

Watching him guzzle the honeyed doughnuts, I felt a wave of affection for the earnest child.

"Once I'm up and about again, what say you to a trip to town? I think it's time to replace the cracked lens in those spectacles of yours."

"Yes please," Tonibler shouted in excitement. Hurling himself atop me, he gave me an enormous hug. As my ribs screamed in protest, Tonibler left a sticky residue of honey and cinnamon all over my pyjama jacket.

# Chapter 27

*Summat in the Water*

A s Sunday dawned, I was relieved that the pain of my cracked ribs had subsided from agonising to a more manageable annoying, though the area was still tender and laughter most definitely not recommended. For once my wife was up with the lark, after enjoying another restful night sleeping alone in the spare bedroom. Thrilled at the thought that she would soon have me upright, she nevertheless doled out a couple of painkillers and absolutely insisted that I remain in bed until Tuesday. Marigold was gripped by the notion that one wrong move would result in a relapse that might prevent me from making it to the vow renewal service on the beach.

It has to be said that after one day of fussing over me endlessly, Marigold's patience was wearing thin, her bedside manner, such as it was, rapidly wearing off. Still, she was in a remarkably upbeat mood as she dosed me up with pills, elated at the prospect of the imminent arrival of Benjamin and Adam, Douglas and Elaine, and her best pal Geraldine.

"I'll have to move back to the marital bed with you tonight," Marigold announced. "I need to make up the spare bedroom for Douglas and Elaine, and the sofa bed for Geraldine. I don't suppose you can give me a hand?"

"Seriously, Marigold. You've just made a whole song and dance of instructing me to stay in bed for the next two days."

"Sorry, I wasn't thinking, dear. Yes, you really must stay put. I've such a lot on my mind with all our visitors arriving today. I'm a bit short of time as I'll be setting off shortly to drive up to the airport to collect Geraldine…"

"Why on earth can't she come down to Meli with the others?" I asked. "They're all arriving on the same plane. Benjamin and Douglas have both arranged to pick up hire cars at the airport. I'm sure one of them can squeeze her in."

"I get to see little enough of Geraldine as it is these days. I'm looking forward to meeting her and having a good old catch up on the drive back. We may even stop for a swim…it's never the same when you tag along."

"I have my uses as the designated driver when the two of you fancy a tipple."

"Well, today I'm looking forward to it just being us girls. Don't think I haven't spotted you rolling your eyes at our chatter."

"As if."

"Anyway, I wouldn't dream of leaving you all on your lonesome, dear. I've had a word with your mother and she's agreed to pop up and look after you whilst I'm out, so you've nothing to worry about."

"Nothing except suffering Violet Burke fussing over me for hours. Don't forget, she's the one that landed me in this predicament."

"It was an accident, Victor. Don't keep bringing it up or you'll only upset your mother. You don't want to go setting her off. I don't want you riling up Violet Burke when I'm going to have to ask her to make those beds up and clean the place. Anyway, I want everyone in the best of spirits for Tuesday."

"Speaking of Tuesday, how are the arrangements going?"

Marigold had taken complete charge of

organising the event, telling me that the only thing I needed to worry about was turning up on the day and reciting my vows. Luckily, she had no idea that my romantic composition was still very much a work in progress.

After much deliberation, Marigold had finally settled on the ideal spot for the momentous occasion; a sandy beach about a forty-minute drive from Meli. Whilst not exactly enamoured at the thought of making a spectacle of myself on a public beach, I had resigned myself to going along with it. I would do my best to ensure that Marigold's special day was perfect for her in every way, creating treasured memories. Perish the thought that the day was a disaster. The last thing I wanted was Marigold organising a repeat performance if anything went wrong.

"The ceremony is scheduled for noon," Marigold revealed.

"Noon. Surely it's not wise arranging it for the hottest part of the day."

"It was a deliberate ploy, dear. Think about it. I felt obliged to invite most of our elderly Greek neighbours to attend but I don't actually want them to turn up. I thought the midday heat would act as an excellent deterrent. I can't see a bunch of pensioners wanting to sit in a stuffy car for the round trip to the coast and then hang around on a beach in the sun without any shade," Marigold said.

The prospect didn't exactly appeal to me either but I wisely kept my own counsel.

"I just know that Kyria Maria and her cronies would do something to ruin the moment," Marigold explained.

"As far as I know, Kyria Maria's only crony is Violet Burke…"

"Yes, well, there's not much we can do about that. Your mother is family after all and we're stuck with her. I'll put Benjamin in charge of Vi on the day…hopefully he can keep his granny in check so that she doesn't embarrass us too much."

"So, let me get this straight. You've extended invitations to our village neighbours in the hope that they will decline and not actually turn up?" Marigold's logic defeated me; it would have made far more sense to me if she simply hadn't invited them in the first place.

"I only want them to decline the invitation to the actual ceremony; they're all welcome to come along to the celebration party afterwards at the taverna. Dina's doing a bit of a spread and Nikos promised to play the *bouzouki*." Seeing that she had failed to convince me, Marigold continued, "It really makes sense, Victor. Most of the oldies don't speak a word of English. I can just picture them interrupting the service and wanting to know what is going on, nosily demanding that we translate every line of our vows into Greek."

"So, who exactly has made it onto your short list of desirables to be welcomed at the ceremony?"

"Do I detect a hint of sarcasm in your words? I just want a small select gathering of family and close friends. In addition to the family, Spiros will be there as the celebrant, and of course, Sampaguita. Then there's Nikos and Dina, Vangelis and Athena, Doreen and Manolis, and Gordon and Moira. I decided against inviting Norman. I thought it might be a bit awkward because Doreen will be there with her beau. I felt obliged to include Edna and Milton but I'm rather hoping they give it a miss."

"Goodness knows how Milton is going to manage on the beach with his walker. He might end up going down in the sand and ending up back in hospital," I groaned.

Ignoring my interruption, Marigold continued, "I must say that I was in quite the quandary about inviting Papas Andreas. Having him there would add some welcome gravitas to the occasion but his mother would be sure to tag along and lower the tone. Luckily, he had a prior engagement, a baptism. And you went and invited Guzim?"

"You told me to."

"I hope you did the right thing." Unbelievably,

she made it sound as though it had been my idea to include the Albanian shed dweller. "Of course, he won't have a clue what's going on."

"He's convinced himself that we are getting married after living in sin all these years," I said.

"Well, I suppose it's too late for you to retract the invitation now," Marigold mused.

"He's actually going above and beyond when you consider how phobic he is about beaches," I confided.

"He has a phobia about beaches?" Marigold parroted.

"And the sea, I think."

"How utterly bizarre. Are there actually words for such phobias?"

"There are indeed and wouldn't you know that they are both derived from Greek…"

"Oh, do tell, Victor. I can see that you're dying to impress me."

"Well, amathophobia is actually a fear of dust but the origin of the word is derived from *ammos*…"

"The Greek word for sand." Marigold sounded very pleased with herself for remembering the word, a remarkable feat considering she had been neglecting her Greek lessons of late.

"And thalassophobia is a fear of the sea…"

"From the Greek word for sea, *thalassa*…"

"Exactly," I confirmed.

"What a peculiar thing for Guzim to be phobic about. Did he offer a rational explanation?"

"Is anything to do with Guzim ever rational?" I quipped. "It was something about being traumatised after swimming in raw sewage in his homeland. Apparently, it left him a gibbering wreck."

"I expect he must have swallowed a mouthful," Marigold shuddered. "Well, at least if the beach makes Guzim feel uneasy, he'll likely keep quiet during the service rather than making a nuisance of himself. Yes, I think you did the right thing to include him, Victor. I mean he has become an integral part of our life in Meli."

"I have to say, I tend to think of him as part of the fittings and fixtures these days," I admitted.

"Oh, good grief, look at the time. I really ought to be making tracks to the airport," Marigold said. "I'm so excited at the thought of having all the family together again. I'll just go and call your mother to come up and look after you. I wouldn't have a moment's peace if I thought I was leaving you to your own devices."

"Another coffee wouldn't go amiss before you leave," I hinted, thinking it might counter the drowsy effect of the pills.

"Really, Victor, do you never listen to a word I say? You can get your mother to make your coffee and do some actual mothering for a change."

Dropping a kiss on my forehead to soften her words, Marigold skedaddled, all consideration of my comfort gazumped by her eagerness to get to the airport to reunite with our visitors.

With nothing else to do, I leafed through the pages of one of Marigold's books on her bedside table. Unsurprisingly, it was yet another tale about a British couple up-sticking to a foreign country, this time France, the pages absolutely littered with irritating and superfluous exclamation marks. Throwing the book aside in annoyance, it just missed clipping Violet Burke on the head as she barged into the bedroom. I must confess that I was actually pleased to see her, thinking a bit of company might relieve the monotony of lying abed with nothing to do.

"Well, I have to say you've got a bit more colour in your cheeks, lad, even if you are looking a bit vacant, like."

"Those pills have knocked me for six and I need a strong coffee to perk me up. I'll be much more with it if you could just brew me a pot…"

"That wife of yours said nowt about me running around pandering to your every whim. She's only paying me to do some cleaning and make up the guest beds," Vi retorted.

"But you're my mother," I said in exasperation. "Did you seriously expect Marigold to offer to pay you to mother me and make the odd coffee? I thought you'd be happy to have the opportunity to finally try out a bit of parenting. Don't forget, I'm only stuck in this bed because of you."

Looking rather shamefaced, Vi replied, "And I suppose you're never going to let it drop. I've noticed how you do like to hark on about things. You're forever going on about that damn bucket I dumped you in."

"Can you blame me? Surely you realise that being abandoned in a bucket left emotional scars."

"You don't hear me complaining about losing the use of my bucket. I never did get it back and it was a right good galvanised one," she snapped. "Now, I reckon I can do you a coffee but don't go taking liberties. Marigold's left me a list of chores an arm long, as if that daft Geraldine will be impressed that the place has had a good bottoming."

When my mother returned with a mug of undrinkable, weak, cheap instant coffee, I bit my tongue, presuming she would consider I was taking liberties if I asked her to replace it with a cafetiere of my usual aromatic brew. Goodness knows where she even found a jar of nasty instant; even Marigold refused to give the stuff houseroom.

"Right, now that you've got your coffee, I'd better make a start on stripping the bed in the spare room. It won't make it itself and that wife of yours is too bone idle to strip off her own mucky sheets."

Against the backdrop of Violet Burke clunking about, I heard the sound of someone arriving at the house. Crossing my fingers, I hoped that in her haste to leave for the airport, Marigold hadn't neglected to pass on to my mother the list of undesirables that I had decreed must be refused admittance.

I groaned inwardly as Violet Burke ushered Milton into my bedroom: he was top of the list. Shuffling in on his walker, the local porn merchant clasped a large bedraggled bunch of flowers that he'd likely filched from the graveyard. He certainly didn't have the wherewithal to be splashing out on floral bouquets.

"Hope you're up for visitors, old chap. I brought you these…"

Before he could complete his sentence, Violet Burke snatched the floral offering out of his hands.

"You'd better not let that drippy wife of yours know that you're bringing me flowers. I can't be doing with another one of her jealous tantrums," Vi declared before marching out, muttering under her breath. "I don't know how that Milton thought he'd impress me with mite infested, wilting weeds."

"I say, those flowers were meant for the patient…" Milton's protestation was not only too late, but insincere. I hadn't failed to notice the look of gormless devotion on his face when he looked at my mother. It was clear that the reality of Violet Burke in the flesh had done little to snuff out the idealised image of her which he had carried in his heart for the last six decades.

"I hope Edna doesn't get wind of my giving flowers to your mother," Milton said, sinking into the chair by my bedside and looking at me with rheumy eyes that reminded me of the stubborn hen. "I say, terrible thing you being mugged like that, old chap. One would never imagine such a thing happening in Meli. I've told Edna that she mustn't think of leaving the house on her own until your assailant is safely behind bars, what."

Clearly the account of how I incurred my injury had undergone a few exaggerated permutations when spread by the village gossips. I wouldn't put it past Violet Burke to have invented a mugger in order to deflect attention from herself.

"You've got the wrong end of the stick. My mother accidentally caused my injury. There was no random mugger."

"Are you sure? I can't believe such a wonderful and fine figure of a woman as Violet could harm as much as a fly."

"When it comes to my mother harming flies, she's an expert. Whether it's blasting them with fly killer of pulverising them with a fly swatter, she shows no mercy. She's well up on the hygiene risks of flies contaminating food…they'll happily regurgitate their saliva and lay their eggs on any food left exposed in the kitchen…"

"Ought to get Violet round to our place then if she's a dab hand with the fly swatter. Dratted nuisance, the flies, what. Whole clouds of the things sometimes, get everywhere. Can't imagine what attracts them."

"What do you expect when you encourage stray cats that have been rooting around in the bins?" I pointed out, wondering how I could rid my bedroom of the unwanted visitor.

As though she'd read my mind, Violet Burke returned and started on Milton. "If you're making a nuisance of yourself, you'll have to go. Marigold left strict instructions that Victor has to rest." Turning to me, she added, "I only let him in 'cos he said he had something right important to ask you. Just say the word and I'll turf him out on his ear, lad."

As she stomped off to the kitchen, I reluctantly asked Milton, "What's so important?" Whatever it was, I hoped he'd keep it short and not go off on one of his usual long-winded tangents.

"It's Edna. The date has finally come through for her cataract op up at the hospital, what. The old girl will be in for two nights. I can't bear the thought of leaving her there to cope on her own, but if I stay at the hospital with her, there's the matter of the cats. Can't leave them to their own devices, what. Thought I'd ask if you could see your way to housing a few of them…"

"It's out of the question," I firmly refused. There was no way I would allow any of Edna's flea ridden adopted strays to come and holiday in the Bucket household. As far as I was concerned, we had quite enough cats underfoot with Catastrophe, Clawsome, and Pickles. "I'm afraid that Marigold's imported domestics are terribly territorial, they'd never tolerate any new feline additions."

"Ah, odd that. Edna's always bringing new strays into the house and they all have to muck along together."

"That's as maybe. Marigold's cats are of a certain pedigree and were purchased from a reputable pet shop, not rescued from the public bins," I said, neglecting to mention that their actual pedigree was a tad dubious. "Catastrophe has been very highly strung ever since she had to have part of her tail removed after Kostis took a pot shot at her with his gun. And of course, Clawsome has never quite recovered from the trauma of being ravaged by Cynthia's mutant cat."

"Ah, got you. Some of ours have had run-ins with Kouneli. I don't like to speak ill of cats, but that dratted mutant of Cynthia's is a bad 'un and no mistake."

"You should ask Doreen to take your cats in," I suggested, hoping that Milton would vacate his seat by my bedside and dash over there immediately.

"She's already turned me down, old chap. Reckons they wouldn't be safe with Norman in the house…"

"You could ask Sherry…"

"She offered to take one… but that still leaves dozens…I may have to implement plan B…"

"Which is?"

"I thought of offering to let my new chum Kyriakos move into our place while we're at the hospital. He could look after the cats and it would give him the chance to get away from the intolerable living situation in his own home. The way that his mother and wife continually snipe at one another gets the poor chap down, what. It's relentless."

"An excellent idea. You should pop over and put it to him right now," I encouraged.

Violet Burke's immediate return led me to assume that she must have been hovering outside the bedroom, ready to turf Milton out. "Right, let's be having you out. My Victor needs his rest."

Relieved to be shot of Milton, I had to admire the no-nonsense way that my mother disposed of unwelcome visitors. She certainly wasn't afraid to get handsy with Milton, though the daft sap probably enjoyed the experience. Whilst Violet Burke resumed the housework, I must have dozed off again. The next thing I knew, I woke up to discover Norman sitting by my bedside holding a plate of profiteroles. Cursing my mother for admitting the traffic cone bore to the Bucket bedroom, I made no pretence of being polite, curtly telling Norman that I was in too much pain to cope with visitors.

"I thought you might appreciate a profiterole treat," Norman said.

"Very thoughtful of you, I'm sure, but Marigold's the one with the sweet tooth," I said, wishing he'd take the hint and leave.

"So, you're not up for visitors?"

"No, afraid not. The doctor ordered complete bedrest and lots of sleep."

"What a pity. I wanted to ask your advice…"

"About what?" I asked, realising he would never make a move until I'd heard him out.

"Well, it's a bit delicate."

"Perhaps you'd be better off having a word with the pharmacist then," I quipped.

"What?"

I might have known my witty sally would fall flat since Norman is not renowned for his sense of humour.

"Just spit it out, Norman. What's the problem?"

"Well, you know how Doreen has gone and got herself a new boyfriend?"

"It hasn't escaped my notice," I confirmed.

"She's awfully smug about it. Anyway, it got me thinking…"

"For goodness' sake. Get to the point, Norman."

"I was thinking about venturing onto the dating scene myself. I wondered if you had any tips on how to date women?"

The sharp pain shooting through my ribs made me instantly regret my uncontrollable laughter.

"Are you out of your tiny mind? The last time I went on a date was over thirty-eight years ago. Why on earth would you think I'd know anything about dating?"

"Here, you want to put a sock in that laughter, lad. You'll do your ribs another injury," Violet Burke proclaimed marching into the bedroom yet again.

"Norman wants to start dating," I chortled.

"Dating what?" Vi spluttered.

"Mrs Burke…" Norman began to say.

"You what?" Vi exclaimed incredulously. Grabbing Norman by the ear, Violet Burke yanked him to his feet. "You're wanting to date me are you, you dozy muppet? Just because Panos went and snuffed it doesn't mean that I'm in the market for new suitors, you cheeky apeth. I don't know what it is today, first Milton hanging around and trying to woo with me his poxy flowers, now this gormless bugger thinking I'd look twice at him. I reckon there must be summat in the water what makes me irresistible to men."

# Chapter 28

*Feeling Left Out*

Plese don't make me laugh, Benjamin. It hurts too much," I begged.

"So much for laughter being the best medicine. I can't believe that granny broke your ribs, Dad. She's such a character." I detected a note of admiration for his granny in Benjamin's tone.

"Whatever you do, don't let her demonstrate her Heinz Manure on either of you," I warned my son and his life partner, Adam.

"Fancy her saving Guzim from death by choking," Adam said. "Vi really is remarkable."

Benjamin and Adam were the first of our guests

to arrive in Meli. Although they had been on the same flight as my half-brother, Douglas, and his wife, Elaine, each couple had hired a car for the drive from the airport whilst Marigold was ferrying Geraldine home in the Punto. The boys were staying at Barry's but had made the Bucket household their first port of call. Having already caught up with Marigold at the airport, Benjamin was keen to be reunited with his old Dad. The boys were a real tonic, filling me in on all their news.

"So, you're stuck in bed for the next two days, Dad?"

"Yes, your mum refuses to let me out in case I exacerbate my injury before her big day."

"Well, we can keep you company…"

"I wouldn't dream of it. You didn't fly all the way over here to be stuck in my bedroom. You want to make the most of your week in Greece. Go out and explore, make the most of the glorious weather, and spend some time with your Mum. Nothing would make her happier."

"I can't stay the full week," Adam said apologetically. "I have to fly back on Wednesday. Work calls."

"You're here for the ceremony, that's the main thing," I assured him.

Adam went off to brew a pot of decent coffee, leaving me alone with my son. "I have a bit of a problem, Ben," I confided. "I still haven't written my vows but it isn't through want of trying. Your mum will have a fit if I come up blank on the day."

"For goodness' sake, Dad. As an aspiring author, surely you can cobble a few romantic lines together."

"My writing leans more to the comedic than slushy. I really don't think your mum would appreciate my coming out with anything remotely humorous. She's taking it all very seriously," I said.

"You've still got two days to come up with something..."

"Yes, but I'm dosed up on painkillers that make my head woolly..."

"Luckily for you, I sometimes dabble in a bit of romantic verse. Adam adores it when I declare my love in smoochy rhyming couplets. Leave it with me and I'll pen you something that will be sure to sweep mum off her feet," Benjamin offered.

"You're a lifesaver, Son. Just avoid making it too amatory or soppy."

When Douglas and Elaine arrived at the house, Benjamin and Adam headed over to Barry's to unpack. It still felt quite surreal to be in the company of a half-brother whose existence I had known nothing about for most of my life, yet in no time at all we found ourselves reconnecting and bolstering our brotherly bond. Douglas confided that he had rather reluctantly, and under duress, visited our reprobate half-brother, Terrance, in Strangeways. Whilst I had every intention of continuing to avoid having anything to do with Terrance, I was pleased to hear that he had promised Douglas that he planned to turn over a new leaf on his release from the big house. I couldn't help wondering if perchance Douglas was being a tad gullible when he mentioned that Terrance's resolution had been inspired by his discovering religion. I'd read about the con of convicts getting religion to con the parole board into thinking they were reformed characters, in the hope of an early release.

Elaine told me that they had met Geraldine on the flight over and that the two women had bonded over Elaine's diet plan, Geraldine becoming an instant convert. I was relieved to hear that the two women were on good terms since they would both be staying in the Bucket household for the next few days. In my enfeebled state, I don't think I could have coped with endless bickering.

Despite the excitement of receiving such welcome visitors, I must have dozed off again. The next time I opened my eyes, it was to discover Geraldine and Papas Andreas making eyes at one another across my bed. The way in which the unsuitable pair were exchanging electrifying looks put me in mind of the risk of a static shock from Marigold's old brushed nylon sheets.

"Are you here to pray for my speedy recovery?" I asked Andreas.

"I am off the duty and here as the neighbour," he replied, jocularly adding, "There is no the point in waste a good prayer on the non-orthodox heathen like you."

I didn't know whether to take offence that I wasn't worthy of his supplication or feel relieved that I didn't have to endure one of his long incomprehensible prayers intoned in Ancient Greek.

When Geraldine started prattling on about Elaine's wondrous weight loss diet plan, demanding to know how many calories there were in each of the dishes she'd be tucking into at the taverna that evening, I feigned sleep.

Over the course of the day, one or other of our visitors from England took turns to pop in on me, a practice they went on to repeat the next day. By that evening, I felt quite left out when Marigold announced that she was off to the village taverna with all our visitors. Even Violet Burke deserted me, preferring to glue herself to Coronation Street downstairs, leaving me bedbound with only the cats for company.

Marigold breezed in before they left to ply me with pills that made me instantly drowsy. "Don't worry, darling. You have a good sleep and I'll leave you something to eat for later."

Marigold was as good as her word. When I woke up, I was touched to see that my wife had left a tray on my bedside table. My heart sank when I removed the cover to discover a plate of *chtapodi kokkinisto*, octopus in tomato sauce, no doubt the home cooked sick-bed offering of Athena. Already feeling below par with my abused ribs, I dared not risk a likely dose of food poisoning from consuming defective octopus cooked in Athena's kitchen and garnished with hair.

Abandoning the food, my stomach rumbled in protest but I didn't want to risk putting pressure on my ribs by heading to the kitchen in search of something edible. Preparing to sleep without any supper, I was moved beyond measure when Violet Burke crept in, announcing, "I'm not stopping, lad. I just popped up with a sneaky Fray Bentos. Best if you don't go letting on to that wife of yours. I can never fathom why she's such a snob when it comes to tinned pies."

Much later, returning from the taverna, Marigold disturbed me as she climbed into the marital bed. After turfing the cats off her pillow, she noticed the untouched tray of octopus still by the bed.

"Surely you haven't gone to bed hungry, darling." Being somewhat tipsy, Marigold must have overlooked the fact that I hadn't actually gone to bed since it was my second full day of confinement. Neglecting to mention that I had greedily scoffed Vi's sneaky Fray Bentos, I reminded Marigold that I considered Athena's octopus to be inedible unhygienic slop that was only fit for the cats.

"You daft thing," Marigold chided, placing a pillow between us to protect my delicate ribs. "I binned Athena's food, just as you told me to. The octopus dish I left you this evening was made especially for you by Litsa. You know what a fabulous cook she is."

# Chapter 29

*Barefoot and Suited in the Sand*

"G ood grief, Marigold's gone a bit over the top," I said as Barry and I traipsed across the sand towards a net strewn plastic arch decorated with floral blooms, erected within spitting distance of the sea. "She never mentioned she was organising anything quite so fancy."

"I don't know, aren't those the net curtains you used to have back in Manchester? I recognise that stain that wouldn't come out after Kimberley threw that beetroot at me," Barry said, referencing his first wife.

"Good grief, I think you're right. I know she's

always harping on about repurposing fabric, but that takes the biscuit. Fancy dragging beetroot-stained net curtains all the way to Greece."

"She must have been listening when you told her that she had to watch the cash because of the renovation," Barry said, before reminding me, "Don't forget to ditch your shoes and socks."

His words echoed Marigold's reminder as she'd given me the once over before I left the house. Examining me in my new blue suit, she'd adjusted my tie, cooing, "You do look smart, darling. There's more than a hint of Richard Burton about you."

"Before he got all rumpled, I hope," I'd quipped. Personally, I considered the tie a tad superfluous since I would be eschewing my shoes and socks in order to fulfil Marigold's fantasy of exchanging our vows barefoot on a sandy beach.

"I tell you what, Victor, I'll take mine off too so you won't feel so self-conscious." I can always count on my brother-in-law to come through for me. Even though I had belatedly in life discovered that I had three half-brothers, I would always think of Barry as my true brother even though he isn't a blood relative.

Just feet away from my feet, the sea lapped gently against the sand, the sparkling blue water reflecting the colour palette of the sky. The heat of the sand scratched my feet and the heat of the sun threatened to boil my head. Glancing across the beach, I spotted sun hats galore adorning tourist heads and wished I had something practical to keep the sun off my pate. I briefly considered spreading my handkerchief over my head but I could only imagine Marigold's reaction if I greeted her at the arch decked out with the proverbial knotted hanky on the head.

"I thought Spiros would be here by now," I said, thinking if Spiros managed to muck up his role as celebrant, I would end up in the doghouse along with the undertaker.

"I wonder what's keeping him. It's only a half-hour till kick-off," Barry said as the two of us stood under the arch feeling more than a tad conspicuous. I couldn't fail to notice that we attracted more than a few curious stares from beachgoers relaxing on their sun loungers. I certainly felt overdressed in my suit, not to mention overheated, when everyone else on the beach was sporting swimwear.

"And you've got your vows written down?"

"Yes." Patting my top pocket, I sighed in relief at the way Benjamin had come through for me, churning out some romantic guff that would be right up Marigold's alley.

"Barry. Victor. *Ela.*" We both turned at the sound of Spiros yelling our names and waving to attract our attention. As Spiros approached, I spotted he was directing a couple of waiters carrying chairs from a nearby taverna. With the waiters following his lead, Spiros was busy laying an improvised path of rattan beach mats across the sand. I was relieved to see that Spiros had dressed for the part in his smart undertaker's suit and tie, his bushy eyebrows looking groomed, the overpowering whiff of cheap aftershave drowning out any lingering scent of embalming fluid.

"How many the chair you need for the guest?" Spiros asked.

"I don't know. Marigold invited quite a lot of the villagers but she hoped they wouldn't turn up. I think she's expecting about twenty guests to turn up."

"Twenty," Spiros repeated incredulously, before barking at the waiters to go and fetch more chairs.

"We can only spare the dozen. We need them for the lunchtime rush," one of the waiters shrugged.

"Okay, we can to sit the woman. The man must to stand behind," Spiros decided, just as the first of the guests began to arrive on the beach.

"Stand, stand, not to sit. Only the woman to sit," Spiros barked, ousting Nikos, Vangelis, Douglas, Manolis and Adam from the seats they'd just claimed and lining them up behind the women.

Even from a distance, I could hear Doreen complaining about being separated from her love. Her whining turned to outrage when Christos and Norman turned up together, having apparently joined forces in mutual annoyance at their brother and spouse. I hoped that Marigold wouldn't spot the pair of gate crashers since she'd excluded them both from her invite list.

I noticed that Marigold's cunning ploy had worked, most of our elderly neighbours absent from the beach, leaving a gathering of just family and close friends. I was delighted for Marigold's sake that in spite of the casual setting, all our guests had made an effort to turn out in their finery. Positively glowing with happiness, Dina looked radiant in a frock the exact same blue as my suit. Even Guzim had dressed up in my old button down that he'd stolen from the scarecrow, pairing it with a pair of sharply creased trousers that actually fitted him and looked suspiciously new. Admittedly his choice of flip flops didn't really compliment his outfit, but what did I know? After all, I was the one feeling like a plonker, barefoot in a suit.

"Your mother looks a picture," Barry observed as Violet Burke made her way ploddingly across the sand, her bulbous form supported by Sampaguita and Geraldine. Having squeezed her bulk into one of the relics from her Warrington wardrobe, my mother could barely draw breath in the overly tight fitted shift dress that she insisted on calling her Jackie O.

"She's certainly a vision in lemon," I agreed, shielding my eyes against the glare of vibrant yellow.

"Well, she'll be all right if she gets a bit peckish," Barry chuckled. "She can snack on those grapes hanging off that boxy hat."

"It's a pillbox and the grapes are plastic. I don't think I could cope with another choking emergency."

"Do you reckon your mother's head used to be smaller?"

"What?"

"Well, she usually turns out in a monstrous hat that's too big for her head, but today her head's too big for her hat."

"She's certainly a sight but don't let on."

"As if."

Joining us beneath the arch, Spiros said, "It is the good that the Marigold want me to marry you, Victor. I would have to offer to be your the *koumbaros*, but I knew you would to choose the Barry because he is to you like your the brother."

"*Koumbaros*?" Barry questioned.

"It's the best man," I reminded him. "But Barry isn't acting as my *koumbaros*, Spiro, because this isn't a wedding and Marigold told me I couldn't have a best man. She isn't having any bridesmaids because it's not a wedding, even though it put Geraldine's nose out of joint."

"Then why's she dressed Anastasia up as a flower girl?" Barry asked. "She looks beyond adorable in her fancy frock; it must have set you back a packet though."

Cringing at the thought of the expense, I reflected that this was the first I'd heard of a flower girl. Still, Anastasia was our darling niece and she deserved to play a special role in Marigold's day, even if an actual flower girl was surplus to normal vow renewal requirements. At least Marigold had made an effort to cut costs by decorating the bridal arch with old net curtains.

"I think the everyone the here except the Marigold," Spiros observed, shuffling his feet impatiently. I supposed that his usual clients, being dead, weren't in the habit of keeping him waiting.

"Marigold will want to make a dramatic entrance," I said, reflecting that she'd certainly have an audience. The arrival of our guests had attracted yet more curiosity from the beachgoers, quite a number of them gathering round to watch what was going on. I supposed we made quite a spectacle. I wouldn't be surprised if the gawping tourists expected to see a wedding on the beach. What with the decorated arch, the improvised path along the sand, and the seated guests all dressed up to the nines, if I was an onlooker, I would most definitely think a wedding was about to take place.

Casting my eyes over the curious onlookers, I recognised a familiar face in the crowd but struggled to place him. As I pondered where I knew him from, it came to me: it was John Macey, barely recognisable to me in nothing but a pair of indecent budgie smugglers, the proverbial hanky on his head to protect his sensitive scalp. Pretending I hadn't seen him, I reflected that it was a good job I hadn't resorted to protecting my own head with my hanky. It really wasn't a good look.

Nudging me in my bruised ribs, Barry announced, "Marigold's here, I'd best leave you to it. Good luck." After formally shaking my hand, Barry scooted off to join the others.

Even though it wasn't an actual wedding, Marigold had set her heart on walking across the beach towards me as though replicating her original steps down the aisle thirty-eight years ago. As all heads turned to watch Marigold approach, my heart swelled with love when I caught my first glance of my beautiful wife. She looked every inch the blushing bride in a floor-length, cream lace dress with a subtle slit, a delicate sweep train brushing the sand. The design was simple yet exquisite on my wife, featuring a V-neckline that was plunging yet tasteful, framed with ruffled cap sleeves.

Marigold held onto Benjamin's arm as he walked beside her, little Anastasia toddling along behind them and scattering rose petals on the sand. Reaching the arch, Benjamin kissed his Mum's cheek and took Anastasia's hand, leading her back towards the guests. Gazing into Marigold's eyes, my heart jumped for joy and I reflected that my idea for the two of us to renew our vows had been a stroke of genius after all.

"Darling, why on earth are you barefoot?" Marigold asked, a lilting tinkle in her voice.

"You must have told me a hundred times that your vision was for us to be barefoot on the beach…"

"After the ceremony, Victor, not during it. I sometimes think that you never listen to a word that I say."

"Well, if you'd like to read me your vows, I promise to listen to every word."

"Do put your shoes on first."

The ceremony went off without a hitch, Spiros' role of celebrant another stroke of genius because of the personal touch he brought to the occasion. I am delighted to report that Marigold's eyes filled up as I read my vows, my voice choked with emotion. As

Marigold and I exchanged a romantic kiss and the well-wishers burst into spontaneous applause, I heard my name shouted with a hearty bellow.

"What on earth?" Turning towards the sea where the disturbance was coming from, I spotted a familiar figure diving into the water from a fishing boat.

"Is that your Captain?" Marigold asked as the figure paused in the water to yell out "Beautiful Towel."

"I didn't invite him," I said as Captain Vasos erupted onto the sand. Enveloping me in a smothering hug that threatened to set back my ribs, the good Captain left a distinct wet patch on my suit.

"The more the merrier," Marigold assured me, whispering now was the moment to lose our shoes. Taking my hand, she pulled me along the shoreline, her train trailing in the water. "This is just how I imagined this moment, Victor. The two of us carefree and barefoot in the sand after promising to spend the rest of our days together."

"I think there's about to be three of us," I warned her, watching in disbelief as a familiar Labrador came bounding towards us. Thinking Marigold's idyllic moment would be ruined if Percy Bysshe started humping my leg, I exhaled in relief as Captain Vasos threw himself in the path of the charging Lab, offering his own leg up as a sacrificial sexual limb.

# Chapter 30

*Marigold Springs a Surprise*

T he celebration party at the taverna was in full swing, our family, friends and neighbours throwing themselves effusively into the festivities; fraternising, feasting, and frolicking on the makeshift dance floor. All of our Greek guests remained convinced we had just got remarried, unable to grasp the foreign concept of Marigold and I simply reaffirming our lifelong commitment to one another. After one too many exuberant hugs from our guests had played havoc with my dodgy ribs, Spiros had thoughtfully penned a sign which he pinned to my suit, reading '*min* angizeis' meaning 'don't touch.'

After saving me from the indignity of being humped by Percy Bysshe, naturally we insisted that Captain Vasos join the party. His turning up in the sea in the middle of our ceremony turned out to be nothing more than a happy coincidence. Enjoying a rare day off from Pegasus, Vasos was taking a joy ride in the fishing boat of an old friend from his navy days, when he spotted me on the beach. Naturally we included his old sea dog friend in the invitation to party. Despite the language barrier, the aged, weather-worn sailor appeared to be getting on like a house on fire with Violet Burke.

After donning some clothes, John Macey had approached me on the beach where he had been enjoying a spot of sunbathing with Penny, the owner of the out-of-control Labrador. Convinced by our public display that the Buckets had just tied the knot, he offered his hearty congratulations before telling me that in a matter of months we would be neighbours, his offer on the house in Meli having been accepted. It seemed churlish not to invite him to join our party in the circumstances since we would, after all, soon be living cheek and jowl, though I drew the line at inviting Percy Bysshe. My leg was altogether too much of a desirable temptation to the dog.

Norman and Christos appeared to have

established an unlikely rapport. Eavesdropping on their less than riveting conversation, I wasn't too surprised to hear Christos complaining about Manolis, and Norman grumbling about Doreen. Amused that their antipathy for their respective housemates had drawn them together, I was tempted to suggest to Norman that since he was keen to start dating, he should consider coupling up with the oily Greek. There again, Norman is not renowned for his sense of humour.

Having no desire to risk any additional blows to my ribs, I contented myself with watching the celebrations continue from the side-lines. As the evening drew on, the Bucket family came over to join me, Marigold looking especially radiant. Naturally she was in her element, surrounded by Barry, Benjamin, and Adam.

"I have a special surprise for you, Victor," Marigold gushed. "I've been waiting until it was just close family together before I sprang it on you."

"I'd better fetch granny then," Benjamin said, rushing over to rescue Vi from Captain Vasos, Vasos stoically enduring Violet Burke's swollen feet trampling his much daintier ones as they danced.

"There's no need to include your granny," Marigold called after Benjamin.

My wife's features took on a resigned expression as she realised her words had fallen on deaf ears, Violet Burke already limping towards us, arm in arm with her grandson.

"I can't believe my feet haven't exploded from all this dancing," Vi groaned, sinking into a seat and swiping away a dangling plastic grape that threatened to put out her eye.

"Well, your feet have been threatening to explode forever but they still look pretty intact to me," Benjamin joshed.

"You needn't jest, young Ben. 'Appen you'll go and inherit my swollen trotters," Vi warned. I was familiar with her prediction, my mother forever taunting that her swollen feet were hereditary and would one day be my lot. "Now, what's this about a surprise?"

"It's my surprise gift to Victor," Marigold trilled, barely able to contain her excitement as she grasped my hand. "Darling, I'm taking you away on a second honeymoon."

"A second honeymoon. And how much has that set my credit card back?" I blurted, belatedly realising my words were a tad insensitive. "Sorry, darling, you just took me completely by surprise. Where are you whisking me off to? I'm not sure my battered ribs could cope with international travel."

"Don't worry, I haven't gone overboard. Because you have to be back at work next week, I just booked a simple four-day mini-break in Greece. We leave in the morning and you don't need to worry about long-haul flights as we'll be heading off in the Punto." I sighed in relief, thinking my ribs ought to be able to cope with that as long as Marigold could be persuaded to take the wheel. "And there's more."

"More?"

"Well, since it's such a treat to have Benjamin and Adam here in Greece with us, I booked for the four of us to go together."

"You want to take the boys along on your second honeymoon," Barry guffawed.

"Well, why not? Benjamin did come along on our original honeymoon, in a manner of speaking," I said, alluding to the fact that Marigold had been pregnant at the time.

"I'm sorry to put a damper on your plans, Marigold," Adam said apologetically. "I have to fly back tomorrow, I'm due at work on Thursday evening."

"Oh, no. I did think of checking with you first but I so wanted to surprise Victor, that I didn't want to risk one of you boys blabbing."

"Benjamin can still go," Adam said, squeezing Benjamin's hand.

"But surely I'll be a gooseberry," Benjamin worried.

"Will you heck, lad. 'Appen I'll come along

instead of Adam then you won't be end up being one of them third wheels. I've never been on a second honeymoon," Violet Burke piped up. "You don't mind sharing a room with your old granny, do you, Benjamin?"

# A Note from Victor

I hope you enjoyed this latest Volume in the
Bucket saga.

All reviews gratefully received, even a word or
two is most welcome.

Please feel free to drop me a line if you would like
information on the release date of future volumes
in the Bucket to Greece series at
vdbucket@gmail.com
or via Vic Bucket on Facebook.

I am always delighted to hear from happy readers.

Printed in Great Britain
by Amazon

75719396R00214